Critical Praise for the First Edition

"Eva and Jan have organized an amazing breadth of resources available on the Internet. No financial professional should try to do research without reviewing this book. It will make your research more efficient and expansive if you use the sources highlighted here."

Z. Christopher Mercer
CEO, Mercer Capital

"Through years of financial research and training, these two highly talented and skilled professionals have provided not only a broad listing of available sites, but also a carefully selected and thorough menu to direct practitioners to essential data for their research engagements...This book serves as a highly useful and practical tool for every valuation practice, helping all analysts to better understand the enormous research possibilities available to them through the Internet. With thoughtful, quality guidance, it will help you overcome your research obstacles and maximize your valuable research time."

James L. (Butch) Williams,
CPA/ABV, CVA, CBA
Chairman of the AICPA Business
Valuation Subcommittee, Dixon
Odom PLLC

"This is a highly practical reference tool for any business appraiser or financial advisor. The authors are two of the best-known business valuation research professionals in the United States."

Shannon Pratt, CFA, FASA, MCBA
Managing Director
Willamette Management Associates

BEST WEBSITES FOR FINANCIAL PROFESSIONALS, BUSINESS APPRAISERS, AND ACCOUNTANTS

BEST WEBSITES FOR FINANCIAL PROFESSIONALS, BUSINESS APPRAISERS, AND ACCOUNTANTS

EVA M. LANG
JAN DAVIS TUDOR

John Wiley & Sons, Inc.

For general information on our other products and services, or technical support, please contact our Customer Care Department within the United States at 800-762-2974, outside the United States at 317-572-3993 or fax 317-572-4002.

Wiley also publishes its books in a variety of electronic formats. Some content that appears in print may not be available in electronic books.

For more information about Wiley products, visit our web site at www.wiley.com.

Lang, Eva M.
  Best websites for financial professionals, business appraisers,
and accountants / Eva M. Lang, Jan Davis Tudor.— 2nd ed.
     p. cm.
Includes index.
  ISBN 0-471-33338-7 (pbk. : alk. paper)
  1. Business—Computer network resources—Directories. 2. Web
sites—Directories. 3. Internet addresses—Directories. I. Tudor, Jan
D. II. Title.

 HF54.56.L36 2003
 025.06'65—dc21

                         2003006628

Printed in the United States of America

10 9 8 7 6 5 4 3 2 1

Eva:
To Scott

Jan:
To Tim Berners-Lee, for creating the World Wide Web

CONTENTS

Preface xxi

Acknowledgments xxv

About the Authors xxvii

Chapter 1	**Searching the Internet**	**1**
	Search Results and Paid Placement	**8**
	The Invisible Web	10
	Searching Tips	**12**
	Use That Advanced Search Feature	12
	What about Those Meta Search Engines?	15
	Put Google on Your Toolbar!	16
	Fee-Based Sources	17
	Conclusion	**19**
Chapter 2	**Portals and Vortals**	**21**
	Portals	**22**
	About.com	22
	AccountingWEB	23
	Business.com	23

CorporateInformation.com   24

The Dismal Scientist   24

FindLaw   26

FirstGov   27

Google News   28

Hoover's Online   29

Librarian's Index to the Internet   29

State Search   29

Publist.com   30

Statistical Resources on the Web   30

ValuationResources.com   31

Yahoo! Finance   31

Vortals   **32**

How Do I Find a Vortal for a Particular Industry?   34

Caveat Emptor   35

Chapter 3   **Websites for Conducting Economic Research**   **37**

First and Foremost   **38**

Bureau of Labor Statistics   38

Economagic   39

Economic Report of the President   40

Economy.com   41

Federal Reserve System   43

Fedstats   46

Global Insight   46

National Bureau of Economic Research   47

U.S. Census Bureau   49

Best of the Rest   **50**

Bank One Corporate Economics Group   50

Bureau of Economic Analysis   51

Conference Board Business Cycle Indicators   51

Congressional Budget Office Projections   51

Consensus Economics   52

EconBase   52

EconData   52

Econometrics Laboratory at the University of
California, Berkeley 53
Economic Information Systems 53
Economic Policy Institute 53
Economics Research Network 53
The Economist 54
The Financial Forecast Center 54
Government Information Sharing Project 54
Haver Analytics 55
IDEAS 55
Resources for Economists on the Internet 55
STAT-USA 56
Wachovia 56
Yardeni's Economics Network 56

Chapter 4   **Industry Sites**   **57**

First and Foremost **59**
Dialog Open Access 59
ECNext Knowledge Center 60
First Research Industry Profiles 61
Integra Industry Reports 62
MarketResearch.com 64
Thomson Research 65
Trade Association Directories 66

Best of the Rest **68**
Bizminer 68
Economy.com Industry Reports 69
Financial Times Surveys 69
Frost & Sullivan Research Publications 69
Harris InfoSource 70
Hoover's Industry Snapshots 70
IBIS World 70
IRS Market Segment Specialization Program (MSSP) 70
ITA Basic Industries 71
Manufacturing Marketplace 71

MindBranch   71
MoBDN Industry-at-a-Glance Reports   72
Plunkett Research Online   72
U.S. Census Bureau: Industry Resources   72
ValuationResources Industry Resources Report   73
WetFeet.com   73

Chapter 5   Market Data   75

Betas   75
Alacra   75
Multex Investor   76
Wall Street Research Net   77

Bonds and Interest Rates   77
Bondtrac   77
Federal Reserve Board   77
Yahoo Bond Center   77
T-Bills, Notes & Bonds Online   78

Earnings Estimates   79
Alacra   79

Open- and Closed-End Mutual Funds   79
CBS Marketwatch   79
Morningstar   80
Yahoo! Finance Mutual Funds Center   80

Stock Quotes   81

Stock Quotes—Historical   81
Yahoo! Finance   81
Wall Street Research Net   82

Chapter 6   Public Company Data   83

First and Foremost   84
10k Wizard   84
CorporateInformation   84
EDGAR-Online   86

EDGARScan   86
FreeEDGAR   88
Hoover's Online   88
LIVEDGAR   90
Multex Investor   92
Mergent Online   93
MSN Money Central   93
One Source Business Browser   94
SEC Info   94
Wall Street Journal Briefing Books   95

Best of the Rest   **96**
144A/Private Placement Database   96
eLibrary   96
Goldman Sachs Research on Demand   96
IPO.com   97
SEDAR (System for Electronic Document Analysis
    and Retrieval)   97
Value Line   97
Wall Street City   97

Chapter 7   **Sites for Private Company Analysis**   **99**

First and Foremost   **99**
Business Filings Databases   99
CorporateInformation   100
CorpTech   100
Dun & Bradstreet   101
Experian (formerly TRW)   102
Forbes Magazine and the Forbes Private 500   103
Hoover's Online   103
Inc. Magazine and the Inc. 500   104
Integra Information   105
Thomas Register of American Manufacturers   106

Best of the Rest   **107**
A.M. Best Insurance Company Directory and Reports   107
Business CreditUSA.com   107

EDGAR   107
eLibrary   108
Ex-Exec Tracker   108
Franchise 500   108
TechSavvy   108
Vault Reports   109
zapdata.com   109

Chapter 8   Salary and Executive Compensation Surveys   111

First and Foremost   112
Abbott, Langer & Associates, Inc.   112
America's Career InfoNet (ACINet)   114
Best Jobs USA Salary Survey   115
Bureau of Labor Statistics   115
CareerJournal   117
eComp Executive Compensation Database   118
Economic Research Institute (ERI)   118
JobStar: California Job Search Guide   119
LIVEDGAR   120
SalariesReview.com and SalaryExpert.com   121
Salary.com   121
Trade Associations   123
Wageweb   123

Best of the Rest   124
Business Magazine Special Issues   124
CompGeo Online   124
Executive Compensation Advisory Services   125
Hewitt Compensation Center   125
The Institute of Management and Administration (IOMA)   126
Risk Management Association (RMA) Annual
   Statement Studies   126
William M. Mercer – Mercer Human Resource Consulting   126
WorldatWork   127

Chapter 9   Websites for Conducting Merger and Acquisition Research   129

First and Foremost   130

Alacra   130

Bizcomps   131

Business Valuation Market Data   132

Corporate Growth Deal Retriever   134

The Daily Deal at The Deal.com   135

Done Deals   136

EDGAR Databases   138

Global Securities Information's Mergers
    & Acquisitions Database   140

Mergerstat   141

NVST.com   141

SNL Securities   143

Thomson Financial Investment Banking/Capital
    Markets Group   144

Securities Data Company Worldwide M&A Database   144

Best of the Rest   145

American Society of Association Executives' (ASAE)
    Gateway to Associations   145

Dealogic   145

Ingenta   146

Institute of Business Appraisers Market Database   146

International Business Brokers Association   146

Investment Dealers Digest   147

Kagan and Associates   147

Mergers & Acquisitions Report   147

Merger Central   148

Merger Market   148

MergerNetwork   148

Thomas Register of American Manufacturers   149

Webmergers.com   149

Chapter 10   Websites for Intellectual Property Research   151

First and Foremost   152

Delphion Intellectual Property Network   152
The Intellectual Property Mall   154
The Intellectual Property Transaction Database   155
Law.com Intellectual Law Practice Center   157
MicroPatent   158
Patent Café Intellectual Property Network   159
Thomson & Thomson   161
The United States Copyright Office   161
United States Patent and Trademark Office   163
University of Texas Copyright Crash Course   165
World Intellectual Property Organization   166

Best of the Rest   168

ABA Intellectual Property Law Section   168
Association of Research Libraries Copyright and IP Center   169
BizFindLaw Intellectual Property Center   169
Copyright Clearance Center   169
Copyright Website   170
Department of Energy Patent Database   170
European Patent Organization ESP@CENET   170
Get the Patent   170
The Intellectual Property Law Server   171
Intellectual Property Rights Helpdesk   171
IP Menu   171
Intellectual Property Owners Association   172
International Trademark Association   172
Questel   172
RoyaltySource   173
RoyaltyStat   173
SurfIP   173
Trademark.com   174
The Watch File at the University of Texas   174

Chapter 11   Tax and Accounting Sites   175

First and Foremost   177

American Institute of Certified Public Accountants   177
Big Four Major Accounting Firm Sites   178

Bureau of National Affairs 180
Commerce Clearing House (CCH) 182
CPA Journal 183
Electronic Accountant 184
Internal Revenue Service 185
Kleinrock's Tax Expert Online 186
RIA and RIA Checkpoint 187
SmartPros 187
Tax Analysts 189

Best of the Rest 190
Accounting Research Network 190
Accounting & Tax Database 190
AccountingWeb 191
AuditNet 191
CFO.com 191
Comperio 192
Federal Tax Law 192
FTA State Tax Rates 192
PPCnet 193
Regulations and Standards 193
Writing Skills for the Tax Professional 194

Chapter 12 Websites for International Business Research 195

First and Foremost 196
American Chambers of Commerce Abroad 196
Bureau van Dijk 197
Commercial Service—U.S. Department of Commerce 198
CorporateInformation 199
Datamonitor 200
Datastar 201
Economist/Economist Intelligence Unit 202
ELDIS Country Profiles 203
Euromonitor 203
European Union Business Resources 204
globalEDGE 204
Global Business Opportunities (GLOBUS) and
  the National Trade Data Bank (NTDB) 206
Global EDGAR 206

Global Insight   207
International Business Resource Connection   208
International Trade Center   209
Kompass   209
U.S. Department of State Business Center   210
Wall Street Journal Online   210
World Factbook   212

Best of the Rest   **213**
AllAfrica   213
Bank Hapoalim   213
Basic Guide to Exporting   213
BolagsFakta   213
Business Europe   214
China Big   214
China Online   214
Company Records On-Line (CAROL)   214
Consensus Economics   215
DATAINTAL   215
EDGAR Online Global Reports   215
EUbusiness   215
Europages: The European Business Directory   216
Europrospectus   216
Federation of International Trade Organizations
    International Trade/Import-Export Portal   216
Forbes International 500   216
Global Business Centre   217
HierosGamos: The Comprehensive Law and
    Government Portal   217
Hoover's Online   217
International Finance Corporation   217
International Statistical Agencies   218
Latin American Network Information Center   218
Latin Focus   218
Lex Africa Business Guides   219
Mbendi: Africa's Leading Website   219
MenaBusiness   219

New Zealand Companies Office Database   220
Planet Business   220
System for Electronic Document Analysis and
    Retrieval (SEDAR)   220
Thomas Register of European Manufacturers   220
Webstat   221

Chapter 13   Public Records   223

First and Foremost   224
Choicepoint   224
KnowX   225
NETROnline: Real Estate Information and Public
    Records Research   225
Public Records Sources   227
search systems Public Record Locator   227
USSearch   228

Best of the Rest   228
Discreet Research   228
National Association of Unclaimed Property
    Administrators (NAUPA)   229
Merlin Information Services   229
National Criminal Justice Reference System (NCJRS)   229
National Public Records Research Association (NPRRA)   230
U.S. Death Records   230

Index   231

Preface

This book is aimed primarily at the accountant or financial analyst who is engaged in consulting work—such as business appraisal, financial planning, and management consulting. The consulting area is the most rapidly growing area of accounting practice, and financial professionals in this area can benefit significantly from the increase in information available on the Internet.

As in the first edition, the sites included in this book are the result of years of collective Internet research, and we are sharing the sites we consider the cream of the crop. By learning and bookmarking these selected sites, you will be off to a great start with your research projects. In addition, as can be expected, there has been some fallout on the Internet. Some excellent sites simply lost their funding, some were acquired and changed missions, and those with less-valuable content folded. It appears that the strong sites just keep getting stronger.

In the first edition of this book, Eva began Chapter 1 with the sentence, "I have yet to meet an Internet user who did not have a horror story about the difficulty of finding information on the Internet." Well, two years later, we can still make this exact same statement. Yet despite its continued growth, the Internet *has* gotten a little easier to search. We just need to change our thinking about *how* to search the Internet. And we need to stop relying on search engines and directories and realize their limitations. Sure we still have to use them—a lot! But we also need to think about portals, the "invisible Web," and fee-based services.

We've identified three major trends in Internet research:

- Information *wants* to be free but can't.
- Search engines are getting better.

- Fee-based, value-added services save time and money, and in many cases are the *only* sources of certain types of data.

TREND #1: THERE'S LESS OF A FREE LUNCH ON THE INTERNET

In the early days of the Internet, it seemed that just about whatever information we found on the 'net was free. Well, that is changing. In some cases, banner advertising-related-revenues for commercial Websites decreased, and the site owners found they needed to start charging for their data in order to stay afloat. But in most cases, Website owners simply need to recuperate some of the money invested in running their Websites. A good example of this is *American Demographics*, one of the first trade journals to appear full-text online. About five years ago the magazine provided an archive of its articles for free. Today most of the articles are $2.95.

Just a couple of years ago, more researchers had several options for free EDGAR (Electronic Data Gathering, Analysis, and Retrieval) filings; today, just a couple of free sites exist. Even trade associations have found a willing market for their in-house reports and have started charging for them. Why not? According to the market research firm IDC, "the market for online content is being driven by businesses and consumers that are increasingly willing to pay for reliable sources of timely, accurate and complete information." The firm forecasts that aggregate worldwide spending for online content will exceed $50 billion in 2002 and $108 billion in 2006.[1]

The Online Publishers Association concurs. Their report, "Online Paid Content: U.S. Market Spending," shows that U.S. consumer spending for online content in the first quarter of 2002 was $300 million—an increase of 155 percent from the first quarter of 2001. 12.4 million U.S. consumers paid for online content in the first quarter of 2002—an increase from 5.3 million U.S. consumers in the first quarter of 2001.[2]

Not only does it appear that paying for data on the Internet is the trend, but we also believe in compensating those who gather information and add value to it by putting it in searchable, database form. A good example of this is merger and acquisition (M&A) data. It is impossible to do a good transaction (M&A) search on the Internet without paying for the data. Why? The data takes time and expertise to gather and review, and in many cases adds value by calculating multiples. So, while you can access the Done Deals, Pratt's Stats and Mergerstat databases on the Internet, you have to pay for the data.

---

[1] "Demand for Online Content Prompts IDS to Launch New Continuous Intelligence Service." Press Release. IDC. October 22, 2002. Available at: www.idc.com.

[2] Online Publishers Association. "Online Paid Content: U.S. Market Spending Report." August 2002. www.online-publishers.org/.

TREND #2: SEARCH ENGINES ARE GETTING BETTER

The various search engines are in competition with each other—big time. They want to be the biggest and fastest Internet database while returning the most relevant search results. Search engines, such as AltaVista, are also being redesigned to meet searchers' needs. Chapter 1 contains more detailed information about the current state of search engines.

While the results generated by search engines are becoming more relevant, it is unfortunately getting harder to tell which results are the "real" results generated by your search and which results are paid for by advertisers. While we have no problem with search engines selling "sponsored" links, they must be clearly identified as such. Google is an example of a search engine that does an excellent job of clearly identifying these ads by segregating them in a colored box and clearly labeling them "Sponsored links." Other search engines do not make this distinction so clearly. Some include the advertisers links at the top of the search results without clearly marking them with different fonts or colors and, worse, some refer to the advertisers' links as "Featured listings." "Featured" is not a synonym for "sponsored," and this can be misleading. So look carefully when you click on that first search result, to understand what you are getting.

TREND #3: VALUE-ADDED OR FEE-BASED SERVICES—THEY ARE WORTH THEIR WEIGHT IN GOLD!

There is a common myth that every bit of information you need to find is on the Internet, and it is free. Wrong. Yes, you can find a lot of great information on the 'net for free. Sometimes the data exists on the Internet, but in a fee-based database like LexisNexis. And sometimes the information you need is in the local library and not on the Internet at all!

In many cases, it may be worth your while to pay for information from a fee-based service simply because it is much cheaper time-wise to go directly to a service and pay $2.95 for an article rather than spend 30 minutes looking for it "for free" on the 'net. In addition, information specialist Mary Ellen Bates recently wrote "the high-priced value-added information services such as LexisNexis, Dialog, and Factiva are incredible tools for in-depth research. You'll find content there that will never appear on the Web—articles from industry newsletters, market research reports . . . . and financial information on companies from around the world."[3]

The playing field has been leveled in terms of services that were once accessible only to research departments of large companies or by those

---

[3] Bates, Mary Ellen. "Ferrari Searching on a Volkswagen Budget." SearchDay, December 4, 2002. Available at: http://searchenginewatch.com/searchday/02/sd1204-budget.html.

willing to fork over hefty annual subscription fees. Many of the professional online services offer pay-as-you-go pricing plans and have developed user-friendly interfaces to the systems. If you think you've "done your research" make sure you've considered fee-based services, especially in a litigation-support situation.

While we will include information about the major commercial information providers such as Factiva (formerly Dow Jones Interactive), OneSource, Alacra, LexisNexis, and Dialog, and financial data services like Bloomberg, Factset, and Securities Data, we not go into detail about them. Still, we strongly encourage you to consider subscribing to one of these services if you find that your information needs are increasing and can no longer be met by free and low-cost Websites.

It is important to reiterate that, despite popular belief, everything ever published is *not* available on the Internet, and that all information on the 'net is free. In addition, because our time is valuable, it may make more sense to spend five minutes on a fee-based service and pay for the data rather than spend hours trying to find it for free on the 'net.

If you wonder why just a handful of sites are suggested for a specific subject, it is most likely because the site mentioned is considered a "portal." In order to keep visitors on their sites, and hopefully increase profitability and brand recognition, Internet companies are converting their sites into portals, or "one-stop-shopping" sites for researchers. Portals have become so popular, and such great time-saving tools for researchers, we've dedicated an entire chapter to them.

Finally, while every attempt was made to provide up-to-date information, the rapid pace of change on the Internet makes that virtually impossible. Be aware that Website addresses may have changed along with the amount and cost of the content on each site.

Memphis, Tennessee and Portland, Oregon
February 2003

Acknowledgments

Eva:

A special note of thanks to the executive board of the Financial Consulting Group for their support and encouragement as I worked on this manuscript. I am especially grateful to a number of people at Christ United Methodist Church in Memphis, Tennessee, including the Messengers Sunday School class for their prayers and Jo Ellen Druelinger and the Communications Office for their encouragement.

I want to thank Barbara Walters Price, Vice-President of Marketing for Mercer Capital, and my family—the Bradys, the Kuhlmans, and the LeMays. I am also deeply indebted to my husband and partner, Scott LeMay, without whom this book, and most of the good things in my life, would not exist.

Jan:

To my dear friends Roxana Bassi and Martin Jauregui for their home and friendship while working on this book.

About the Authors

Eva M. Lang, CPA, ASA, is a nationally recognized expert on electronic research for business valuation and litigation support services. She is a frequent speaker to national groups on technology issues and conducts Internet training seminars for corporations and trade associations. Eva has been involved in numerous projects in the areas of business valuation, financial analysis, and technology consulting. She has served as member of the Business Valuations and Appraisals Subcommittee of the AICPA and on CPA committees at the state level in the areas of estate planning, litigation services, and management consulting services. She has written for numerous financial publications including the *AICPA CPA Expert*, the *Practicing CPA*, and the *Journal of Accountancy*.

Eva currently serves as chief operating officer of the Financial Consulting Group, the largest alliance of business valuation and consulting firms in the United States. She writes and publishes the *FCG Buzz* electronic newsletter, maintains the Business Valuation Blog, and edits the FCG print newsletter *Building Value*.

Jan Davis Tudor is president of JT Research, located in Portland, Oregon. Jan coordinates a team of trained information specialists to provide business professionals with the data they need in a timely and cost effective manner. Jan considers herself a freelance research librarian, and while her business caters to business appraisers, she researches a wide variety of subjects. She received her Masters in Library and Information Studies from the University of California at Berkeley, and is a member of the Association of Independent Information Professionals and the Special Library Association. Jan contributes regularly to *Online* and *Searcher* magazines. She has been a speaker on research strategies and the Internet, both nationally and internationally.

CHAPTER 1

Searching the Internet

Efficient and effective Internet research depends on the skill of the researcher. It takes time to develop a "feel" for the Internet, as well as know where to turn for information. Even though we devote a lot of our time to research, we still find it challenging to "keep up" with the changes in sources as well as search tools and techniques. Because it is so important to know how to use the tools that will help you find information on the Internet, we've started out this book with a chapter on search engines. While you may bookmark many (if not all!) of the sites in this book, chances are that you will still need to use search engines and directories to find additional material for a specific research project.

We've said it before and we'll say it again, search engines and search directories aren't the same! Directories or portals, such as Yahoo!, are smaller subsets of the entire Internet. Each site on a portal is hand-selected by a human, and in Yahoo!'s case, classified into hierarchical subject categories. On the other hand, search engines such as Google offer much larger portions of the Internet, because search engines attempt to index as much as they can from the entire World Wide Web.

What does this mean to searchers? Well, if you are doing a comprehensive search on revenues and forecasts for the turnaround management consulting industry, for example, you'll probably get much better results from using a search engine, because it is searching more of the Web. However, if you are simply trying to find the address of the secretary of state's office in Oregon, Yahoo! is probably a better place to begin your search because the search is much more specific.

For better search results:

- Use search directories for broad, general searches.
- Use search engines for more specific, comprehensive searches.

- Use unique words whenever possible.
- Use "advanced search" features such as phrase searching.

Not all search engines are the same, and we recommend using more than one search engine for comprehensive searches. Many searchers tend to think that if they don't find what they are looking for on the 'net on Google, the information doesn't exist. The iProspect survey mentioned on page 9 shows that 52 percent of survey respondents use only one, favorite online search engine, and 35 percent alternate between favorites.[1] This is a disturbing trend because all search engines have their limitations.

It is important to keep in mind that each search engine searches differently, and therefore retrieves different search results. Greg Notess, librarian at the University of Montana and Internet search engine expert, performs periodic surveys of the overlap of search results among search engines. In March 2002, Notess found that "almost half of all pages found were only found by one of the search engines, and not always the same one. Over 78 percent were found by three search engines at most."[2] What this means to searchers is that if we don't find what we are looking for using one search engine, we should try the search in a different search engine. If you are doing a comprehensive search on a particular topic, be sure to use at least three different search engines.

In March 2002, Notess also performed an analysis of the 10 different search engines using 25 single-word queries. The results of his survey indicate that Google found more total hits than any of the other search engines, and placed first on 23 of the 25 searches. WiseNut came in second place and found more hits than Google on two of the searches. In terms of total hits retrieved from his searches, the top 7 search engines are:[3]

1. Google (www.google.com)
2. alltheweb (www.alltheweb.com)
3. AltaVista (www.av.com)
4. WiseNut (www.wisenut.com)

---

[1] "Search Engine Users Seek Instant Gratification." *BizReport*, December 3, 2002. Available at: www.bizreport.com.

[2] Notess, Greg. "Search Engines Statistics: Database Overlap." *Search Engine Showdown: The User's Guide to Web Searching*. March 2, 2002. Available at: www.searchengineshowdown.com/stats/overlap.shtml.

[3] Notess, Greg R. "Search Engine Statistics: Database Total Size Estimates." *Search Engine Showdown: The User's Guide to Web Searching*. December 31, 2002. Available at: searchengineshowdown.com/stats/sizeest.shtml.

5. Hotbot (www.hotbot.com)

6. MSN Search (search.msn.com)

7. Teoma (www.teoma.com)

Search engines are constantly changing. Google still dominates the search engine market, and we'd like to point out a couple of unique things about the search engine. As Google crawls the Web and indexes pages, it makes a copy of each page in case the original page is unavailable. Each site listed in the list search results has a link for "Cached" and "Similar pages" (see Exhibit 1.1). If we click on the "Cached" link, we can see the Web page as it was originally indexed by Google. The importance of this feature is that many Web pages disappear because the site owners have taken them off the Internet. But Google has kept a copy for us!

Exhibit 1.1   Google

Teoma and WiseNut are new search engines trying to usurp Google's market share. Like Google, Teoma has no banner or pop-up ads. On the other hand, Teoma has indexed far fewer pages than Google. Still, what we like about Teoma is that, in addition to ranking pages according to relevancy based on the searcher's keywords, this search engine also tries to determine the authority of a site's contents (see Exhibit 1.2). According to the folks at Teoma, the search engine "ranks a site according to the number of same-subject pages that reference it, not just general popularity, to determine the site's level of authority."

Teoma gives the searcher three responses to each search: "Results: Relevant web pages," "Refine: Suggestions to narrow your search," and "Resources: Link collections from experts and enthusiasts." Because of the links to authoritative sites, such as those from trade associations and trade publications, Teoma is especially effective for searching industry information (see Exhibit 1.3).[4]

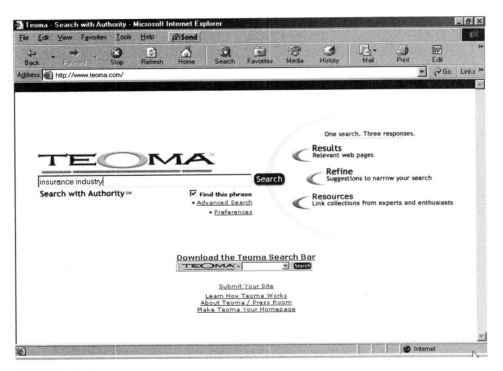

Exhibit 1.2   Teoma

---

[4] http://sp.teoma.com/docs/teoma/about/searchwithauthority.html.

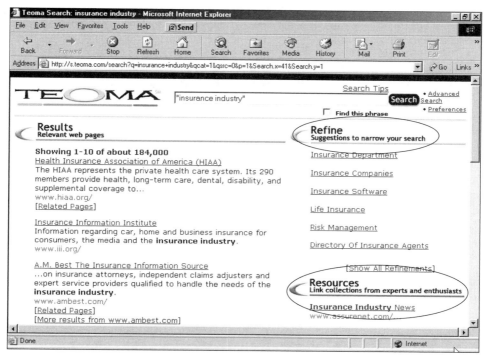

Exhibit 1.3   Teoma Search Results

WiseNut claims its search results are more relevant than Google's because of its "context-sensitive ranking algorithm." Google ranks its retrieved sites in order of how many links the site has from other pages. WiseNut, on the other hand, examines a site by how many links it has *and* the text on the page, then compares the two and places the most relevant sites at the top of the list. Like Google and Teoma, WiseNut has a very plain and simple home page. WiseNut also provides WiseSearch, its advanced search option.

Alltheweb claims to be the biggest Internet search engine, searching 2,095,568,809 indexed Web pages, compared with the 2,073,418,204 Web pages listed on Google's home page.[5] Searchers can now customize the presentation of their search results on alltheweb. For example, search terms can be highlighted in the search result, only one site from each domain will be displayed, and a "Search Tip" can be displayed in a panel to the right of the search results (see Exhibit 1.4).

---

[5] "Fast's alltheweb.com Dethrones Google as the World's Largest Search Engine." Press Release. June 17, 2002. Fast. Available at: www.fastsearch.com/press/press_display.asp?pr_rel=137.

Exhibit 1.4   alltheweb

AltaVista has reinvented itself in an effort to recapture its role as a leading search engine. According to AltaVista, "While recognizing that the relevancy of results is even more important than index size, AltaVista has crawled over five billion pages and eliminated duplicate pages, dead links, and spam to create an even better experience for users.[6]

---

[6] "AltaVista Advances Internet Search With New Features and Functionality for 'Power of Precision' Searching." Press Release. AltaVista. November 12, 2002. Available at: www.altavista.com/about/prelease?yr=2002&dt=111202.

There are so many excellent search engines that books have been written about them. We recommend Randolph Hock's *The Extreme Searcher's Guide to Web Search Engines,* (Medford, NJ: CyberAge Books-Information Today, 2001). In addition, two renowned Websites are dedicated to discussing the various search engines in detail. For a list of the available search engines and detailed information about searching them, see *Search Engine Showdown: The Users' Guide to Web Searching* (http://searchengineshowdown.com) (see Exhibit 1.5) and Search Engine Watch (www.searchenginewatch.com) (see Exhibit 1.6).

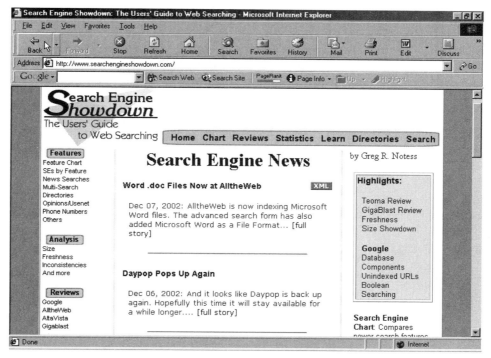

Exhibit 1.5 Search Engine Showdown
http://searchengineshowdown.com.

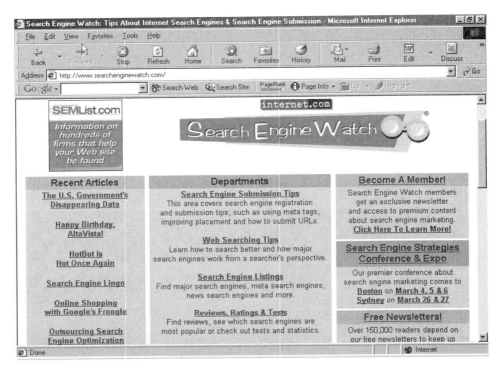

Exhibit 1.6   Search Engine Watch

SEARCH RESULTS AND PAID PLACEMENT

In order to stay afloat financially, most search engines and directories, such as AOL, Yahoo!, and MSN, are accepting payment from Website owners to ensure that their sites are ranked higher in the list of returned search results. Laurianne McLaughlin reports in the July 2002 issue of *PC World* that from the list of retrieved results from an MSN search, the "Featured Sites are a combination pages from three sources: advertisers who have paid to be there; other sites that, like MSN, are owned by Microsoft; and sites that are just plain useful. MSN doesn't identify which links come from which category. Sponsored Sites consist entirely of spots paid for by advertisers."[7]

---

7 McLaughlin, Laurianne. "The Straight Story on Search Engines." *PC World*, July 2002. Available at: www.pcworld.com/news/article/0,aid,97431,00.asp.

For example, if Jan paid Yahoo! somewhere between $50 and $300 per month, her company's Website, www.jtresearch.com would supposedly be placed at the top of the search results, as a "sponsored site" for a search such as "valuation research." What this means though is that your search results are skewed. Say you did a search on the trucking industry, and the top 10 sites returned to you were paid-for or sponsored sites; you would mostly likely need to look further down your list of search results for relevant pages.

It is interesting to note that according to a 2002 survey by iProspect of Internet users in the U.S., 78 percent of Internet searchers will "abandon a search engine site if they do not find their desired result on the first three pages."[8] Yikes! If you are like one of the Internet users surveyed by iProspect and only look at the first three pages, you may walk away from your computer thinking there is nothing on the Internet on your topic. However, because of paid placement you need to look at more than the top 10 results. Some search engines clearly identify which sites have been "sponsored," in other words, paid for higher placement. Other sites don't.

Make sure you know which sites that are retrieved are paid for and which aren't. Google prominently lists its sponsored sites on the right-hand side of the screen in a highlighted box (see Exhibit 1.7). AltaVista, on the other hand, puts its sponsored sites at the top of each list of search results. McLaughlin's article, "The Straight Story on Search Engines" (www.pcworld.com/news/article/0,aid,97431,00.asp) provides an excellent summary of each search engine and how to identify their paid placement sites.[9]

While search engine providers are under some pressure from consumer action groups to be more up front about sites that are sponsored, we will continue to see more and more paid-for sites. For example, AltaVista recently reported that the company has "eliminated pop-up and pop-under ads on its U.S. site in August of this year, and will continue to phase them out from its other country sites over the next several months. The company has also phased out the 'skyscraper' ads that were located on the right-hand margin of the search results pages, replacing them with additional paid listings."[10]

---

[8] "Search Engine Users Seek Instant Gratification." *BizReport*, December 3, 2002. Available at: www.bizreport.com.

[9] McLaughlin, Laurianne. "The Straight Story on Search Engines." *PC World*, July 2002. Available at: www.pcworld.com/news/article/0,aid,97431,00.asp.

[10] "Altavista Advances Internet Search With New Features and Functionality for 'Power of Precision' Searching." Press Release. Altavista. November 12, 2002. Available at: www.altavista.com/about/prelease?yr=2002&dt=111202

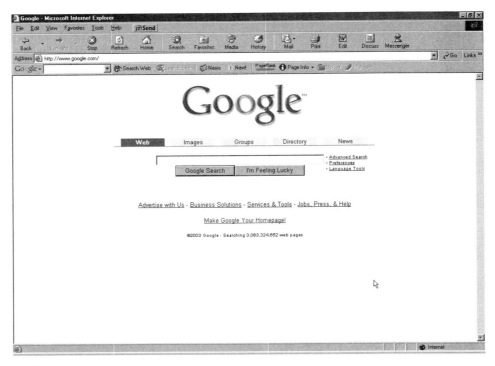

Exhibit 1.7   Google Search

The Invisible Web

When we sit down at our computers and type a few keywords into a search engine such as Google and look at the search results, it is easy to think we've searched the 'net. Unfortunately, it isn't that simple. Many of the pages on the Internet are inaccessible for a number of reasons, and unfortunately many of these pages contain valuable and authoritative information.

BrightPlanet reports that the invisible Web is approximately 400 to 550 times bigger than the Internet as we know it, and is the fastest growing category of new information on the Internet. The company also reports that 97.4 percent of the invisible Web is free.[11]

---

[11] Pedley, Paul. "Why You Can't Afford to Ignore the Invisible Web." *Business Information Review*, March 2002.

So what exactly is the invisible Web? Those Internet pages ignored by search engines, which include:

- Pages "deep" into a site
- PDF or PostScript files (Google and AltaVista are now indexing this format)
- Compressed files
- Content-rich databases and dynamically generated pages
- Password-protected pages

According to Internet search experts Chris Sherman and Gary Price, some of the top invisible Web categories include data commonly needed by financial and valuation professionals:[12]

- Historical stock quotes
- Company directories
- Economic information
- Public company filings
- Basic demographic information

So how is the invisible Web created? First of all, search engines build their databases by periodically "indexing" the Internet. Each search engine sends out crawlers, or spiders, to index each page. Search engine consultant Avi Rappoport describes this process well: "Crawling" is the process of following links to locate pages, and then reading those pages to make the information on them searchable."[13]

Most, if not all, search engines crawl only a portion of a site, and the amount crawled differs among search engines. So, if a site is huge, which many sites are, some of the pages "deep" into the site will not be included in a search engine's database. For instance, Google "stops indexing a Web page after indexing 101k of content," says Gary Price.[14]

Also, many search engines have a difficult time indexing .pdf files. Because so much information is published on the Internet in .pdf these days, we need to emphasize this point. Take for example all of the data on U.S. government sites that is in .pdf, such as census material. When we do a search on MSN for example for construction permits, the MSN search engine won't

---

[12] Sherman, Chris and Gary Price. *The Invisible Web: Uncovering Information Sources Search Engines Can't See.* Medford, NJ: CyberAge Books, 2001.

[13] Rappoport, Avi. "Anatomy of a Search Engine: Inside Google." *SearchDay*. October 30, 2002.

[14] The Virtual Acquisition Shelf and News Desk. Posting by Gary Price on Wednesday, September 18, 2002, available at http://resourceshelf.freepint.com/archives/2002_09_01_resourceshelf_archive.html/#85464374.

retrieve the data that the U.S. Census Bureau publishes because the engine doesn't index the .pdf files containing the data.

Google has been the most successful in indexing .pdf files, and AltaVista and alltheweb are now indexing .pdf files as well. While it is possibly a matter of time before all of the search engines can index .pdf files, we should make sure to use the Google, AltaVista, or alltheweb search engines for our searches.

Search engines also have a hard time indexing sites that require passwords, so the engines just pass them by. Just think of all the sites where we've had to enter information about ourselves in order to gain access to the site's data. I can think of many, for example, Jupiter (www.jup.com), a marketing research firm that often provides great bits of data in the summaries of their research reports. On their Website is a summary of their "Home Networking" survey, which I could not retrieve from the search engines because the page exists on a site requiring a password.

Another example of Web pages missed by search engines are those created "on the fly," or those that exist in databases. For example, the database ingenta (www.ingenta.com) contains citations to thousands of journal articles. From the search page on ingenta, a database of thousands of academic and trade journal articles found at www.ingenta.com, we can enter keywords and retrieve citations to articles that we may not find anywhere else on the Internet.

For more detailed information about the invisible Web, we recommend *The Invisible Web: Uncovering Information Sources Search Engines Can't See* by Chris Sherman and Gary Price, (Medford, NJ: CyberAge Books, 2001).

What the significance of the invisible Web boils down to is that there is a lot of good information that we can't find via search engines, so we need to go directly to the sources of that data. But how does one find the sources? Several Websites exist to help point us in the right direction. For example, Sherman and Price publish The Invisible Web Directory at www.invisible-web.net. The directory is organized by broad subject headings. The Librarian's Index to the Internet (described in detail in Chapter 2) is a good site to add to your research strategy. Portals, discussed in detail in Chapter 2, are also excellent places to gain access to the invisible Web.

SEARCHING TIPS

Use That Advanced Search Feature

Most people simply put their search terms in the box presented on the first page of the search engines' home page. We used to promote Boolean searching, that is, the use of "and," "or," and quotation marks. While searchers can still use these Boolean terms for more precise searching, it is just as easy to use each search engine's advanced search feature (see Exhibit 1.8). In fact, the search engine developers prefer it. Search directories, such as Yahoo!, also have advanced search options (see Exhibit 1.9).

So what does "Advanced Search" mean? The advanced search page of a search engine provides you with a template that allows you to create a specific search query that usually results in more relevant search results. You can search for a phrase, such as "restaurant industry," add the word "forecast," and limit your results to those pages added to the Internet in the six months after the first of the year, in the United States (see Exhibit 1.10).

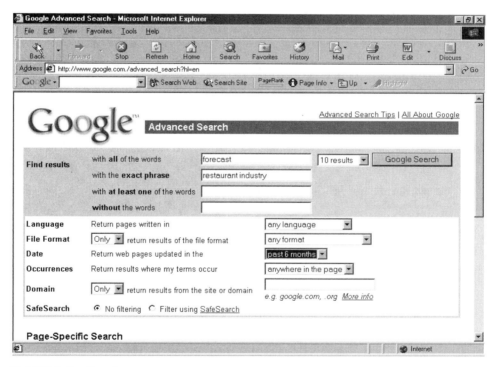

Exhibit 1.8   Google

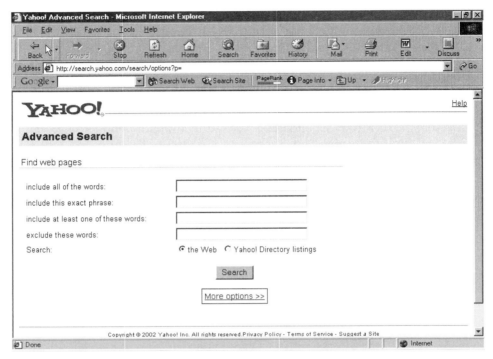

Exhibit 1.9   Yahoo! Advanced Search
Reproduced with permission of Yahoo! Inc. ©2003 by Yahoo! Inc. YAHOO! and the YAHOO! logo are trademarks of Yahoo! Inc.

Another interesting way to limit your search results is by domain type. Say, for instance, you want to find government information on agency spending on outsourcing for information technology. By selecting .gov (for government), you will limit your search results to government sites. If you are unfamiliar with the appropriate domain code, each search engine's advanced search template offers an index from which you can choose.

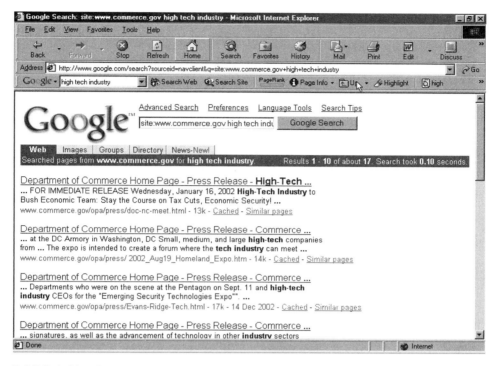

Exhibit 1.10   Google

What about Those Meta Search Engines?

Meta search engines are tools that search multiple search engines simultaneously. Lots of meta search engines exist, but the editors of *SearchDay* (searchenginewatch.com/searchday) report that InfoSpace is "the industry gorilla," because it operates the two best known meta search engines, Dogpile and Metacrawler. It is interesting to note that results from both Dogpile and Metacrawer are identical, but with one big exception. Webcrawler results are ad free and banner free.[15]

---

[15] "The Big Four Meta Search Engines." *SearchDay*, September 17, 2002, Number 357.

According to InfoSpace's York Baur, Dogpile is "designed as a mainstream consumer site, with a simple presentation." Search results are grouped by the search engine from which they were found. Says Baur, "This presentation makes it easy to compare and contrast results from different search engines for the same query, and is one of Dogpile's most useful features." On the other hand, "Metacrawler is a hardcore site for the sophisticated searcher," states Baur. Instead of grouping results by search engine, Metacrawler merges results based on relevancy and performance.[16]

According to search engine expert Chris Sherman, three convincing reasons exist for using a meta search engine:[17]

- For "quick and dirty searches," because if you want an answer fast, you may have better luck querying multiple engines simultaneously.
- For broad and shallow searches, that is, if you are trying to obtain an overview of a topic.
- To learn of potential keywords for an unfamiliar subject. For example, a search across several search engines using the keyword "microbrew" may come up with other industry terms such as "craft brew."

While Dogpile and Metacrawler are definitely valuable search tools, several other meta search engines are worth checking out. In September 2002, *SearchDay* published a "Meta Search Engine Roundup," based on Search Engine Watch's (www.searchenginewatch.com) pick of the "top choices" of meta search engines for searching the Web.[18]

You may ask why we recommend using several search engines for a comprehensive search topic when we could just use a meta search engine. Well, metasearch engines only provide a portion of each search engines's results, perhaps the first 10 to 50 sites retrieved from each search engine. With many search engines giving priority to paid placement sites, the results of a meta search engine may not be helpful.

Put Google on Your Toolbar!

If you do a lot of searching and love Google, then there is no reason *not* to put Google on your tool bar. It takes just a few seconds, and once it is installed, the Google toolbar automatically appears along with the Internet Explorer (IE) toolbar. What we love about this is that we don't have to go to the Google site every time we want to do a search. We can type our keywords directly into the

---

[16] Ibid.

[17] "Meta Search Engine Week!" *SearchDay*, September 16, 2002, Number 356.

[18] "Meta Search Engine Roundup." *SearchDay*, September 18, 2002, Number 358.

box. However, if we want to take advantage of the site's Advanced Search feature, we need to start our search directly from the Google site.

Having Google on our toolbars means we can also use Google's search technology within a site. For example, if you are on a huge site, say the U.S. Department of Commerce (DOC), and you want to look for what the Department has to say about the high-tech industry, you can put in the keywords "high tech industry" in the Google tool bar, and Google will search the DOC site. In many cases, it is much more effective to use Google's search technology than the site's own search capability.

If you are a Teoma fan, you can add the Teoma toolbar to your Internet Explorer toolbar. With Teoma's toolbar you not only access Teoma from any Web page, but also look for a word in a dictionary, highlight your search terms as they appear on the page, and email the page you are on to a friend or colleague.

Fee-Based Sources

Fee-based services, such as Factiva (formerly Dow Jones News Retrieval), LexisNexis, Alacra, and Dialog, aggregate and provide uniform and value-added access to databases containing financial data and analysis, current and archived news and journal articles, merger and acquisition data, private company directories, market research and industry reports, investment bank reports, historical and current betas and earnings estimates, shareholding and bondholding data, and mutual fund performance information.

Fee-based services often provide information not found elsewhere; they allow for precision searching, such as the use of controlled vocabulary. They allow for Boolean and/or complex search statements, and are better organized and quicker to use than the free Internet sources, and often contain historical data. On the other hand, they can be expensive to use and do have a learning curve.

Alacra adds value to the databases it provides by presenting them in terms of research subject or concept. The Alacra home page provides a search feature that allows researchers to search across the entire 80+ databases simultaneously (see Exhibit 1.11). A unique and extremely useful feature of Alacra is the incorporation of Portal B- the company's database of the best business-related Websites culled from the bookmark files of information professionals in the field as well as from Alacra's staff. In other words, a search across the Alacra system of 80+ databases will also retrieve relevant Websites. Now called "The Business Web," these hand-selected sites, each summarized and indexed, are from the Websites of business and law schools, governments and associations, and commercial enterprises.

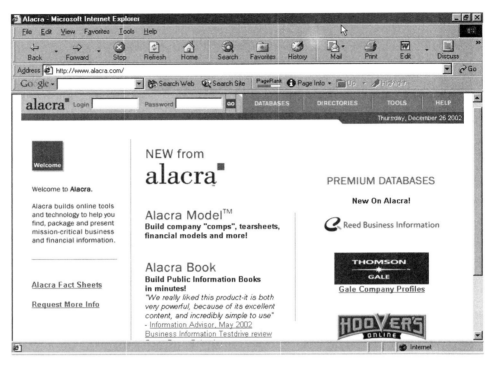

Exhibit 1.11 Alacra

Alacra charges users a set subscription fee of $150 per seat per month. A lot of free information is provided before paying for additional information from the premium content.

Factiva (see Exhibit 1.12) is a Dow Jones & Reuters Company that is used by thousands of information professionals, researchers, and business professionals throughout the world. The database provider gives access to national and international content, including the Dow Jones and Reuters newswires and *The Wall Street Journal*. Factiva contains nearly 8,000 sources, many of which cannot be accessed in other database services. Factiva has several pricing plans designed for corporate customers, such as a Standard Flat Fee based on usage of articles and an Enterprise Flat Fee for a minimum of 50 users. However, currently there is no pay-per-article plan for Factiva.com.

LexisNexis is a well-known database provider of authoritative legal information, news, public records, and business information, including tax and regulatory publications. The service has been around for a long time and is used by lawyers, business professionals, and librarians throughout the world. The company provides a variety of pricing plans, including a pay-as-you-go plan that allows you to search for free with easy-to-use search forms and pay only for the articles, cases, or documents you view.

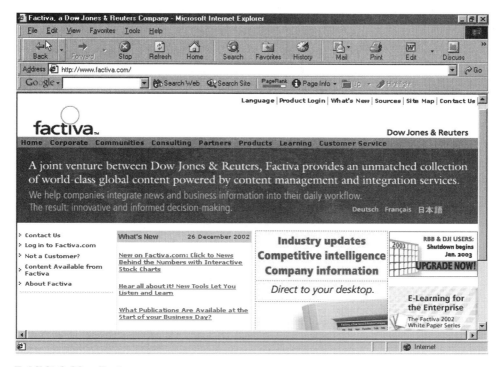

Exhibit 1.12   Factiva

CONCLUSION

We have more sophisticated ways of searching the Internet, yet we must be aware of the 'net's limitations. Where we begin our research is important, as well as how we search for the information we need. In many cases more than one search engine needs to be used, and in other cases, a fee-based service should be used instead a free one.

We can no longer expect information on the Internet to be free. Just as we don't expect the magazines and books we find in bookstores to be marked "free," we can't expect the data we find on the 'net to be free either. Data providers, companies, and trade associations are putting a lot of effort into publishing information on the 'net, and they deserve to be compensated for it. And as more and more information is available on a pay-as-you-go basis, the expectation that you will *use* the fee-based services increases as well.

CHAPTER 2

Portals and Vortals

As mentioned in Chapter 1, commercial Websites are under pressure to be profitable in order to keep their existence on the 'net. In order to do so, Websites want their sites to be "sticky," that is, they want you to stay on their site. Therefore, dozens of portals are licensing and providing data from a variety of sources in order to create brand awareness, increase site traffic and stickiness, and generate revenues. Portals are important Internet research tools because individuals or companies have gathered in one place links to the most relevant Websites for a given subject.

The original portal is Yahoo! It was designed to serve as a good starting point to the vast quantity of data on the 'net and was organized in subject categories to achieve that purpose.

Now, subject specific portals are the new wave, with the best example being Hoover's Online. If you are researching a particular company and begin your search at Hoover's Online, you will not only be presented with Hoover's analysis of the company, but also with links to additional information about the company provided by different sources, such as NewsEdge, Harris Info-Source, Dun & Bradstreet, BizMiner, and ValuEngine. An even more specific portal is Jerry Peters' ValuationResearch.com, a portal for business appraisers.

A recent article in *I/S Analyzer* says "Information, too little, too much, in too many nooks and hidden crannies with little to differentiate one source from the other, is a constant problem in today's business world."[1] Well, portals definitely help with this information challenge because portals save Internet searchers a lot of time by providing a good place to begin a research project.

---

[1] "Portals Combat Information Overload." *I/S Analyzer*, 2002.

In this chapter, we will introduce our favorite research portals. While each of these portals are mentioned in other chapters, because they are so useful as gateways to subject-specific information we want to highlight them here. In this chapter, we will discuss only those portals we consider "first and foremost."

PORTALS

About.com

www.about.com (Exhibit 2.1)

Free site

About.com is a directory of 700 specialty Websites on a single topic and grouped into 23 channels and over 700 topics written and maintained by paid "guides" from all over the world. About.com also has "more than 50,000 subjects with over 1 million links to the best resources on the Net and the fastest-growing archive of high quality original content."

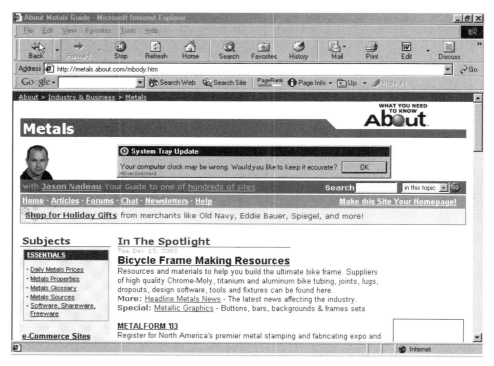

Exhibit 2.1 About.com

About.com calls itself "the Human Internet" because it uses human beings to do a job often performed by computers. About.com's paid guides develop original content for their specialty "subject" site; maintain Internet directories; email newsletters, bulletin boards, and chat rooms in their topic area; and provide links to additional sites that they consider worthwhile.

The coverage in any area is dependent on the existence and quality of a guide. As of this writing, there is no site for accounting, but a site for taxes exists at http://taxes.about.com/mbody.htm. There are a number of industry sites with excellent guides and great content. For example, the Metals Industry site at http://metals.about.com/mbody.htm and the construction industry at http://construction.about.com/mbody.htm have knowledgeable guides with relevant industry experience who have compiled useful collections of information about their respective industries (see Exhibit 2.1).

AccountingWEB

www.accountingweb.com

Free and fee-based site

AccountingWEB is an accounting portal whose "approach is to use the best of the Internet technology available today, and mix it with some good old-fashioned human insight to help direct you to the information and resources you need to stay informed."

Accounting-related news is provided for free, but subscribers gain full, unrestricted access for one year to all premium areas of the AccountingWEB portal, which includes feature articles, special discount offers, software tips, human resources trends, marketing features, technology resources, practice management ideas, communication and personal development strategies, vendor offers, and archived material.

Business.com

www.business.com

Free site

Business.com is a very popular business information portal developed by industry experts and library scientists. It contains more than 400,000 listings within 25,000 industry, product, and service subcategories. Business.com is a good place to begin research on a particular industry because it provides a wide range of links to organizations, associations, business-to-business sites, and company Websites.

There is a lot of data on this site, so it makes sense to take the time to learn how the site is organized. For example, a keyword search on the "fragrance industry" provided links to listings found in the site's Cosmetic Index, Flavor and Fragrance Suppliers, and Beauty and Personal Care Product Publications, to name a few areas. Or, one could begin the search by browsing through the site's subject categories, such as Chemicals. Be advised that Business.com has Standard and Featured Listings placement programs, which results in lots of listings for company Websites, so check the Categories and Resources of each major category to find links to noncompany sites.

Business.com is also a great place to start your research on publicly traded companies, as well as issues relating to management, financial services, advertising and marketing, and computers and software.

CorporateInformation.com

www.corporateinformation.com   (Exhibit 2.2)

Free site, registration required

Corporateinformation.com is a good starting place for international company data. The site is provided by Wright Investors' Service (WISI), a Connecticut-based investment management and financial advisory that provides "detailed analysis of over 20,000 companies," 8,000 of which are U.S.-based and 16,000 of which are international. From the home page, researchers can look for a company by country, U.S. state, company name, or ticker symbol.

Once a company name is entered, links to a variety of sources of information regarding that company are provided. For example, when privately held company Kinko's is entered, links to Business Wire company reports, Hoover's Company Capsule, Vault Report Employer Snapshot, ZD Company Finder, and Virtual job fair are shown (see Exhibit 2.2).

The Dismal Scientist

www.economy.com/dismal/

Free and fee-based site

Looking for economic data but not sure where to start your search? Well, The Dismal Scientist can help you. The portal provides daily coverage of macroeconomic trends. According to the site, "Chief Economist Mark Zandi leads a dedicated and experienced staff of researchers, economists, and online producers who create our proprietary Web content and databases."

Exhibit 2.2   CorporateInformation.com

Real-time coverage of over 100 economic indicators for 13 countries, the Euro Zone, and OECD is provided for free. It provides not only well-known indicators, such as the consumer confidence and consumer price index, but also more industry-specific indicators such as "oil and gas inventories" and "chain store sales."

As a subscriber, a researcher will find more detailed data. The subscription rate is reasonable and worth it if you need current economic information on a state, national, or international level. Business Outlooks and forecast tables are also provided.

Economy.com is also a great portal for international economic information. Current economic profiles are available for any one of eight countries, and GDP figures for 176 countries; it also provides International Business Forecasts that include a detailed forecast table that indicates both historical and forecasted real GDP growth for the world, 7 major regions, and 33 individual countries.

FindLaw

www.findlaw.com (Exhibit 2.3)

Free site

FindLaw has won numerous awards for being the best portal for legal resources on the Internet. The site provides a most comprehensive collection of legal resources on the Internet for legal professionals, businesses, students, and individuals, such as cases and codes and legal news. Findlaw provides links to primary sources (e.g., codes, cases, statutes) and secondary sources (e.g., law journals, commentary), as well as links to a number of specialty guides on topics such as cyberspace law.

Law Crawler, found at http://lawcrawler.findlaw.com, is a powerful Web search tool that reaches beyond Find Law and searches additional law-related sites such as those from law schools and governments. You can narrow your search results by limiting the search by site type and/or geographic by clicking on "More Searches and Databases" at the search box.

Exhibit 2.3 FindLaw

The "Find a Lawyer" tool, from West Legal Directory, is available at http://directory.findlaw.com. You can search for law firms and lawyers by name, state, and practice area.

The FindLaw for Business section at http://biz.findlaw.com/ is devoted to the legal issues of concern to business owners. Articles and guides are available on topics such as Small Business Legal Concerns, Business Operations, Debt and Bankruptcy, and Human Resources, to name a few (see Exhibit 2.3).

FirstGov

www.firstgov.gov   (Exhibit 2.4)

Free site

FirstGov is "the official U.S. gateway to all government information." The site is a search engine and topical directory to millions of Web pages from the federal government, local and tribal governments, and foreign nations around the world. The site organizes information by subject, rather than by agency (see Exhibit 2.4).

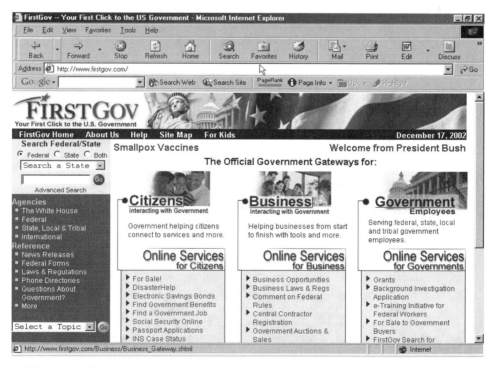

Exhibit 2.4   FirstGov

Google News

http://news.google.com   (Exhibit 2.5)

Free site

The best place to go for current news is a news portal. In the past, we may have thought of checking CNN.com or even the news posted on Yahoo! or MSN. However, there is now a better place to go for news from a variety of sources, thereby giving us news from a variety of viewpoints. Google News gathers news from over 4,000 sources worldwide.

According to the folks at Google "Google has developed an automated grouping process for Google News that pulls together related headlines and photos from thousands of sources worldwide"—enabling you to see how different news organizations are reporting the same story. You pick the item that interests you, then go directly to the site which published the account you wish to read.

The site is organized by broad subject categories, and is searchable by keyword (see Exhibit 2.5).

Exhibit 2.5   Google News

Hoover's Online

www.hoovers.com

Free and fee-based site

Hoover's is "a portal that provides more than 3 million businesspeople with timely and reliable information and research tools." Hoover's is well-known for its cleverly written business descriptions of public and private companies. Hoover's own business description states: "Hoover's wants to be the business world's homepage. The company offers proprietary business information through the Internet, wireless devices, and co-branding agreements with more than 30 other services."

Hoover's claim to fame is a database of information on more than 12 million corporations and organizations, more than 18,000 of which are profiled by Hoover's staff.

Librarian's Index to the Internet

www.lii.org

Free site

Sometimes we need to find information that is just out of the realm of what we are normally used to searching. In these cases we recommend the Librarian's Index to the Internet. Dubbed "Information You Can Trust" and sponsored by the Library of California, the site "is a searchable, annotated subject directory of more than 10,000 Internet resources selected and evaluated by librarians for their usefulness to users of public libraries."

State Search

www.nascio.org/statesearch

Free site

State Search, provided by the National Association of State Chief Information Officers, is a portal to information published by state governments. Therefore, it is a great place to start your research on a state's economic condition or find data published by a state's transportation or health department.

Publist.com

www.publist.com

Free site, registration required

> Publist.com is a portal to information about publication information for over 150,000 domestic and international print and electronic publications, including magazines, journals, ejournals, newsletters, and monographs. The site is searchable by publication title, subject, publisher, and ISSN. Searches can also be limited by country. Journal articles may be ordered through the site's online document delivery service.

Statistical Resources on the Web

www.lib.umich.edu/govdocs/stats.html   (Exhibit 2.6)

Free site

> Finding statistics on a given topic can be one of the most difficult research projects to accomplish on the Internet. Grace York, coordinator of the Documents

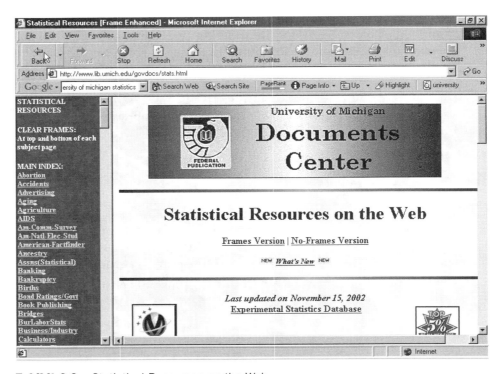

Exhibit 2.6   Statistical Resources on the Web

Center at the University of Michigan, has developed and maintained this site for years. This portal, which in our opinion serves as *the* starting point to finding statistics, is divided into 24 major categories, such as Agriculture, Health, Military, Energy, and Transportation. Like most portals, the site doesn't provide the actual data, but rather, links to sources that do (see Exhibit 2.6).

ValuationResources.com

www.valuationresources.com (Exhibit 2.7)

Free site

We agree with the site's founder and editor, Jerry Peters, CPA, ASA , ABV, and CBA. ValuationResources.com "is a valuable resource for business appraisers, CPAs, and other parties interested in business valuation. Subjects covered include valuation publications, economic data and forecasts, industry overviews, issues, and trends, industry outlooks, and forecasts, financial benchmarking, compensation surveys, public company information, transaction data, valuation discounts and premiums, legal and tax resources, online business research, company profiles and credit reports, trade association directories, appraisal associations, valuation newsletters, and valuation forums."

While ValuationResources.com is a great starting point for information on business valuation, it excels as a starting point for industry information. Organized by SIC code, links are provided to appropriate trade associations, compensation data, trade publications, and benchmarking data (see Exhibit 2.7).

Yahoo! Finance

Finance.yahoo.com (Exhibit 2.8)

Free site

We could probably write a book about all of the information provided on Yahoo! Finance. The site is a personal finance portal—one of the best. Not only does Yahoo! Finance provide current financial news, but it also provides updated industry news, analysis, and profiles. It is also a great starting point for beginning research on stocks, bonds, mutual funds, options, and the international stock market. Finally, like many business portals, Yahoo! Finance provides a wealth of information on publicly traded companies (see Exhibit 2.8).

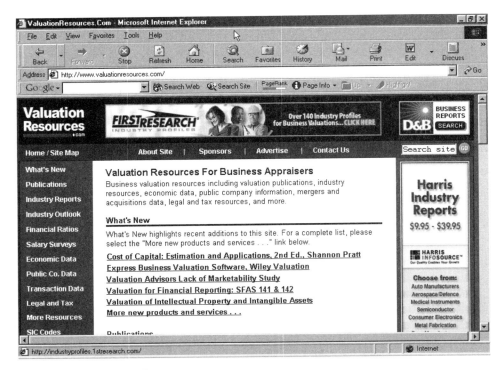

Exhibit 2.7   ValuationResources.com

VORTALS

While many of us think of the Internet as a B2C (business-to-consumer) marketplace, many Internet analysts believe the future of the 'net lies in the B2B (business-to-business) arena. As companies take advantage of the growing B2B infrastructure by participating in industry-specific vortals, information professionals are provided with another source of industry data. Vortals provide information and resources for a particular industry. In most cases vortals are developed so that companies can easily participate in B2B activity—buyers and sellers looking to do business. Hundreds of vortals exist for diverse industries from steel manufacturing to trucking to dentistry.

Vortals have taken off because they can save companies money. Instead of paying a middleperson up to 40 percent to sell its goods, a company pays the portal around 10 percent for the transaction. Vortals are also an advertising channel, giving participating companies a wider market reach.

Exhibit 2.8 Yahoo! Finance
Reproduced with permission of Yahoo! Inc. ©2003 by Yahoo! Inc. YAHOO! and the YAHOO! logo are trademarks of Yahoo! Inc.

Why should financial professionals be interested in vortals? As the author of Fuld & Company's *CI Strategies and Tools* writes, "wherever money is exchanged, so is information."[2] In addition to providing a venue for buyers and sellers, vortals can also serve as a hub for peer discussions, current industry and company news, buyers' guides, job listings, trade show data, interactive catalogs, and employee training courses—all potential sources of data.

However, not all information on a vortal is available for public viewing. Because many vortals are integrated with participating companies' back-end systems or intranets, a lot of the data is proprietary. If you are looking for a quick industry overview or forecast, it is probably more fruitful to search a database of trade journal articles or find the relevant trade association. However, for more in-depth competitive intelligence or industry analysis projects, vortals may provide some interesting data.

Here are some sample industry research projects that may require a visit to a vortal:

---

[2] Fuld & Company, Inc. *Competitor Intelligence Book.* Retrieved from www.fuld.com/tindex/ CIBook/chap01.html.

Industry analysis. While trade journal and news articles provide excellent, often summarized industry information, researchers often need to glean less-publicized trends from other sources. For example, the very fact that a particular company or group of companies is selling their products through a vortal tells us that the Internet is a distribution channel for that industry, and that barriers to entry may be decreasing because of the Internet. Observing the information posted by a company on a vortal may provide insight into that company's strategies, and the number of companies participating in a vortal may also indicate an interesting trend.

Compiling a buyer's list. When Bruce Liebman, an information professional with Houlihan Lokey Howard and Zukin is asked to compile an initial list of possible acquisition candidates, he first looks for a buyers' guide. "If I get my hands on one of those I pass it on to the client and they go to town" because they are so comprehensive, vortals are excellent places to find buyers' guides (see discussion on Industryclick.com below). When a buyers' guides aren't available, researchers can check the companies listed on vortals to make their own list. For example, I typically use the Thomas Register to find manufacturers of a particular product. Yet I found additional manufacturers that I didn't find in the Thomas Register on a couple of vortals.

Identifying products. Vortals can be a great place to find information about what products are currently being bought and sold, or new products offered within an industry. Looking at the sellers' areas of a vortal can provide information about a product line's depth, options, and intellectual property issues.

How Do I Find a Vortal for a Particular Industry?

To find a vortal for an industry I'm researching I usually start with Business.com (reviewed on page 23). I locate that industry from Business.com's home page, then select "B2B Markets." For example, Business.com provides links to 17 vortals, or B2B markets, for the restaurant industry, such as Restaurantmarket.com and FoodGalaxy.com. There appears to be a vortal for just about any industry where buying and selling goes on. ChooseEnergy.com is one place for consumers and buyers to purchase energy, and ChemEtrade.com exists for those interested in trading specialty and fine chemicals.

Another favorite Internet site for locating industry vortals is Industryclick.com. Industryclick.com, organized by industry, provides the content from 90 technical and trade magazines published by Primedia, job listings, and supplier directories. The supplier directories are gold mines, because they contain hundreds of company listings from the combined printed buyers' guides of the Primedia publications. Having access to the Primedia magazines is nothing to skim over. We're talking data-filled publications that we can search by industry and keyword for free full-text articles.

Caveat Emptor

Let the researcher beware. Keep in mind that most vortals are established to serve as a distribution channel for companies within an industry—as a way for buyers and sellers to meet and conduct business. Each vortal is unique, many are membership-based, and the amount of information available to the nonmember researcher can range from a gold mine to zilch.

While some vortals like RestaurantMarket.com provide nonmembers free registration on the site, users are asked to check boxes indicating their interest in buying or selling equipment. In all honesty I couldn't check these boxes, so I was unable to access the "Equipment Market" portion of the site. However, a keyword search on the "Industry Search" page led me to information about equipment manufacturers. I'm not sure if it is the same information that members receive.

CHAPTER 3

Websites for Conducting Economic Research

The Internet is a rich source of economic statistics. Both government and private industry delight in measuring every component of modern industrial production and in turning those measurements into statistics. The sites discussed in this chapter include both government- and private-industry-sponsored repositories for those statistics.

Many of the sites here contain the same core statistical information. However, there is significant variation when it comes to the scope of the statistics presented, the presentation and output options, and the extent of value-added features such as analysis, discussion, and interpretation. Sites profiled here range from those offering only raw statistical data to those offering the detailed analyses of some of the largest economic data services in the world.

The majority of the economic data sources in this chapter compile data on the national or regional level. If you are looking for information on local economic conditions, consider searching the articles in a local newspaper or business journal. Frequently, an area business journal will run articles about important economic developments. At year end, most do a special "looking back at events in our area in the past year" article. To find a listing of local newspapers, many of which have their own Websites, check a media list like Newslink at http://newslink.org/. This site links to hundreds of local newspapers and even includes listings of "alternative" and campus papers. The Newslink section on Business Newspapers, http://newslink.org/biznews.html, links to business journals in many U.S. cities.

Another option for local information is the Chamber of Commerce, but keep a skeptical eye out for boosterism! The information available from Chambers of Commerce varies widely and the quality of the material available is not necessarily directly related to the size of the area. The U.S.

Chamber of Commerce site at www.uschamber.com has a directory of Chambers by state with links to the local chamber Website.

If you are doing regular economic research, we urge you to "test drive" a number of the sites to find the format that works best for you. Some sites allow data to be downloaded into an Excel spreadsheet, while others present the data only in a plaintext format. Your needs will dictate which site to choose among those with similar data.

Be sure that you are using the information obtained from a site in a manner consistent with the user guidelines. Some companies restrict the commercial use of data obtained from their sites.

The sites listed in the "First and Foremost" section of this chapter are those that we have found to be reliable sources of statistics and analysis presented in easily accessible format. Sites offering all or part of the data for free will be rated higher than a site that offers similar data for a fee. "Best of the Rest" sites may focus on a niche area, be fee-only, or have limited navigation and output features.

FIRST AND FOREMOST

Bureau of Labor Statistics

http://stats.bls.gov   (Exhibit 3.1)

Free site

The Bureau of Labor Statistics (BLS) site is the major repository of employment statistics on the Internet. This site is filled with hundreds of pages of statistics and publications. As a navigation aid, the BLS has segregated some statistics into the "Most Requested Series" section, www.bls.gov/data/top20.htm. This section includes civilian labor force and unemployment statistics along with productivity measures and consumer price index data. Regional employment statistics are located at www.bls.gov/bls/regnhome.htm (see Exhibit 3.1).

What can you expect to find?

- Virtually any statistic related to employment in the United States as well as foreign labor statistics and international price indices
- Publications including *BLS Bulletins, Issues in Labor Statistics, National Compensation Survey, Occupational Outlook Handbook,* and the *Monthly Labor Review*
- Research papers, statistical papers, and economic working papers

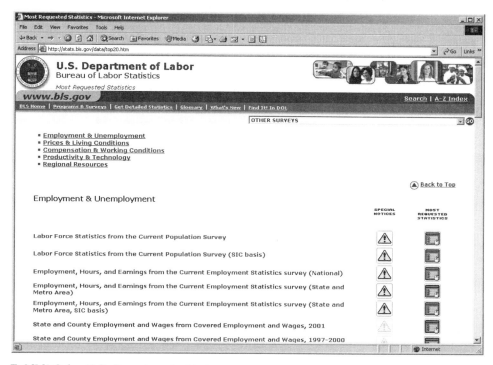

Exhibit 3.1 U.S. Department of Labor

Economomagic

www.Economagic.com

Free and fee-based site

Economagic gathers and manipulates statistics from government agencies in the United States, Canada, and Japan, as well as trade associations and private companies. The data can be displayed as plain numbers, in charts, or in spreadsheets, where the data can be analyzed and downloaded.

Most of the data on Economagic is available at no charge, but some features, such as forecasting, are only available to subscribers. Most of the data, such as employment statistics from the Bureau of Labor Statistics, interest rates from the Federal Reserve System, and building permit data from the Census Bureau, are available on other sites discussed in this chapter. The advantages of the Economagic site are having easy access to more than 100,000 data files on a single site, the capability to view them in multiple formats, and the option to download information directly into a spreadsheet.

What can you expect to find?

- Statistics in graphical or numeric formats
- Data from the Federal Reserve System, Department of Commerce, Bureau of Labor Statistics, Census Bureau, Bank of Canada, and Bank of Japan
- Interactive charts of data series

Economic Report of the President

http://w3.access.gpo.gov/eop   (Exhibit 3.2)

Free site

The Council of Economic Advisers (www.whitehouse.gov/cea/index.html) is responsible for producing the annual Economic Report of the President. This 400+ page document is published each February by the Government Printing Office.

Approximately 75 percent of the report is devoted to detailed analyses of economic conditions. The real treasure in the Economic Report of the President lies in the Appendix to the Report: the Statistical Tables Relating to Income, Employment, and Production. The tables cover all aspects of the economy from income to population to corporate profits to agriculture. Historical data are presented so trends can be plotted over the last 40 or 50 years. Most of the data are aggregated annually, and for some statistics more recent data are presented monthly or quarterly. A searchable index of the Economic Report of the President for each year since 1995 is available on the Government Printing Office site.

The Council of Economic Advisers is also responsible for submitting a monthly report of economic statistics. *Reports of the Council of Economic Advisers to Congress* dating back to April 1995 are available from the Government Printing Office (www.access.gpo.gov/congress/cong002.html). These reports are typically about 40 pages long and contain only tables and graphs. All the major economic indicators, such as gross domestic product, income measures, price indices, employment data, credit market data, and some international statistics, are included (see Exhibit 3.2).

What can you expect to find?

- More than 100 pages of statistical tables relating to income, employment, and production in the United States from the current report in Adobe .pdf format and in a spreadsheet format
- Full text of all Economic Reports of the President since 1995

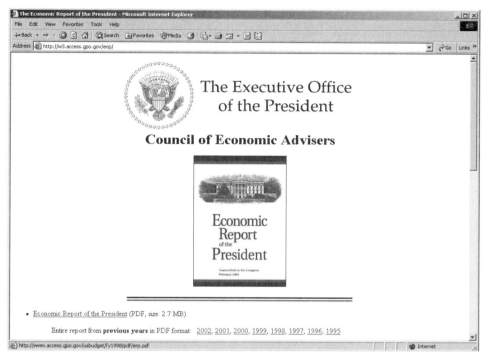

Exhibit 3.2   The Executive Office of the President, Council of Economic Research

Economy.com

www.economy.com   (Exhibit 3.3)

Free and fee-based site

Economy.com, Inc. is an independent provider of economic, financial, and industry research for businesses, governments, and professional investors. Economy.com's products cover country analysis, financial markets, industrial markets, and regional markets.

The Economy.com family of products is comprehensive in its coverage of economic data. If you are seeking an economic data item not collected by Economy.com, you don't need it. For example, the *Data Buffet* product is a database of 40 million (yes, that is 40 million) historical time series that cover all aspects of the U.S. economy. This includes broad detail on consumers, industry, demographics, financial markets, prices, flow of funds, trade, housing, and the National Income and Product Accounts. Data for county, metro, state, and U.S. geographic levels as well as zip code and city are contained in the U.S. dataset. The international dataset contains approximately four million time series and offers extensive coverage of all major industrialized countries.

All this data doesn't come cheap. A subscription for both the U.S. and international datasets runs well into five figures.

At the other end of the spectrum, from a cost perspective, is the Economy.com site, FreeLunch.com. The FreeLunch site limits access to a mere 900,000 economic and financial data series, but all the data is free. Users can search the databases and download data directly into Microsoft Excel.

FreeLunch is not considered a separate product by the company, but rather one of the four components of the Economy.com Network. The other sites are Economy.com (the parent site), the Dismal Scientist (a provider of economic analysis), and DismalMarket.com (Think it would be fun to have an insulated lunch bag emblazoned with the FreeLunch URL? This Website and $12.95 will get it for you.).

Economy.com does have 20 other products in addition to the Data Buffet. They include the County Forecast Database, the Detailed Employment & Output Forecast Database, the Housing Market Monitor, the Industry Forecast Database, the Macro/Financial (U.S.) Forecast Database, the Metro Forecast Database, the Regional Financial Review, the State Forecast Database, and more.

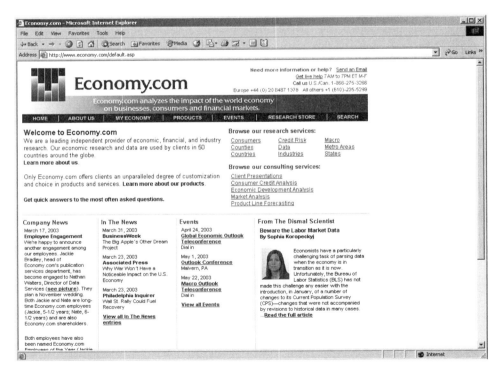

Exhibit 3.3 Economy.com

While most of the products mentioned above dance around in the five-figure price range, Economy.com offers the Précis series of data products for just $200 each. The Précis series includes an Industry report covering economic conditions of 60 U.S. industries, a Metro report on current and expected economic conditions in U.S. metropolitan areas, and a State economic report (see Exhibit 3.3).

What can you expect to find?

- The ability to purchase every economic data item known to man
- Expensive economic data (Data Buffet), moderately priced economic data (Précis), and free economic data (FreeLunch)

Federal Reserve System

www.federalreserve.gov (Board of Governors – Federal Research primary site)   (Exhibit 3.4)

www.federalreserve.gov/otherfrb.htm (Links to Federal Reserve Banks)   (Exhibit 3.5)

Free sites

The Federal Reserve System collects and disseminates a variety of monetary statistics, including interest rates, money supply, and foreign exchange rates. Through its network of 12 Federal Reserve District Banks, the Fed also provides detailed regional economic analyses.

In the Economic Research and Data section of the Federal Reserve site, you will find links to current and historical monetary statistics, including selected interest rates and commercial paper yields. The Federal Reserve also publishes a number of surveys, studies, reports, and working papers that are also available on the site.

Eight times a year, the Federal Reserve publishes a compilation of reports on economic conditions in each of the 12 Federal Reserve Bank districts. In this publication, known as the Beige Book, the Fed gathers anecdotal information on current economic conditions in each district from interviews with key business contacts, economists, market experts, and other sources. Copies of the Beige Book, starting with the October 1996 issue, are available at www.federalreserve.gov/FOMC/BeigeBook/2003/. A searchable index of the Beige Book series, beginning with the first issue in 1970, is available from the Federal Reserve Bank of Minneapolis at http://minneapolisfed.org/bb (see Exhibit 3.4).

The Federal Reserve System site includes a map of all 12 Federal Reserve Banks (FRBs), with links to each bank's Website. The amount and accessibility of information varies among FRB Websites because there is no standard format

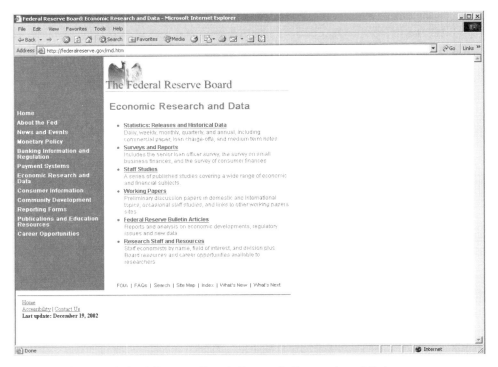

Exhibit 3.4   The Federal Reserve Board, Economic Research and Data

for the data. Typically, you will find background information on each FRB, along with information on the workings of the Fed, publications produced, economic analysis sources, and regional economic data (see Exhibit 3.5).

Each of the Federal Reserve Banks produces an economic analysis publication:

- FRB Atlanta *(EconSouth)*
- FRB Dallas *(Southwest Economy)*
- FRB San Francisco *(Western Economic Developments)*
- FRB Minneapolis *(The Region)*
- FRB Kansas City *(Regional Economic Update)*
- FRB Chicago *(Chicago Fed Letter)*
- FRB St. Louis *(Regional Economist)*
- FRB Richmond *(Region Focus)*
- FRB Cleveland *(Economic Trends)*
- FRB Philadelphia *(Business Outlook Survey)*
- FRB New York *(Regional Trends)*
- FRB Boston *(New England Economic Review)*

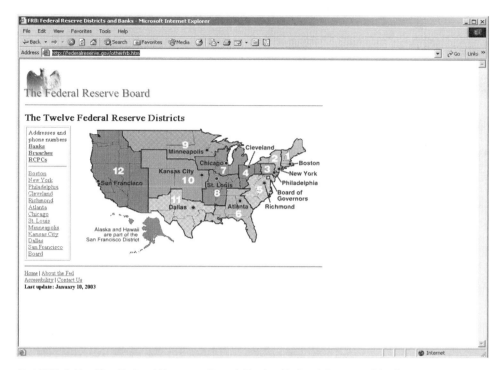

Exhibit 3.5   The Federal Reserve Board, Twelve Federal Reserve Districts

In addition to the regional economic research done by each FRB, some of the banks also collect and publish data on the national economy. The FRB St. Louis is home to the FRED (Federal Reserve Economic Data) database of economic statistics at http://research.stlouisfed.org/fred. The extensive FRED database covers hundreds of national and regional economic statistics, from housing starts to interest rates to unemployment rates. Many of the statistics date back 40 years or more.

FRB Kansas City established the Center for the Study of Rural America in 1999, and its Website is at www.kc.frb.org/RuralCenter/RuralMain.htm. The Center collects statistics on rural economic and agricultural conditions and publishes the *Main Street Economist*, a newsletter featuring commentary on the rural economy.

What can you expect to find?

• Statistics on banking, interest rates, and money supplies and articles relating to the U.S. banking system and monetary policy

• Current and historical coverage of the 36 selected interest rates published in the H.15 Interest Rate Release

- Data on consumer credit and the household debt-service burden
- Regional economic analysis and publications, including the Beige Book with more than 30 pages of economic discussion and analysis by Federal Reserve district

Fedstats

www.fedstats.gov

Free site

This site is a compendium of a wide variety of links to statistics collected by more than 100 agencies of the U.S. federal government. Fedstats is not a comprehensive collection of every statistic available from every agency, but it does pull together hundreds of statistics into one easy-to-search site.

Many of the statistical series focus on health, safety, and education, but there are also a number of economic and demographic statistics. These statistics include labor data from the Bureau of Labor Statistics, the Employment Standards Administration, and the Employment and Training Administration. Economic statistics are collected from the Census Bureau, the Department of Commerce, the Economics and Statistics Administration, the U.S. Army Corps of Engineers, and the Small Business Administration.

Unlike sites that take government issued statistics and recast them, Fedstats merely links to the data on the sites of the respective government agency.

What can you expect to find?

- Alphabetical listing of government agencies with descriptions of the statistics they provide and links to their Websites, contact information, and key statistics
- Published collections of statistics available online, including the Statistical Abstract of the United States

Global Insight

www.globalinsight.com/

Fee-based site

Global Insight, Inc. was formed by combining two of the most well-known economic data and forecasting entities in the United States, Data Resources (DRI) and WEFA (formerly known as Wharton Economic Forecasting Associates).

Global Insight provides the comprehensive economic coverage of countries, regions, and industries. Global Insight collects financial information and delivers it to clients, and also provides a broad range of consulting services.

The company has organized its products and services into four areas: Countries and Regions (country analysis, forecasts, economic data, and consulting expertise), Consulting Services, Industry Expertise (comparative industry rankings, data, and analysis), and Data and Software (global economic, financial, and industry data).

The economic and financial data available from Global Insight are impressive. There are more than 90 historical databases covering global financial markets, international economies, and U.S. national, regional, and industrial markets. Global Insight data are accessible through the information service FactSet.

When DRI and WEFA merged in September 2001, the new entity was known as DRI-WEFA. While not an exciting name, DRI-WEFA was immediately identified with its respected antecedents. It was not until October 2002 that DRI-WEFA was renamed Global Insight, trading all their brand equity for a name that is an overused cliché.

What can you expect to find?

- Detailed economic and financial data for U.S. and global markets
- Industry analysis
- Brief collection of free articles and sample reports to those who register as a guest on the site

National Bureau of Economic Research

www.nber.org (Exhibit 3.6)

Free and fee-based site

The National Bureau of Economic Research (NBER) is a private, nonprofit, nonpartisan organization bringing together research conducted by more than 500 university professors in the United States. Clearly, some of the brightest minds in the country are contributing to the development of economic theory at NBER. They are especially proud that 12 of the 31 American Nobel Prize winners in Economics have been researchers at the NBER.

Publications produced by the NBER and available from the Website include working papers, *NBER Digest*, and the *NBER Reporter*. NBER researchers initially report their findings in scientific papers aimed at other professional economists in academic institutions, business, government, and the business media around the world. Nearly 500 NBER working papers are published each year, and many subsequently appear in scholarly journals. Working papers are available for purchase. Users can access a searchable index of the working papers for free at http://papers.nber.org/papers.html.

The *NBER Digest* is a monthly publication that summarizes recent and newsworthy NBER working papers. The summaries are written by professional journalists for a nontechnical audience. The *Digest* is available on the site at www.nber.org/digest.

The *NBER Reporter* covers the workings of the NBER on a quarterly basis. Each issue includes a full list of all new working papers, along with coverage of NBER conferences and other research activities. The *Report* is available online at www.nber.org/reporter (see Exhibit 3.6).

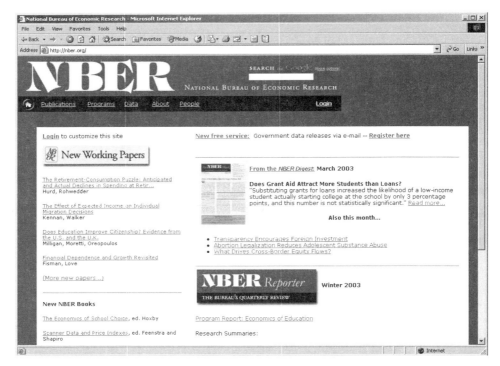

Exhibit 3.6   National Bureau of Economic Research

U.S. Census Bureau

www.census.gov (Exhibit 3.7)

Free site

The Census Bureau is not limited to collecting and disseminating information about the U.S population every 10 years. The Bureau also conducts the lesser-known, but no less important, Economic Censuses and Census of Governments. These surveys are the cornerstones of U.S. economic statistics, providing five-year benchmarks on businesses, industries, and nonfederal governments.

The Bureau also maintains a section on its Website devoted to current economic indicators. The Economics Briefing Room at www.census.gov/cgi-bin/briefroom/BriefRm has collected the major current economic indicators on a single page. Each indicator is displayed with a brief description of the indicator, a thumbnail version of a chart of the indicator over time, and comparative information.

For those looking for in-depth information not available to the general public, the Census Bureau has established the Center for Economic Studies (CES) at www.ces.census.gov/ces.php/home. The CES serves researchers and policy makers in government, academia, and business who need access to Census Bureau records for model-based statistical research.

The U.S. Census Bureau has a listing of Census Bureau Economic Programs at www.census.gov/econ/www/. This site provides links to economic statistics collections including data by industry sector, the annual survey of manufacturers, building permits, retail e-commerce sales, current industrial reports, and more.

For a listing of data extraction tools on the U.S. Census Bureau site see www.census.gov/main/www/access.html.

The U.S. Census Bureau has also developed an interactive Website called American FactFinder to disseminate data from the decennial census, at http://factfinder.census.gov. Users can browse the Bureau's data warehouse from this site to search, view, print, and download reports and tables to come up with their own customized statistics (see Exhibit 3.7).

What can you expect to find?

- Statistical data, including detailed information from the 2000 U.S. Census in the areas of population, housing, and income
- Current population estimates for U.S. cities, counties/parishes, and states
- Detailed reports from the Economic Census covering business and industry statistics
- Detailed press releases on current economic indicators

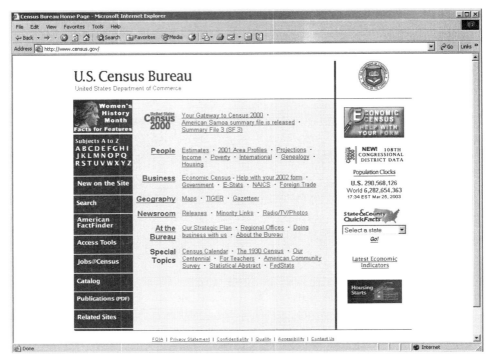

Exhibit 3.7   U.S. Census Bureau

BEST OF THE REST

Bank One Corporate Economics Group

www.bankone.com

Free site

The Bank One Corporate Economics Group (CEG) is staffed with full-time economists who gather economic data and publish a number of weekly and monthly economic and industry updates. Publications available free include the "Outlook-at-a-Glance," weekly economic forecast, and "One View" monthly economic forecast. "Outlook-at-a-Glance" is a six-page Adobe .pdf publication that covers the business cycle outlook, inflation, monetary policy, the stock and bond markets, international issues, labor, housing, transportation, and energy, as well as a brief regional round-up. "One View" is a monthly update on economic conditions in the U.S. and key regional economies.

Bureau of Economic Analysis

www.bea.doc.gov

Free site

> The Bureau of Economic Analysis (BEA) is an agency of the U.S. Department of Commerce and is one of the world's leading statistical agencies, producing some of the most closely watched economic statistics. The BEA's primary focus is on the calculation of estimates of gross domestic product (GDP) and related measures. The BEA is also the publisher of the popular *Survey of Current Business*, a monthly publication presenting analyses of current U.S. business conditions, available online at www.bea.doc.gov/bea/pubs.htm. The BEA Regional Economic Measurement Division publishes *BEA Regional Facts* (BEARFACTS), which consist of narrative discussions of personal income data for states, counties, and metropolitan statistical areas. BEARFACTS can be downloaded at www.bea.doc.gov/bea/regional/bearfacts/index.htm.

Conference Board Business Cycle Indicators

www.conference-board.org

www.tcb-indicators.org

Free and fee-based sites

> The Business Cycle Indicators database includes data on the economic indicators that have proven to be most useful in determining current conditions and in predicting the future direction of the economy. More than 250 economic data series are in the BCI dataset. They cover most major aspects and sectors of the U.S. economy, including the composite leading indices, coincident indices, and lagging indices, as well as the underlying data series or indicators used to construct these three indices.
>
> The Conference Board does more than just publish Business Cycle Indicators. The Conference Board is a respected, not-for-profit, nonpartisan organization disseminating knowledge about business, economics, and management. Their Website provides information on the Conference Board's publications such as the *Consumer Confidence Survey*, *Across the Board* magazine, and research reports on issues of corporate governance and management.

Congressional Budget Office Projections

www.cbo.gov

Free site

> The Congressional Budget Office (CBO) publishes Current Economic Projections which forecast the major macroeconomic variables extended 18 to 24

months into the future. Selected projections are extended out to 10 years. These free forecasts of GDP, unemployment, treasury bill rates, and other data items were shown in a recent survey to be just as accurate as those costing thousands published by the private sector.

Consensus Economics

www.consensuseconomics.com

Fee-based site

Consensus Economics is an economic survey organization that polls hundreds of economists monthly to obtain their views on the economic situations in more than 70 countries. The forecasts are compiled into a series of publications covering estimates for the principal macroeconomic variables (including growth, inflation, interest rates, and exchange rates).

EconBase

www.economicsdirect.com

Fee-based site

This site provides access to the Econbase database of economics and finance journals. The database covers 79 journals and provides access to more than 60,000 online papers on a variety of economic-related topics. It is fully searchable by Title, Author, Keyword, and Full Text. Full-content articles are available in .pdf format.

EconData

inforumWeb.umd.edu/Econdata.html

Free site

Gratuitous statistics—that's what you will find on EconData site at the University of Maryland. Several hundred thousand economic time series produced by a number U.S. government agencies are distributed in a variety of formats. The EconData site was developed by Inforum, a research organization at the University of Maryland, with a focus on business forecasting and government policy analysis. Don't confuse this site with Econdata.net at www.econdata.net. While the names are similar, the sites are not related. Econdata.net does not have any original content, but it is an extremely well organized collection of links to more than 500 economic sites.

Econometrics Laboratory at the University of California, Berkeley

http://elsa.berkeley.edu/eml/emldata.html

Free site

> The Econometrics Laboratory is a unit of the Institute of Business and Economic Research in the Department of Economics at the University of California, Berkeley. The Laboratory's focus is in the field of computationally intensive econometrics. The site allows access to detailed economic statistics and specialized software tools to assist in complex analysis.

Economic Information Systems

www.econ-line.com

Free and fee-based site

> Economic Information Systems is a value-added reseller of economic data. They offer the *Economic Insight Report*, which contains charts and analyses for approximately 300 business and economic indicators. State, Metro, and County Editions of the *Economic Insight Report* are also available. The cost to purchase the State and Metro Edition runs several thousand dollars for the full series with underlying data, but selected items, including summary versions of the other Insight products, can be downloaded for free.

Economic Policy Institute

http://epinet.org

Free and fee-based site

> The Economic Policy Institute (EPI) is a nonprofit, nonpartisan think tank focusing on the economic condition of low- and middle-income American families. EPI conducts original research and publishes studies, papers, and periodicals, including *The State of Working America* and the *State Resources Guide*. The EPI DataZone (http://epinet.org/datazone) presents aggregate time series data that document historical labor market trends on a state and national basis.

Economics Research Network

www.ssrn.com/ern/index.html

Free site

> A resource for academic working papers on economic research is the Economic Research Network and its sister organization, the Financial Economics

Network (www.ssrn.com/fen/index.html), part of the Social Science Research Network (SSRN). Accessible in the SSRN Electronic Library are abstracts of over 17,000 scholarly working papers and the full text of another 5,000 documents.

The Economist

www.economist.com

Free and fee-based site

The *Economist* is a weekly paper of news, ideas, opinion, and analysis published in London since 1843. Printed in six countries and published on the Internet, more than 80 percent of its circulation is outside the United Kingdom. Economist.com reproduces the editorial content of the *Economist* print edition (including extra articles about Britain that are printed only in U.K. editions). Additional content includes related articles, background information, and unique content, including the "Cities Guide," "Country Briefings," "Global Executive," and "Diversions." The parent company of the *Economist* also owns the Economist Intelligence Unit, a business information provider, and *CFO* magazine. There is a wealth of free information on the *Economist* Website, including data on global markets, country-specific research, and in-depth articles on current economic conditions.

The Financial Forecast Center

www.forecasts.org

Free and fee-based site

Applied Reasoning Inc. developed the Financial Forecast Center to publish the forecasts produced by their cutting edge neutral network software. The forecasts are extensive. The forecasted economic indicators include inflation, gross domestic product, housing starts, and oil prices. A variety of interest rates are forecasted including the prime rate, treasury rates, and LIBOR. Short-term forecasts for all these indicators and more are available for free. Access to longer-term forecasts requires a $29.95 annual subscription.

Government Information Sharing Project

http://govinfo.kerr.orst.edu

Free site

The Government Information Sharing Project is an Oregon State University project designed to bring together demographic, economic, and educational data. You will find population estimates, regional economic information, and demographics by county. This is a repackaging of information found elsewhere on the Internet, but it is nicely organized and easy to navigate.

Haver Analytics

www.haver.com

Fee-based site

Haver Analytics offers detailed economic and financial information to subscribers only. The site provides access to more than 100 databases of economic and financial data covering housing, construction, industrial production, interest rates, money supply, federal receipts and outlays, wholesale and retail trade, manufacturers' shipments, inventories and orders, employment, productivity, population, international trade, and business cycle indicators. Haver databases also contain international data, industry information, and regional U.S. data.

IDEAS

http://ideas.repec.org/

Free site

IDEAS is a bibliographic database of economic resources. The database contains more than 180,000 research items that can be browsed or searched, and more than 90,000 full text records are available for downloading. The Department of Economics of the University of Connecticut maintains the IDEAS site, which uses the "Research Papers in Economics" (RePEc) database. RePEc is an internal name for a group working on the provision of electronic working papers. This site is part of a large volunteer effort to enhance the free dissemination of research in economics. The EconPapers site at http://econpapers.hhs.se/ also provides access to the RePEc database.

Resources for Economists on the Internet

http://rfe.org

Free site

This guide is sponsored by the American Economic Association and edited by Professor Bill Goffe of the State University of New York. It lists more than 1,000 resources available on the Internet of interest to academic and practicing economists, and those interested in economics.

STAT-USA

www.stat-usa.gov

Fee-based site

Sponsored by the U.S. Department of Commerce, STAT-USA is a fee-based service giving users access to U.S. business, economic, and trade information from the federal government. The site contains current and historical economic and financial data for the domestic economy and international market research, trade opportunities, and country analysis from the National Trade Data Bank.

Wachovia

http://wachovia.com/corp_inst/page/0,,13_54,00.html

Free site

Wachovia acquired the Economics Group of First Union in a 2001 merger. The new Wachovia economics department publishes a variety of publications including *Economic Indicator Analysis* (in-depth analysis on economic indicators), *Weekly Economic Commentary* (insight into current events that affect the economy and financial markets), *Monthly Economic Forecast* (a commentary and forecast table on U.S. and international economic conditions with projections for financial markets), *Country Reports* (timely commentary on issues affecting individual countries), and *Regional Economics* (economic analyses with a regional focus, such as gross state product, state outlook projections, and state employment data).

Yardeni's Economics Network

www.yardeni.com

Free site

Dr. Ed Yardeni is the Chief Investment Strategist, and a managing director of Prudential Securities Incorporated. His Website is built around the publications and topical studies that he writes for Prudential and includes *Investment Strategy*, his weekly market analysis publication. There are also other Prudential analytical research papers that can be downloaded from the site, including topical studies and strategy alerts. In addition to this original research, Dr. Yardeni has assembled an extensive set of links to economic indicators and has created an impressive collection of charts.

Industry Sites

Financial professionals are frequently faced with the need to understand industry issues. Whether in our own industries (accountants found it impossible to escape news of change in their profession in 2002 and 2003) or the industries of our clients, understanding the dynamics of an industry is valuable to many financial professionals. Business appraisers have no choice but to delve into the industries in which their clients operate. Revenue Ruling 59-60 lays out the factors necessary to consider when performing a business valuation for estate or gift tax purposes. It instructs the appraiser to consider "the economic outlook in general and the condition and outlook of the specific industry in particular."

A complete industry analysis usually includes a review of an industry's recent performance, its current status, and the outlook for the future. There are many sources of industry information, including business and trade periodicals, consulting firms, trade associations, private research firms, investment firms, and government agencies. A thorough industry analysis will draw from a variety of these sources.

Given that all these sources of industry data are available on the Internet, it is necessary to have a plan of approach. An effective plan will work from the general to the specific and will include a number of sources. Start with sites that provide information on a variety of industries, such as First Research Industry Reports. Identify trade associations and check to see if they collect and distribute industry information. If there are publicly traded companies in the industry, then check for reports from investment analysts available through sources like Multex. Search for articles in trade periodicals and the general business press. Check with market research firms about industry reports. The sites listed here will cover all these areas. Because there are hundreds of industries, it is beyond the scope of this chapter to list them all. We will focus on sites that provide access to information on multiple industries and selected major industry sites.

Sometimes, while researching an industry, you may encounter an industry portal. These are often maintained by a trade association or industry consulting firm and contain links to firms and resources in a specific industry. An example is the HVAC portal for the Heating, Ventilation, and Air Conditioning industry at www.hvacportal.com. This portal's purpose is to "Help HVAC professionals find the best of the Internet." The portal has links to publications, industry organizations, educational resources, career information, bidding opportunities, and codes and standards. Another example is the Tobacco Industry Portal which is hosted by the Tobacco Merchants Association. This portal has news, statistics, market share, tobacco leaf production data, and more.

To locate trade publications, try a periodical directory such as Media Finder (www.mediafinder.com). Media Finder's online search function allows users to see listings of publications in over 260 categories. For example, searching the accounting category will provide the name and a brief description of 199 accounting industry publications. Also check the Websites of trade magazine publishers such as Reed Business Information (formerly Cahners Business Information). On the Reed Business Information Website (www .reedbusiness.com), you can find descriptions of the more than 135 business-to-business publications they produce along with links to the industry Websites they design.

Whether you are a financial professional in solo practice, with a small group, or a very large firm, you will benefit from making a librarian your partner in industry research. Large firms typically have in-house libraries staffed by special librarians. If you are fortunate enough to be in this position, your first step in industry research will be to visit your in-house library and learn about the resources available. Chances are that your firm will have subscriptions to information services such as LexisNexis, Proquest, or Dialog that will give you access to industry information.

If you are solo or in small practice, the best Website for you may be the one for your local library. Your local public or university library will almost certainly offer access to some business databases. Check with your local public library to see if you can access online databases through the library Website using your library card number for access. As an example, check the list of 44 databases that patrons of the St. Paul Public Library can access online at the St. Paul Library Website: www.stpaul.lib.mn.us/databases/alphabet.htm. You need only a valid library card to access these databases for free. A list of links to local public libraries is available at http://sunsite.berkeley.edu/Libweb/Public_main.html.

The sites listed in the "First and Foremost" section of this chapter are those that we have found to be reliable sources of industry information. They offer valuable content in a well-designed and maintained site. Sites are presented in alphabetical order. Sites offering all or part of the data for free are considered more desirable than sites offering similar data for a fee. "Best of the Rest" sites may focus on a niche area, be fee-only, have limited navigation and output features, or be limited in some other way.

FIRST AND FOREMOST

Dialog Open Access

http://openaccess.dialog.com/business/

Fee-based site

Dialog, created in 1972, was the world's first online information retrieval system and has long been the primary tool of professional researchers. Since 1972, Dialog has amassed a collection of 900 databases covering a vast array of topics: intellectual property, government regulations, social sciences, food and agriculture, news and media, business and finance, reference, energy and environment, chemicals, pharmaceuticals, science and technology, and medicine.

However, it was not until 1999 that Dialog became a practical option for end users. Prior to that, mastering Dialog's complicated search syntax required special training and the subscription cost was prohibitive for most low-volume searchers. In 1999, Dialog (now owned by the near-monopoly Thomson Corporation) launched Dialog Open Access. An alternative to subscription service, Open Access has no passwords, monthly fees, or minimum charges. Users have access to a large portion of the Dialog service using a simple form-based interface, paying by credit card only for documents downloaded. Databases in the following categories are available through Open Access: business and news, chemistry, engineering, environment, government, intellectual property, medicine, and pharmaceuticals.

One of the excellent databases accessible through Open Access is ABI/INFORM. This database has substantive abstracts and full-text articles from more than 1,100 leading business and management publications providing in-depth coverage of business conditions and trends, management, marketing, advertising, accounting, finance, company, trade and industry news, corporate strategies, brand and product information, business technology, and more.

Other databases accessible through Open Access include the Gale Group Trade and Industry Database, a multi-industry database covering international company, industry, product, and market information and Gale PROMT a database of abstracts and full-text records from trade and business journals, local newspapers, regional business publications, research studies, investment analysts' reports, corporate news releases, and corporate annual reports.

What can you expect to find?

• Dozens of business and financial databases offering the full text of articles from business and financial journals, as well as financial data

ECNext Knowledge Center

www.ecnext.com/commercial/knowledgecenter.shtml

Fee-based site

The International Market Research Mall (IMR), a collection of reports from several market research providers, has morphed into the ECNext Knowledge Center. In addition to the database of IMR reports, the ECNext Knowledge Center also sells commercial newsletters, country reports, company profiles and financial reports, and trade journals.

The ECNext Knowledge Center offers users market intelligence from over 500 leading publishers and over 250,000 sources, covering every major industry and country. The products fall into four general groups: Market Research Reports, Trade Newsletters, Company Profiles, and Country Reports.

The market research reports are the core of the site and include both general industry overviews and niche market analyses. The reports are generally large documents, containing very detailed information regarding the history, current situation, and future of products, services, countries, and industries. Most reports can be purchased by the chapter or by the full document. ECNext has agreements with a number of respected market research vendors, including MarkIntel and Investext.

The trade newsletters are topical or industry-focused newsletters. Articles are often time-sensitive and provide information about new advances, technology, or current events on the particular topic or industry. The ECNext Newsletter collection also includes articles from Gale Group's Newsletter *ASAP*.

The ECNext company profiles provide an overview of a particular company, with heavy focus on the most recent financial statements and current events. The profiles, some of which are provided by Investext, are generally 1 to 4 pages in length.

The Country reports focus on the business environment in a particular country, including government, current events, and other issues that affect business conditions within the country or region.

What can you expect to find?

- Thousands of detailed, but expensive, market research reports
- Market research reports for individual purchase—no subscription necessary
- Access to specialized industry newsletters

First Research Industry Profiles

www.1stresearch.com   (Exhibit 4.1)

Fee-based site

First Research publishes summary industry analyses on a wide variety of industries. The reports focus on understanding industry dynamics relative to suppliers, customers, and competitors. The reports are updated quarterly and are, on average, about 15 pages long. The reports cover industry trends, challenges, and opportunities, and provide links to industry-related sites.

The reports are organized under the headings of Quarterly Industry Update, Industry Overview, Call Preparation Questions, Credit and Business Risk Issues, Business Trends, Industry Opportunities, News & Media Information, Financial Information, Web Site Links, and a Glossary of Acronyms.

The quality of the reports provided is excellent. In charge of industry analysis for First Research is Ingo Winzer, a noted analyst whose views on industry and real estate have been quoted by CNBC, *Barron's, The Wall Street Journal,* and in other media. Mr. Winzer, an MIT graduate, has conducted financial investment and strategic corporate research for more than 20 years.

These reports are downloadable from the site to subscribers who pay an annual fee. Subscribers can then download an unlimited number of reports making the cost per report very low for heavy users. Individual reports are available for purchase from AccountingWeb at www.accountingweb.com/firstres/ (see Exhibit 4.1).

What can you expect to find?

- Detailed downloadable research reports on more than 140 industries

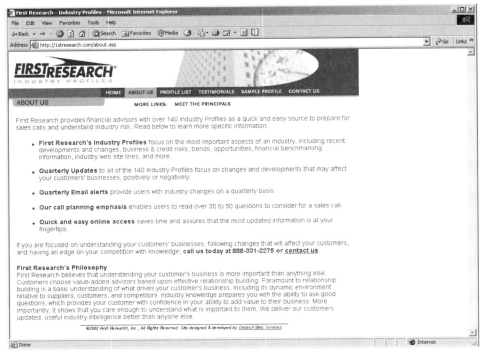

Exhibit 4.1   First Research

Integra Industry Reports

www.integrainfo.com/products/industrydata/
frprodindata.htm   (Exhibit 4.2)

Fee-based site

Integra collects U.S. government data on private companies and industries primarily from the Internal Revenue Service and the Department of Labor, and combines it with proprietary data. From this combined database they offer benchmarking data for private companies. Integra primary industry reports are: the Three-Year Industry Report, the Five-Year Industry Report, and the Industry Growth Outlook Report. The Three-Year and Five-Year reports contain the following items for each selected industry:

- Historical financial statement data
- Graphs of key operating trends
- Selected financial ratios and industry growth rates

The Five-Year Industry Report has an expanded ratio section and cash flow information. The Industry Growth Report is a one-page graph of historical and forecasted industry growth compared to the growth of the entire U.S. economy. Interga also sells a five-page Industry Narrative Report. The Industry Narrative Report, a custom report based upon the industry sector specified, can be ordered online to be mailed to the customer (see Exhibit 4.2).

What can you expect to find?

- Benchmarking data by industry

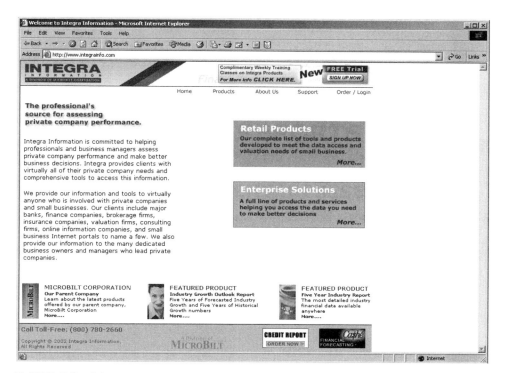

Exhibit 4.2 Integra

MarketResearch.com

www.marketresearch.com   (Exhibit 4.3)

Fee-based site

MarketResearch.com (formerly Kalorama Information) is a distributor for hundreds of other market research report publishers, including Frost & Sullivan, Freedonia, Euromonitor, and BCC, as well as its own products, which include Packaged Facts, FIND/SVP, Specialists in Business Information (SBI), Kalorama Information, and KidTrends. MarketResearch.com has agreements with more than 350 publishers to provide access to 40,000 research publications. Reports can be ordered online, and most can be downloaded in .pdf format; however, some are only available in printed form and will be shipped from the publisher.

Searching the extensive database is free and users can view an abstract of the report and see the table of contents before deciding to purchase the report (see Exhibit 4.3).

The reports available on MarketResearch.com range from inexpensive, short Harris reports for less than $20.00 to the BCC reports that run hundreds of pages and cost $4,000 or more. For example, a search on the retail grocery industry yielded hundreds of reports including:

- "Supermarkets & Grocery Stores in the US" by IBISWorld dated 12/10/2002—41 Pages—$495.00
- "US Grocery Retailing Report 2002" by Snapshots International Ltd. dated 8/31/2002—11 Pages—$225.00
- "Annual Industry Reviews: 2003 Special Report" by Supermarket Strategic Alert dated 1/1/2003—24 Pages—$75.00
- "Supermarket Trends & Predictions: 2003 Special Report" by Supermarket Strategic Alert dated 1/1/2003—17 Pages—$50.00

What can you expect to find?

- Market research reports
- Industry analyses, newsletters, and global market reports

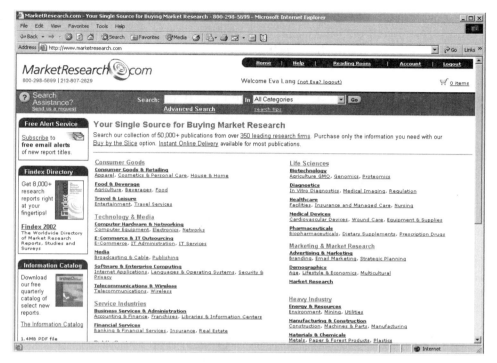

Exhibit 4.3   MarketResearch.com
Copyright © 2002, All Rights Reserved, MarketResearch.com, Inc.

Thomson Research

http://research.thomsonib.com

Fee-based site

Thomson Financial has folded the Investext Research Bank site into a new Web-based product called Thomson Research. Thomson Research combines Thomson Financial's two primary research products: Research Bank Web and Global Access. This new product combines the former Research Bank databases (Investext, MarkIntel, and Industry Insider) with I/B/E/S, Disclosure, and other financial databases.

The Investext database contains analysts' reports from the major brokerage houses like Morgan Stanley and Merrill Lynch. The analysts' reports cover publicly traded companies and the industries in which they operate. Reports are in Adobe Portable Document Format (PDF), which retains original page layout, including tables and charts.

MarkIntel market research reports cover industry concerns such as market size, consumer trends, and competition. MarkIntel reports typically focus on an industry or product and include profiles of key players, market share and demographic trends, forecasts and analyses, and competitive information.

The Industry Insider database is a compilation of information from trade associations. Trade associations compile data on industry growth trends, consumer spending habits, sales figures, manufacturing capacity, product developments, market share rankings, and demographics. The Industry Insider trade association research collection is the only electronic collection of trade association intelligence available. Chief economists at over 200 trade associations worldwide provide valuable analysis, trends, forecasts, statistics, and economic indicators.

The former Global Access databases are primarily financial and include I/B/E/S, (analyst earnings forecasts, historical estimates, and recommendations) and Disclosure (financial information on 12,000 domestic public companies), and Worldscope (international financial information on more than 20,000 active companies).

What can you expect to find?

- Thousands of analysts' reports from major brokerage houses
- Original research from trade associations—many reports not otherwise accessible to nonmembers
- Market research reports on hundreds of industry groups and subgroups
- Financial information on thousands of domestic and international companies

Trade Association Directories

http://info.asaenet.org/gateway/OnlineAssocSlist.html

www.ipl.org/ref/AON

www.marketingsource.com/associations   (Exhibit 4.4)

Free and fee-based sites

The Website of the American Society of Association Executives (ASAE) has complied a free searchable index of more than 6,500 trade associations.

This Association Gateway search page (http://info.asaenet.org/gateway/OnlineAssocSlist.html) allows you to search for a trade association by name, category, or geographic locations.

Associations on the Net, at www.ipl.org/ref/AON, a service of the Internet Public Library, lists only what it considers to be "prominent organizations and associations," so its database of association listings is much smaller that ASAE's.

At the Marketing Source site (www.marketingsource.com/associations) you can purchase an online subscription to their *Directory of Associations* covering 35,000 associations and professional societies, including business and trade associations, 501c nonprofit organizations, and other charity and community associations. You can also search the database for free, but the free interface displays only the Name, City, State, and the Web URL of an association. Paid subscribers can view and download the following information for each entry: Association Name, Key Contact's Name and Title, Street Address, Number of Members, City, State, Zip Code, Conventions/Meeting Information, Phone, Fax, Brief Description of Services, email Address, and Web URL.

The Associations Database at the Training Forum (www.trainingforum .com/assoc.html) includes records for both Chambers of Commerce and trade associations. While the database is large, with more than 10,000 records, only name, address, and phone numbers are provided. There is no link to the association's Website.

The Associations Unlimited database is the most comprehensive. It combines data from the entire *Encyclopedia of Associations* published by the Gale Group with additional IRS information on nonprofit organizations, for a total of nearly 457,000 organizations. Information on this online database is available at www.gale.com/pdf/facts/au.pdf. The database is sold primarily to libraries who usually provide access free to patrons (see Exhibit 4.4).

What can you expect to find?

• Searchable index to trade associations display a minimum of the associations name and location

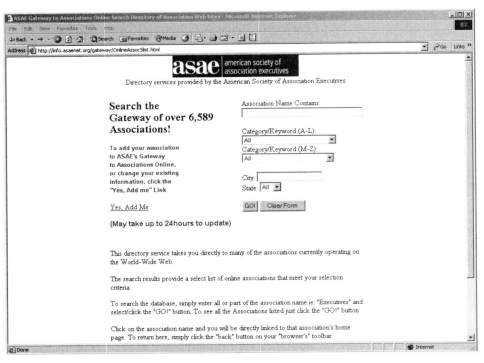

Exhibit 4.4   American Society of Association Executives
Copyright 2002, American Society of Association Executives.

BEST OF THE REST

Bizminer

www.bizminer.com

Free and fee-based site

Bizminer produces statistical Marketing Research profiles on more than 15,000 business segments at national and local levels. Metro Marketing Research Profiles analyze industries in each of 250 U.S. metropolitan areas. Bizminer reports cover data such as the number of businesses in an area and the average sales per employee. The reports are inexpensive, and free samples are available on the site. A selection of Bizminer reports is available for free from *Business Week* Online at www.businessweek.com/smallbiz/bizminer/bizminer.htm.

Economy.com Industry Reports

www.economy.com

Fee-based site

The Economy.com site is primarily known as a provider of economics statistics and analysis, and is discussed in the "First and Foremost" section of Chapter 3. On the Economy.com home page, a click on the Industry link will take users to a list of the Précis Industry reports available for purchase on this site. Précis Industry covers conditions in 60 U.S. industries. Each report includes an analysis of trends, risk factors, and forecasts. All reports include a U.S. Macro forecast summary and outlook, forecast assumptions, general industry outlook, industry indicators for comparisons across industries, and a user's guide. Each report is four pages and is updated three times yearly.

Financial Times Surveys

http://surveys.ft.com

Free site

The *Financial Times* publishes approximately 240 surveys annually, which appear with copies of the newspaper most days of the week. Topics include financial markets, global industries, business management, and developed and emerging countries.

Frost & Sullivan Research Publications

www.frost.com

www.markets.frost.com

Fee-based sites

Frost & Sullivan is a well-respected market research firm that produces meticulously detailed, carefully researched, very expensive reports on thousands of industry topics. A selection of Frost & Sullivan reports can be ordered from the MarketResearch.com site mentioned earlier in this chapter as well as from this site.

The Markets.frost.com site is a listing of the industry portals produced by Frost & Sullivan. These portals offer free access to free content and market intelligence for a number of industries. For example, the Food Industry portal at www.food.frost.com/ has free Market Insight reports and allows users to sign up for free newsletters on food industry topics.

Harris InfoSource

www.harrisinfo.com

Fee-based site

Harris InfoSource industry reports provide profiles of 95 manufacturing industries that include summary statistics for each industry as a whole and a breakdown of each of the SIC and NAICS codes that compose the industry. Each report covers trends in firm count and employment, the industry's regional presence, a list of major companies, product listings, and more. The reports are inexpensive, and before you buy, you can view a complete list of industry sectors, sample report pages, and sample full profile details.

Hoover's Industry Snapshots

www.hoovers.com/industry/archive/0,2048,169,00.html

Free site

Hoovers Online, the respected provider of company information, has a collection of 45 industry spotlight profiles tucked away in its archive. The snapshots are well-written and packed with graphics, photos, and charts. Each has a glossary of jargon, and there are links from the snapshots directly to financial information on the companies discussed.

IBIS World

www.ibisworld.com

Fee-based site

IBIS World Industry Reports provides access to information on more than 250 industries. The reports include key statistics, market size, industry segmentation, and a five-year outlook. The reports may be 30 or 40 pages long and include a review of other major players in the industry as part of the industry overview.

IRS Market Segment Specialization Program (MSSP)

www.irs.gov

Free site

The IRS has developed a series of Audit Techniques Guides to alert agents to specific industry practices and issues. These guides contain examination techniques and examine common and unique industry issues, business practices, industry terminology, and other information to assist examiners. The Audit Guides are lengthy, many exceeding 100 pages.

ITA Basic Industries

www.ita.doc.gov/td/bi

Free site

The International Trade Administration, a part of the U.S. Department of Commerce, runs the Basic Industries program. A broad range of U.S. industries are characterized as basic industries, including motor vehicles, automotive parts and accessories, machine tools, chemicals and pharmaceuticals, construction and mining equipment, forest products, metals and materials, energy, and biotechnology. The mission of the Basic Industries program is to enhance international commercial opportunities for these sectors, thereby creating new jobs in America.

The ITA Basic Industries Website has a collection of industry research resources for each of these basic industry sectors. These resources cover general industry statistics, market research, trade agreements, export data, and trade statistics.

Manufacturing Marketplace

www.manufacturing.net

Free site

Manufacturing.net provides information and services for manufacturing professionals, including a product supplier database, industry-specific news and research, economic reports, editorial content from well-known trade publications, marketplaces for books, and industry standards.

Manufacting.net is a product of Reed Business Information. Reed is a well-known publisher of trade magazines and pulls on content from its magazines such as *Industrial Distribution, Industrial Maintenance & Plant Operation, Logistics Management & Distribution Report, Manufacturing Systems, Material Handling Product News, Medical Design Technology, Modern Materials Handling, Plant Engineering*, and *Warehousing Management* for this portal.

MindBranch

www.mindbranch.com

Fee-based site

MindBranch distributes research from over 300 publishers, research firms, and analysts in 130 industry segments. Products include market research reports, newsletters, directories, subscriptions, and custom research. MindBranch has more than 30,000 reports, company profiles, directories, databases, and newsletters in its database and available on its Website. Searching is free and once a report is identified, users can view a free abstract and choose between ordering a print copy or downloading the report in .pdf format.

MoBDN Industry-at-a-Glance Reports

www.missouribusiness.net/iag/index.asp

Free site

These reports published by the Missouri Business Development Network focus on industries where small so-called "mom-and-pop" businesses account for much of the activity. The reports summarize trends, issues, opportunities, and challenges for 21 industries. While these reports were prepared with Missouri businesses in mind, many issues apply to businesses in other states as well. Reports are downloadable in .pdf format and average about 30 pages in length.

Plunkett Research Online

www.plunkettresearch.com

Fee-based site

Plunkett Research, Ltd., is a consulting firm providing business and industry information to the corporate, library, academic, and government markets. Plunkett industry reports and almanacs cover market analysis, industry information, business statistics, financial histories, technology trends, corporate profiles, and executive contacts.

Some of the industries covered by Plunkett Research are not covered widely elsewhere, making them a good place to check for that "orphan" industry. Subscribers can purchase unlimited online access to the entire Plunkett database or just download individual products or even a section of a product. For example, users can download *Plunkett's Retail Industry Almanac* for $230 or get the 40-page *Plunkett's Retail Industry Trends and Statistics Summary* for $39.95.

U.S. Census Bureau: Industry Resources

www.census.gov/cir/www/

Free site

The Current Industrial Report program at the U.S. Census Bureau provides monthly, quarterly, and annual measures of industrial activity. These reports assess manufacturing activity in important commodity areas such as textiles and apparel, chemicals, primary metals, computer and electronic components, industrial equipment, aerospace equipment, and consumer goods. Each report includes a summary of findings, tables that present statistics on manufacturing and consumption, values, and comparisons with other SIC codes. For each product, Current Industrial Reports typically cite the value and quantity of shipments, together with imports and exports of the product.

ValuationResources Industry Resources Report

http://valuationresources.com/IndustryReport.htm

Free site

The ValuationResources site provides a selection of Industry Resources Reports by SIC code. Each Industry Resources Report is a page of links directing the user to other sites with industry information. The Report for SIC 5812 Restaurants has links to sites, including the National Restaurant Association, First Research Industry Reports, and Economy.com Industry reports. There are also links to compensation data and to financial benchmarking data. Some links, such as the one to Financial Studies of the Small Business, take the user to an order form for a publication.

WetFeet.com

www.wetfeet.com

Free site

Wetfeet, Inc. is a human resources consulting and recruitment firm. The Wet-Feet.com site provides information on companies, careers, and industries for job seekers. The site includes a collection of overviews which cover industry trends and structure along with an outlook for job prospects. The reports are updated frequently. The accounting industry overview section on Big Five firms was updated to Big Four firms before some Andersen partners had cleaned out their desks.

CHAPTER 5

Market Data

This chapter contains sources of data for betas, stock, bond, and mutual fund prices, interest rates, and earnings estimates. The chapter is organized slightly differently than the other chapters. Websites are arranged by subject, then by site. All of the sites in this chapter are considered "First and Foremost."

BETAS

It is possible to find both current and historical betas on the Internet, however historical betas are available only on the fee-based sites.

Alacra

www.alacra.com   (Exhibit 5.1)

Fee-based site

The Alacra online database service provides two sources of historical and current betas, and a subscription to the Alacra service is necessary in order to access the databases. Each database provides beta reports that contain a range of dates defined by the user and can be downloaded into spreadsheet format.

- Barra
  - The *Beta Books for Companies* database contains several risk models. Barra U.S. Equity Small Cap Model provides key risk analysis statistics on over 11,000 publicly traded U.S. companies in 54 industries, and contains records dating back to May 1981. A report covering a range of dates runs $120 per company (See Exhibit 5.1).

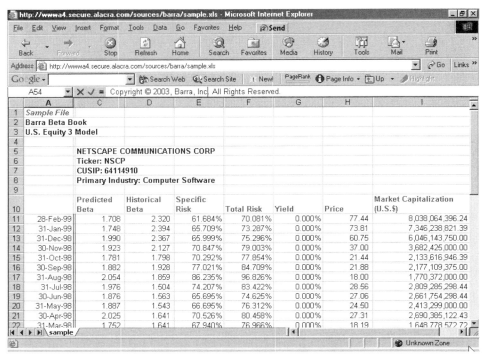

Exhibit 5.1   Alacra/Barra
Barra, Inc., copyright 2003.

- *Beta Books for Industries* database. The Barra U.S. Equity Model provides key risk analysis statistics on 54 industries grouped into 13 sectors, and researchers may select multiple sectors and industries. Beta calculations are based on the Standard & Poor 500 index. Reports for each industry are $120.00 for a single beta and $240.00 for a range of betas.

- *Media General Financial Services* (MGFS) provides financial statistics on over 9,000 publicly traded companies that can be searched either by name or by a variety of performance criteria. The "price history report" provides 60 months (or less) of betas, and runs $2.00 per company.

Multex Investor

www.multexinvestor.com

Free site

After inputting a ticker symbol, the "Snapshot Quote" provides a current beta.

Wall Street Research Net

www.wsrn.com

Free site

After inputting a ticker symbol, the "Company Description" provides a current beta.

BONDS AND INTEREST RATES

Bondtrac

www.bondtrac.com

Fee-based site

Geared towards the investor, Bondtrac subscribers have access to:

- Historical data and trade history for all bond types
- Live yield summary updates for treasury, corporate, agency, and municipal bonds, with corresponding yield charts and histograms
- Extensive portfolio analysis tools

Federal Reserve Board

www.federalreserve.gov/releases/h15/data.htm

Free site

The Federal Reserve Statistical Release "Selected Interest Rates" contains daily interest rates for selected U.S. government securities and private money market and capital market instruments. Published weekly, it provides historical detail back to 1962.

Yahoo Bond Center

bonds.yahoo.com

Free site

This site provides:

- The latest composite bond rates for U.S. Treasury, municipal, and corporate bonds
- Current 10-year Treasury yield

- A Bond Screener that allows users to screen by bond type, years to maturity, amount to invest, and safety level
- "Market Summary," providing commentary and analysis about the bond market
- Calculators

T-Bills, Notes & Bonds Online

www.publicdebt.treas.gov/sec/sec.htm (Exhibit 5.2)

Free site

This data-filled government site provides:

- The "Treasury Bill, Note, and Bond Auction History" section, which provides data for the bills, notes, and bonds auctioned by the federal government since 1980. Users can search by auction date, maturity date, CUSIP, and issue date, and customize the output (see Exhibit 5.2).
- Recent treasury note and bond auction results.

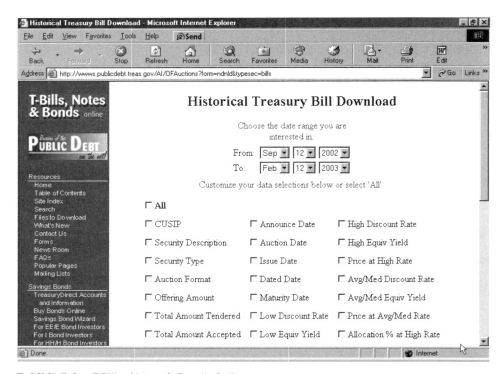

Exhibit 5.2 T-Bills, Notes & Bonds Online

EARNINGS ESTIMATES

Obtaining current earnings estimates for a particular company is easy on the Internet. While all of the major investment portals provide estimates from either First Call, I/B/E/S, or Zack's, some of the best sources are:

- Hoover's (www.hoovers.com) provides current earnings estimates from First Call.
- Wall Street Research Net (www.wsrn.com) provides current earnings estimates from Zacks.
- CBS Marketwatch provides current earnings estimates from I/B/E/S.

Alacra

www.alacra.com

Fee-based site

The Thomson Financial I/B/E/S database provides historical earnings estimates: $50.00 for up to 2 years of estimates, $75.00 for up to 5 years, $100.00 for up to 10 years, and $150.00 for more than 10 years.

OPEN- AND CLOSED-END MUTUAL FUNDS

Current pricing data for closed-end or open-end funds is available for free on the Internet, and it is nice for comparison purposes that two free sites, CBS Marketwatch and Yahoo! Finance, obtain their data from two different sources: Lipper and Morningstar, respectively.

CBS Marketwatch

cbs.marketwatch.com

Free site

CBS Marketwatch licenses their mutual fund data from Lipper, and provides the following from their Website:

- "Fund Profile," which contains a current snapshot of the fund, including a description, NAV chart, holdings, expenses, and links to any related news items.
- With the "Fund Finder," researchers can locate funds by type and fund period.

- A fund comparison tool that allows users to compare several tickers at once by returns, risk, fees, and holdings.
- Lists of top funds.
- Prospectuses.

Morningstar

www.morningstar.com

Free and fee-based site

The Morningstar site provides the following:

- The Morningstar "Quicktake" report contains detailed data about each fund, including performance, Morningstar rating, portfolio analysis, news alerts and opinions, and data regarding fees and management.
- "Quicktake" reports on both open- and closed-end funds contain five years' of historical data.
- Under "Find a Mutual Fund," researchers can obtain a detailed chart of the current top 20 or top 100 closed-end mutual funds. This chart can be sorted by features such as Premiums/Discounts or NAV Return. Each fund listed has a link to more information about that particular fund.
- Morningstar's premium service provides analysts reports on over 2,000 funds, portfolio optimization tools, and an email alert service. The premium services runs $11.95 a month or $109 a year.

Yahoo! Finance Mutual Funds Center

biz.yahoo.com/funds

Free site

With Morningstar data, this Yahoo! Site provides:

- A default current price chart
- A "Profile" that contains background information on the fund and its operations, performance data, and fees and expenses
- A fund screener allows you to screen for mutual funds by category, fund family, performance rank, manager tenure, Morningstar risk and return ratings, performance returns, fees, and holdings.
- Prospectuses for each fund

- Fund calculators
- Lists of top fund performers

STOCK QUOTES

All of the investment portals such as Yahoo! Finance provide stock quotes that are delayed 20 minutes for companies listed on AMEX and the NYSE, and 15 minutes for those quotes from NASDAQ. In addition, each portal offers current high, low, open, last, change price data, % change, P/E 52-week hi/lo prices, as well as a chart. However, the amount and presentation of data depends on each site. In addition, because the portals license their stock quote data from a variety of sources, if you don't find a quote for a company on one of the portals, try your search on a different portal.

For those of you who need real-time stock quotes, MSN Money Central provides free real-time quotes, but registration is required, and registration involves reading and signing various agreements from the stock exchanges saying that you will use the data for nonprofessional use and will not redisseminate the data, and that the site is not liable for trading losses.

The major investment portals and their source of intraday stock quotes are:

- Hoovers.com, (www.hoovers.com), with quotes from Thomson Financial
- Wall Street Research Net, (www.wsrn.com), with quotes from North American Quotation, Inc.
- Yahoo! Finance, (finance.yahoo.com), with quotes from Reuters
- CorporateInformation (www.corporateinformation.com), with quotes from Quote.com
- TheStreet.com, (www.thestreet.com), with quotes S&P Comstock

STOCK QUOTES—HISTORICAL

Yahoo! Finance

Finance.yahoo.com

Free site

Yahoo! Finance provides daily, weekly, and monthly stock price data, adjusted for splits and dividend distributions. Data can be downloaded into spreadsheet format, but the amount of data you are able to download at one time is limited. Both adjusted and unadjusted data are presented.

Wall Street Research Net

www.wsrn.com

Fee-based site

For unadjusted stock price data without the dividend line item, WSRN's "Historical Price Data Spreadsheets" in weekly, monthly, quarterly, and yearly formats are available for $2.50–$5.00. Data is available in a variety of formats, and there is no limit to how much data is presented in one report.

CHAPTER 6

Public Company Data

Financial analysts and business appraisers often need access to public company financial information for a variety of purposes. The investment community has embraced the Internet, and virtually every major brokerage firm has a Website brimming with investment information. Private enterprises are providing free and easy access to the Securities and Exchange Commission (SEC) EDGAR system. Internet portals, such as Hoover's, are aggregating company data from a variety of sources and making it available from one Website.

There is an abundance of public company financial data on the Internet, but its format, and the companies that provide the data, are constantly changing. The sites we've listed in this chapter are those that compile and present information from several sources, add value to the data by presenting sophisticated searching and filtering mechanisms, and are free or reasonably priced. However, we have listed a few premium services, such as Mergent Online, because such services are extremely worthwhile information sources for firms that do a lot of financial analysis.

The sites listed in the "First and Foremost" section of this chapter are those that we have found to be reliable sources of industry information. They offer valuable content in a well-designed and well-maintained site. Sites are presented in alphabetical order. Sites offering all or part of the data for free are considered more desirable than sites offering similar data for a fee. "Best of the Rest" sites may focus on a niche area, be fee-only, have limited navigation and output features, or be limited in some other way.

FIRST AND FOREMOST

10k Wizard

www.10kwizard.com

Fee-based site

10k Wizard is no longer a free site, but it is definitely still worth using. 10k Wizard's robust search engine allows for precise searching and printing. Researchers can search across the entire EDGAR database by SIC code, phrases, names, form types, date, ticker symbol, partial company name, and keywords. The full-text retrieval tool also allows for the use of the Boolean operators And, Or, and Not. This advanced search feature is handy when one wants to find a specific filing for a particular company or the instances of certain keywords within a filing. Subscription fees are $150 per year, $25 per month, or $50 per quarter.

What can you expect to find?

- Real-time EDGAR filings in both Rich Text Format (RTF) and text formats
- Unlimited access and downloads
- Insider trading data from Forms 3, 4, and 144
- Unlimited personal alerting on full text, insider trading, form types, or ticker symbols
- Ability to download tables as Excel spreadsheets
- Client Tracking/Bill Back Feature

CorporateInformation

www.corporateinformation.com   (Exhibit 6.1)

Free, registration required

"Detailed Analysis of over 20,000 companies" from Wright Investors' Service is available on this site. CorporateInformation.com has been providing researchers with a list of comprehensive links to useful public, private, national, and international company Websites since 1997 and contains a lot of very useful, free, and unique information. The site's database contains over 350,000 company profiles and is searchable by company name, ticker, industry, and country. The database also contains over 15,000 research reports.

What can you expect to find?

- The "CI Profile" contains a brief company description, stock chart and recent stock performance, officers, ratio analysis, Wright's rating, and links to historical stock information, SEC filings, news, earnings estimates, patents, and brokerage reports.
- The "Research Report," written by analysts at the Winthrop Corp. and distributed by Wright's Investors' Service, provides a brief analysis of competitors and their recent valuations, sales, profitability, earnings, research and development, inventory, and so forth.
- The "Analysis Summary" provides 10 years' stock price, ratios, equity capital, earnings per share, and dividends data.
- The "Sales Analysis" provides up to 10 years' sales, sales growth, EBITDA, percentage of sales, income before extra, employees, and sales/employees data.
- The "Price Analysis" provides up to 10 years of quarterly stock price data.
- The "Earnings Analysis" provides up to 10 years of earnings per share and dividends data (Exhibit 6.1).

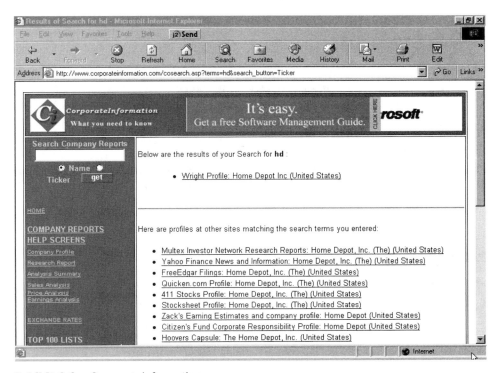

Exhibit 6.1   CorporateInformation

EDGAR-Online

www.edgar-online.com

Fee-based site

In addition to free access to EDGAR filings via the company's FreeEdgar service, Edgar-Online provides reasonably priced access to EDGAR documents with value-added features. Subscription plans exist for individual and professional users, and prices run from $14.25 to $275.00 a quarter, with a limited amount of downloads.

What can you expect to find?

- Template-type forms allow for the ability to search across the EDGAR database using a variety of criteria, including company name, ticker, person's name, filing type, industry, location, and date range.
- Each filing has an integrated table of contents. In the HTML version of the document, each section of the filing is outlined so that users can click to go directly to the section they want to see.
- Import data from any SEC document into Word or WordPerfect format for enhanced formatting including standard pagination, and Income Statements, Balance Sheets, and Cash Flow information into Excel or other spreadsheet programs.
- Links to related company information from other information providers, including quotes from PCQuote, charts from BigCharts, business credit reports from Dun & Bradstreet, and other research from Zack's, Wall Street Research Net, Multex, and InsiderTrader.
- The ability to customize a portfolio of companies, industries, and SEC information one needs to track on a regular basis; order complete printed bound copies of any EDGAR filing and have them delivered to your office the next day, and set up "WatchLists" to be notified of filings based on user-defined criteria.

EDGARScan

edgarscan.pwcglobal.com/servlets/edgarscan   (Exhibit 6.2)

Free site

Provided by PricewaterhouseCoopers, EDGARSCAN "is a program designed to read and analyze SEC EDGAR filings," and focuses on quarterly and annual filings (10-Qs and 10-Ks).

What can you expect to find?

- The ability to search across the 10-Ks and 10-Qs of public companies by SIC code, and rank retrieved companies by financial variables such as net income or current ratio
- The "Benchmarking Assistant," which allows researchers the ability to compare a company with its peers, using up to 144 different financial metrics
- Preformatted documents for easy printing
- Each filing has a table of contents with hyperlinks to different sections of the filing
- Ability to download into spreadsheets
- Summary view of financials
- The "Advanced Filing Search" template, currently in experimental mode, allows researchers to create specific searches by a variety of criteria (see Exhibit 6.2)

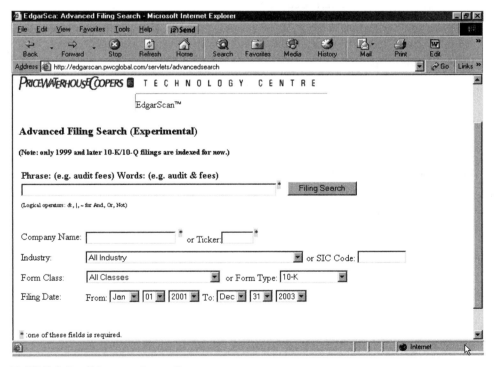

Exhibit 6.2   PricewaterhouseCoopers

FreeEDGAR

www.freeedgar.com

Free, registration required

> FreeEdgar.com is a free and popular source of EDGAR filings. Owned by Edgar-Online Inc. (referenced above), the site provides real-time access to EDGAR documents and is designed for "changed to cater primarily to new and casual users of SEC filings," according to the company. Registered users can search FreeEdgar for free, but the number of documents allowed per month is limited.
>
> The full-text retrieval tool also allows for the use of the Boolean operators "and," "or," and not." This advanced search feature is handy when one wants to find a specific filing for a particular company, or the instances of certain keywords within a filing. EDGAR filings are available in text format.

> *What can you expect to find?*

- The "Search Filings" search allows searches by SIC code, company name, and ticker symbol.
- The ability to define and store one's own portfolio of searches, "Watchlists," which will notify the researcher when a company on the watchlist files with the SEC.

Hoover's Online

www.hoovers.com   (Exhibit 6.3)

Free and fee-based site

> Hoover's is "a portal that provides more than 3 million businesspeople with timely and reliable information and research tools" (www.hoovers.com). Approximately 3 million people use Hoover's every month because the site consolidates a lot of useful company information in one easy-to-use place. Hoover's provides content from a variety of vendors, including Media General, Thomson Financial, NewsEdge, and the SEC. While a lot of information is provided for free on the site, personal and corporate memberships allow access to premium company data.
>
> Those interested in subscribing to Hoover's premium service need to contact a Hoover's representative for pricing information.

> *What can you expect to find?*

- Company "capsules" for approximately 14,000 private and public companies. The level of financial data in each capsule depends on whether the company is private or public.

- Each "capsule" contains a description of the company, its top three competitors, current news stories, financial snapshot, detailed stock quote, links to company press releases, quarterly financials (five quarters), annual financials (3 years), list of other companies in the industry, and links to additional fee-based reports on the company by firms such as Dun & Bradstreet, Experian, and Harris Infosource Reports.

- Member benefits include (in addition to the free resources) a more descriptive company "profile," in-depth quarterly (five quarters) and yearly (3 years) financials, 10 years of income statement and stock history data, the ability to download the financials into an Excel spreadsheet, and the "Business Boneyard," a database of historical information about companies that were "swallowed up in mergers and acquisitions, or were victims of bad management, market trends, or bankruptcy."

- Paying subscribers can also take advantage of Hoover's Advanced Search feature that allows a researcher to search across the database of company capsules by SIC code, financials, number of employees, type of company, and geographic area (see Exhibit 6.3).

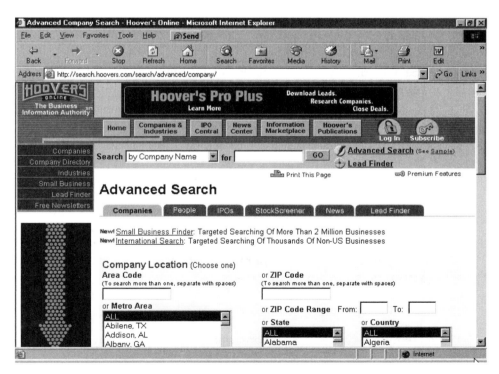

Exhibit 6.3 Hoover's Online

LIVEDGAR

www.gsionline.com   (Exhibit 6.4)

Fee-based site

Global Securities Information Inc.'s LIVEDGAR provides reasonably priced access to EDGAR documents. LIVEDGAR is well known for its sophisticated yet easy-to-navigate search interface and a powerful search engine that allows users to search across the entire EDGAR database by SIC code, phrases, names, form types, date, ticker symbol, partial company name, and keywords. Boolean operators such as "And," "Or," "Not," "To," and the wild cards "?" and "*" can be used. Furthermore, proximity operators such as "W/n" and "P/n" allow researchers to develop very specific concept searches.

LIVEDGAR's latest feature is its "10-K Section Search," which provides researchers with the ability to focus searches on a particular section of the 10-K. The company has broken down the 10-K into 23 unique sections (see Exhibit 6.4). This new ability will allow for more precise searching. A few examples of the searches you can easily execute using the new 10-K Section Search feature include:

- Search 10-K Item 3, "Legal Proceedings," for any court, subject matter, company name, or state.
- Search just the "Notes to Financial Statements" section for tax issues, amortization of goodwill, deferred revenue recognition, or any other term.
- Search Item 10, "Directors and Executive Officers," for any particular name.
- Search Item 14, "Controls and Procedures," for Sarbanes-Oxley compliance language.
- Search "Exhibits," for text contained only in 10-K exhibits.

Attorneys and their staffs find the Research Library provided on the LIVEDGAR site very helpful because it allows them to target specific types of documents easily. Examples of these preformatted searches include "Holding company formation" for corporate structure purposes and "Option Pricing— 10 year report" for proxy proposals.

What can you expect to find?

- Template-type search forms and a variety of ways to access EDGAR filings.

- Global Securities has made links within each filing that allow users to go directly to the section they want to see without having to wade through the entire document.

- Ability to download data into a spreadsheet without any need to format, and download documents into a variety of formats including text, Word, Rich Text Format, and .pdf.

- Ability to save searches and set up "WatchLists" to be notified of filings based on user-defined criteria.

- Additional databases contain content such as SEC No-Action Letters, 26,000+ Non-U.S. Registered Offerings, and SEC Regulatory Content, Releases, Speeches, and Enforcement Actions.

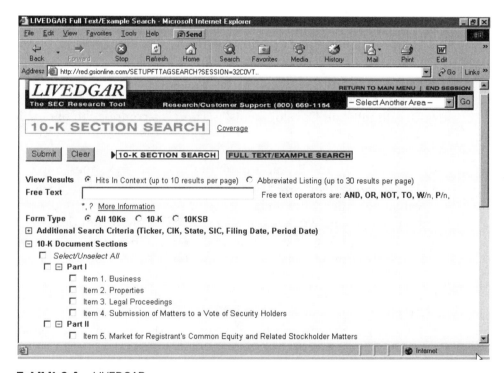

Exhibit 6.4 LIVEDGAR

Multex Investor

www.multexinvestor.com

Free site, registration required

Multex Investor provides detailed company reports for 9,111 public companies. The amount of free and nicely formatted information Multex Investor provides on public companies is amazing. Searching the site is free, but in order to access some of the free detailed stock reports and real-time quotes one must register with the site. The detailed "Learn To Analyze Stocks: Using Market Guide" is also a useful reference tool.

What can you expect to find?

- A detailed description of the company, earnings announcements, and a Daily Checkup that contains real-time quotes, delayed quotes, price charts, news, and significant developments
- Data on officers and directors, including executive biographies, executive compensation, and options
- The "Significant Developments" section is a compilation of detailed paragraphs annotating significant developments for the past two to three years.
- 1-year, 3-year, and 5-year growth rates, 4 years' revenues, and EPS
- Ratios and statistics that include price and volume data, including beta, valuation ratios, share-related items, per share data, dividend information, management effectiveness, financial strength, and profitability
- I/B/E/S earnings estimates, analyst recommendations and revisions, quarterly earnings surprises, historical mean EPS estimate trend, earnings estimates revision summary
- Price performance, institutional ownership, insider trading (previous 6 months), short interest, price history
- Five years' data from quarterly and yearly income statements, balance sheets, statements of cash flow
- NetScreen provides an excellent way to screen the database by SIC code or industry grouping

It is a database of more than 5,500,000 full-text broker research reports from over 850 providers on more than 46,000 companies. The cost of reports range from $10.00 to $150.00. The reports are in .pdf format and include all original text, charts, graphs, tables, color, and document formatting. Using the "Advanced Search Feature," researchers can search for documents by ticker symbol, company name, industry, and research provider.

Mergent Online

www.mergent.com

Fee-based site

A top-of-the-line product, Mergent Online (formerly FISonline) provides access to one of the most detailed and comprehensive global company databases available. Formerly known as Moody's Financial Information Services, Mergent has been publishing detailed business descriptions, corporate histories, and financial statements since 1900, and all modules offer a robust search engine for sophisticated searching. Subscribers can tailor their subscriptions by selecting from a variety of data modules, which include:

- Company Data
- U.S. Company Archives Data
- U.S. Annual Reports International Company Data
- International Company Archives Data
- International Annual Reports
- Institutional Holdings Data
- Insider Trading Data
- FactSheets
- FactSheets Express
- Expanded Long-Term Debt
- D&B Million Dollar Database Plus

MSN Money Central

Moneycentral.msn.com

Free site

The "Investing" section of this site provides a wealth of information on publicly held companies. MSN licenses their data from a variety of sources, such as:

- The "Stock Screener" allows for searching across Media General's database of approximately 10,000 public companies with criteria such as Industry, market cap, and key financial indictors.
- "Company reports" for a particular company contain data nicely formatted from Hoovers.com, including the company description, Quick Facts, stock activity, summary fundamental data, earnings estimates, and institutional statistics.
- Links to more detailed financial data and recent news are also provided.

One Source Business Browser

www.onesource.com

Fee-based site

One Source is a popular aggregator of company data and has been in business for over 10 years. Its *Business Browser* product line "integrates comprehensive and up-to-date business and financial information on over one million public and private companies from more than 25 information providers drawing upon over 2,500 sources of content."

What can you expect to find?

- The Profile Company option allows researchers to identify public or private companies and retrieve reports on their products, competition, corporate structure, industry, executives, current news, articles, and financials.
- With the Find Companies option, researchers can identify companies by a variety of criteria, such as industry, geography, sales, and employment.
- Users can monitor news and industry reports on prospects, customers, competitors, suppliers, and partners using the source's "Track Watchlists."
- Use Find Executives for information on business executives. Researchers can search with this feature by criteria such as name, company, geography, schools, or affiliations.

SEC Info

www.secinfo.com

Fee-based site

SEC Info provides Edgar filings as well as SEDAR filings from the Canadian Securities Administrators. Researchers can search by one of the following criteria: Name, Industry, Business, SIC Code, Area Code, Topic, CIK, Accession Number, File Number, and Zip Code. In May 2003, SEC Info started charging for access. Fees are rasonable: $20 monthly, $45 quarterly, and $120 yearly subscription.

What can you expect to find?

- Linked topics within each document and exhibit, such as Business, Competition, Risk Factors, and Management's Discussion
- The ability to jump around within a document and to documents incorporated by reference
- Indexed exhibits so that you can get directly to Material Contracts, By-Laws, and so on

- Adjustable print quality
- The ability to print an individual page

Wall Street Journal Briefing Books

www.wsj.com

Fee-based site

Subscribers to the online version of *The Wall Street Journal* have free access to the "Briefing Books," reports that contain background and financial information on publicly traded companies. In addition, subscribers have access to the entire Dow Jones Publication Library, which contains current and archived articles from thousands of trade journals and newspapers from around the world.

The Business Briefings are nicely formatted and easy to read. Subscriptions for the online version are $59 a year or $29 a year if one subscribes to the print version. Articles from the Dow Jones Publications Library run $2.95 each.

What can you expect to find?

- A financial overview in both chart and text format
- Stock charts and earnings estimates
- News releases from Dow Jones Newswire
- Links to related news from leading business publications and the *Journal*, press releases, and stock quote details from the Wall Street Research Network

www.wsrn.com

Free and fee-based site

The Wall Street Research Network is a popular site despite its cluttered appearance. Like most financial sites, WSRN compiles a wealth of company information, much of which is free. Financial spreadsheet packages containing 10 years or 13 quarters are available for $24.95 each. Monthly and yearly flat-rate fee packages are also available.

What can you expect to find?

- The free information includes detailed quotes, charts, news, company descriptions, Tear Sheet Fundamentals with 7 years' income statements, balance sheets, ratios, EPS estimates, and company to industry ratios
- Fee-based data includes shares outstanding, shares outstanding chart, annual and quarterly EPS history, historical quotes, dividends and splits history, and the Advanced Searching feature

- One-time research needs, like a download of 10 years' of stock prices, are available for $2.50 to $5.00
- WSRN/BASELINE company profiles are available for $1.99 each

BEST OF THE REST

144A/Private Placement Database

www.gsionline.com

Fee-based site

Global Securities Information Inc. (GSI) offers a database of 144a and Regulation S offering circulars. These documents are gathered from broker-dealers through extensive negotiation on the part of GSI, and are gathered from over 80 countries. The database contains such documents dated from April 1990 to the present.

eLibrary

www.elibrary.com

Fee-based site

Most company portals like Yahoo! and Hoovers contain only 3 months' worth of articles. For $14.95 a month researchers can access years' worth of journal and news articles, books, and television and radio transcripts from eLibrary. Many of the sources included in eLibrary are trade association magazines and newspapers from smaller cities. These types of publications often run stories on local or specialized businesses and can provide more detailed information than might be found elsewhere.

Goldman Sachs Research on Demand

www.gsnews.com

Free and fee-based site

Once registered with the site, researchers can access Goldman Sachs investment reports. Abstracts are free. However, retrieving entire reports requires a subscription.

IPO.com

www.ipo.com

Free and fee-based site

> IPO.com provides data on current IPO filings and pricings. For each IPO the following data is presented: key dates, such as filing data and expected pricing date; offering details, including the share type, proposed ticker, stock exchange, offering amount, and expected IPO price; recent summary financials, names of underwriters, shareholders, supporting companies, and use of proceeds; and summary description of competitors and industry environment.

SEDAR (System for Electronic Document Analysis and Retrieval)

www.sedar.com

Free site

> SEDAR, the System for Electronic Document Analysis and Retrieval, is the electronic filing system for public companies and mutual funds in Canada. The SEDAR Website contains copies of the disclosure documents filed in the system, as well as profiles containing basic information about each company or mutual fund group.

Value Line

www.valueline.com

Fee-based site

> The well-known, reliable, and objective *Value Line Investment Survey* is available online. Users can screen over 1,700 companies using over 250 data fields. The services provide the ability to produce graphs using 25 different variables and up to 5 years history, and compare up to five securities in the same chart.

Wall Street City

www.wallstreetcity.com

Free and fee-based site

> Wall Street City provides much of the same financial information and descriptive information that is available on Hoover's and Market Guide, however it provides technical analysis tools and an array of graphs and charts of interest to investors. On the same page as the financial snapshot for a company, The Last 10 Trades and the prices are posted, as well as the latest news about the company. The company's ProStation product allows for sophisticated charting and real-time quotes.

CHAPTER 7

Sites for Private Company Analysis

Unfortunately, the number of Internet sites in Chapter 6 that are chock-full of detailed information on public companies cannot be duplicated in this chapter. Detailed financial information on privately held businesses is simply not available because private companies are not subject to the same reporting requirements as public companies. The bulk of the sites providing private company data are those of credit reporting agencies, and researchers can screen these databases to get basic financial information, create marketing lists, and research the competition. Nevertheless, many company Websites still provide information about the firm's products, mission statement, personnel, and locations, and sophisticated Internet directories can lead researchers to these sites. Newspapers and magazine articles that typically carry stories about private companies are now available on the 'net for free or a small charge.

The sites listed in the "First and Foremost" section of this chapter are those that we have found to be reliable sources of information presented in an easily accessible format. The "Best of the Rest" sites may focus on a niche area, or have limited navigation and output features.

FIRST AND FOREMOST

Business Filings Databases

www.llrx.com/columns/roundup4.htm

Free site

Seventy-five percent of states in the United States require that some level of business and corporate filings be made available online. Attorney and author

Kathy Biehl developed this site to share with researchers what each state has made available on the Web in terms of corporate and business filings.

What can you expect to find?

- Links to databases of publicly available business and corporate filings, organized by state
- "If a state is not on the list, it has not posted corporate records online"

CorporateInformation

www.corporateinformation.com

Free site

CorporateInformation has been providing researchers with a list of comprehensive links to useful business-related Websites since 1997. After typing in the name of a company, researchers will receive a list of links to related sites about that company. When searching by company name, researchers should enter as many words in the company's name as possible in order to retrieve a relevant list of sites. If the company has two words in its name, type the two words in quotes.

What can you expect to find?

- Links to Websites that contain information about the subject company. For example, the search "Kinko's" retrieved links to a Hoover's capsule, the Vault Report Employee Shapshot, the Virtual Job Fair Company Profile, and some news articles.

CorpTech

www.corptech.com

Free (registration required) and fee-based site

The CorpTech database contains information on approximately 50,000 public and private manufacturers and developers of high-tech products. The companies covered are "primarily emerging small to mid-sized private companies and the operating units of larger corporations." There is no charge to use the site, and basic information is free, however the more detailed reports come with a fee. The database is searchable by location, size, and products, and up to 13 reports can be created.

To access the free data users can search by company name, stock symbol, product, broad industry category, and person's name. In addition, CorpTech provides "10 Fast Finders"—preformatted searches for common uses of the database. These searches include Find public companies and operating units, Find growth companies, Find competitors, Find companies by product, and Find acquisition candidates.

Pay-per-view profiles are available for purchase on an as-needed basis. Subscriptions are available as well. The free report contains ticker symbol(s), company name, address, telephone, Web address, fax, year business began operations, sales, CEO, and business description. The "Standard Profile" ($4.75) contains sales and employment levels, multiple executive names with their titles and responsibilities, and detailed product listings and descriptions. The Power Search allows for very specific searching, for example, by SIC or NAICS codes or revenue size, and is available to subscribers only.

Dun & Bradstreet

www.dnb.com   (Exhibit 7.1)

Fee-based site

Dun & Bradstreet is well known for its credit data, which is used for marketing, prospecting, purchasing, and receivables management purposes. At the company's Website researchers can search the database of more than 75 million companies. Financial data is available for "some" larger private companies and is provided in the "Business Information Reports" and the "Comprehensive Report." D&B obtains its data from company contacts, trade tapes, courthouses, government sources, banks, customers, trade associations, business-to-business publications, and financial institutions. D&B updates the information through interviews, direct mail programs, updates of reported bankruptcies, suits, liens, judgments, UCC filings and payment experiences, and investigations prompted by customers' inquiries.

What can you expect to find?

- The D&B Business Information Report. The Business Summary section displays basic company profile information, such as name, tradestyles, address, phone number, parent company name and location, chief executive officer's name, sales volume, net worth, number of employees, line of business, and the D&B D-U-N-S® Number. Use this summary of the full report to get a quick view of the business and locate areas to investigate more closely.

- A variety of reports are available. See Exhibit 7.1 for a portion of the $130 "Comprehensive Report."

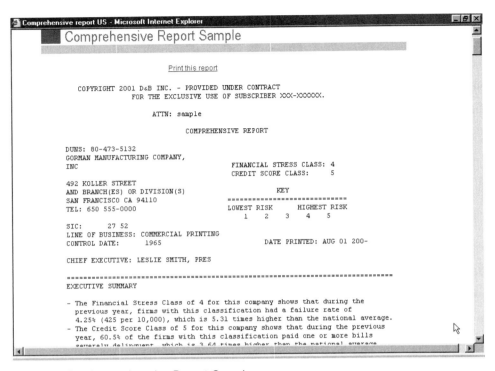

Exhibit 7.1   Comprehensive Report Sample

Experian (formerly TRW)

www.experian.com

Fee-based site

The Experian database contains over 13 million U.S. companies and is used by people who want credit information on a business. Researchers must first register with this site before using it; however, searching the database is free. Unfortunately, in order to find information about a particular company one must enter the company name with its complete address. When comprehensive information is available, Experian provides a full Snapshot report, including a credit risk category, for $19.95. When little information is available, a limited report without the risk category costs $8.00.

What can you expect to find?

- The Snapshot report contains company name and address, legal filings, payment and trend behavior, and company and financial services history.

- The Business Public Records search contains Uniform Commercial Code data, bankruptcy and tax lien information, as well as additional corporate records.

Forbes Magazine and the Forbes Private 500

www.forbes.com/2002/11/07/privateland.html

Free site

Forbes has reported on private companies for many years. Each year *Forbes* publishes "The Private 500," an annual directory of the 500 largest privately held U.S. corporations, "taking into consideration revenues and number of employees."

What can you expect to find?

- An excellent interactive tool to find out more information about each years' list, such as the ability to sort list by company name, state, industry, revenues, and links to related articles
- Extensive database of small companies dating back to 1996
- Current and earlier editions of the "The Private 500"

Hoover's Online

www.hoovers.com   (Exhibit 7.2)

Free and fee-based site

While Hoover's is known for its in-depth profiles of public companies, the site also provides quite a bit of information on selected private companies (see Exhibit 7.2).

What can you expect to find?

- Company "capsules" on private companies contain varying degrees of financial information
- "Key people" in the company
- Competitors
- News and trade publication articles on the company, as well as press releases

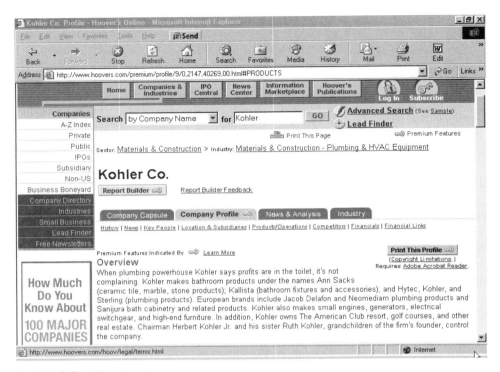

Exhibit 7.2   Hoovers.com

Inc. Magazine and the Inc. 500

www.inc.com/inc500

Free site

Inc. Magazine has always had feature stories on private companies, as well as the yearly "Inc. 500." The "Inc. 500" is an "Annual List of America's Fastest-Growing Private Companies."

What can you expect to find?

- Links to articles about the companies contained in the current "Inc. 500" list
- A free archive of articles dating back from the early 1990s to the present
- The current "Inc. 500" and related articles, as well as a searchable database of the companies included in the "Inc. 500" since 1982

Integra Information

www.integrainfo.com   (Exhibit 7.3)

Fee-based site

Integra provides excellent benchmarking data. The Integra InfoBase is derived from 31 different proprietary and government data sources, all selected and tested for consistency by the Integra Product Team. The names of specific companies are not revealed. Reports are generated by user defined criteria, SIC code, and sales range, and are presented in a variety of formats, including spreadsheet and .pdf.

What can you expect to find?

- The 5-year industry report provides five years of detailed income statement and balance sheet data, over 60 financial ratios. Each report is $140. One page of the report is displayed in Exhibit 7.3.

- The 3-year industry report provides 3-year historical balance sheet and summary income statement information, key financial ratios, and bar graphs of key operating trends. Each report is $70.

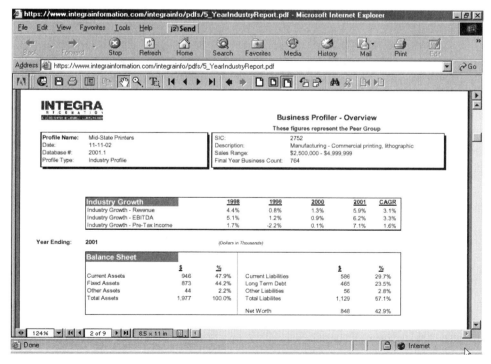

Exhibit 7.3   Integra Information
Integra Information, A Division of Microbilt Corporation.

Thomas Register of American Manufacturers

www.thomasregister.com   (Exhibit 7.4)

Free site

The Thomas Register of American Manufacturers is a well-known and well-established index of manufacturers and is a great source for finding U.S. and Canadian companies, what the company does, or which companies make a certain type of product. The database of 170,000 entries is searchable by company name, product or service, and brand name (see Exhibit 7.4).

What can you expect to find?

- Basic business information such as name and address and number of employees
- Links to company catalogs and Websites are provided for many companies in the database

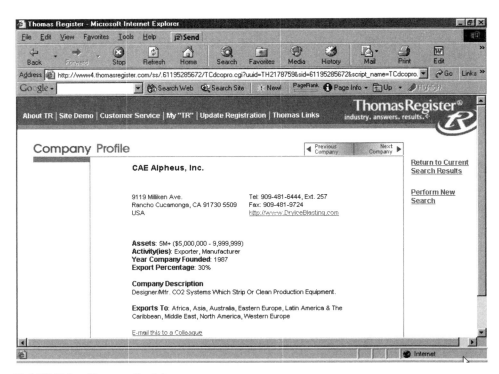

Exhbit 7.4   Thomas Register

BEST OF THE REST

A.M. Best Insurance Company Directory and Reports

www3.ambest.com/ratings/Advanced.asp

Free and fee-based site

An extensive database of nearly 6,000 life/health, property/casualty, and international insurance companies are provided on the A.M Best Ratings and Analysis Website. Researchers can perform searches by using criteria such as company name, type of insurance, and geographic location. Profiles include the company name, address, phone, domicile, affiliation or membership, AMB and NAIC numbers, Web address, ticker symbol, date business commenced, and rating. Researchers may purchase complete company reports.

BusinessCreditUSA.com

www.businesscreditusa.com/index.asp

Fee-based site

BusinessCreditUSA.com is an "Internet business credit portal" that provides business credit reports for public and private U.S. companies and executives. The database currently has 12 million records, and according to the company, approximately 55 percent of the records are from businesses with fewer than four employees. This is a good source for finding fax, telephone, and address data; verifying a business's existence and stability; and generating sales leads. Reports are $5.00. The database is searchable by company or executive name, city, state, telephone number, or ABI number. Each report contains the company name, address, names of select executives, phone, fax, credit rating, number of employees, ticker symbol, SIC code(s), competitors, link to the company's Website, and competitors in the area.

EDGAR

The EDGAR database was discussed in detail in Chapter 6. While the database is composed of detailed information filed by public companies, the possibility exists that you may find information on a particular private company. In certain instances, a public company may have referenced a private company because of an acquisition or licensing agreement. Because the providers of the EDGAR database mentioned in Chapter 6 have developed search interfaces that allow researchers to search by keyword, a quick search on a private company's name as a keyword search may yield some information.

eLibrary

www.elibrary.com

Fee-based site

For $14.95 a month or $79.95 a year, researchers can access journal and news articles, books, and television and radio transcripts that often contain stories on small, local, and private companies. Many of the sources included in eLibrary are trade association magazines and newspapers from smaller cities. These types of publications often run stories on local or specialized businesses and can provide more detailed information than might be found in the more general business publications.

Ex-Exec Tracker

www.thestandard.com/article/display/0,1151,18108,00.html

Free site

Each quarter TheStandard.com publishes and charts "a rundown of who's leaving what company and why (according, at least, to the company's press release)." The chart contains the names of the ex-executives, the date of departure, the to and from companies, their explanation for leaving, time served, and stock market reaction (if the company was public).

Franchise 500

www.entrepreneur.com

Free site

Entrepreneur Magazine offers a database containing information on franchises and their rankings, business descriptions, links to their Websites, an annual breakdown of the number of units owned since 1997, financial information, and additional contact information. You will find the list in the site's "Franchise Zone."

TechSavvy

www.techsavvy.com

Free site

TechSavvy.com "provides a broad base of technical, engineering, design, maintenance and procurement information." Its company directory provides company profiles from Harris InfoSource, a directory of manufacturing companies. For each company, basic contact information is provided along with a detailed company description. In addition, researchers can compile a listing of companies that produce a particular part.

Vault Reports

www.vaultreports.com

Free site

If you want some insider information (or shall we say gossip) on a company, check The Vault. This site is geared towards those looking for a job. Researchers can search for company information by company name, city, number of employees, revenue, and industry. The level and amount of information provided depends on how much the folks at The Vault could compile from surveys, inside contacts, and message boards.

zapdata.com

www.zapdata.com

Free and fee-based site

zapdata.com is an Internet service of Dun & Bradstreet (D&B) Sales & Marketing Solutions. The site contains data on 14 million companies and is an excellent vehicle for creating mailing lists and finding business sales leads. The Company Look Up feature allows researchers to search by company name and location. The basic report is $5.00 and provides information such as address and industry sector and SIC code, annual sales, and number of employees. A variety of additional reports containing more data, such as executive names, are available.

CHAPTER 8

Salary and Executive Compensation Surveys

There are a variety of reasons why financial professionals may need salary and executive compensation surveys. In some cases, boards of directors often need to justify their CEO pay allocations to shareholders, executives wish to assess the adequacy of a proposed compensation plan, or a job seeker wants to know the going salary in her occupation. Business appraisers look for compensation paid to executives at closely held companies in order to determine the compensation adjustment necessary in a valuation analysis.

The Internet has become a very useful tool to help researchers get their hands on the surveys, because it allows trade associations, database providers, and consulting firms a forum in which to make their surveys available. As in other areas, the trend in compensation data is toward fee-based access. There are still a number of free sites, but these tend to be directed more toward job seekers than those doing a financial analysis.

The Internet sites listed in this chapter include both "executive compensation" surveys, which typically provide information on the compensation packages of a company's executives and top managers, and "salary surveys," which typically include the salaries of all workers within an industry, from entry level to the executive.

It is important to remember that these surveys provide not only annual salary data, but also details about the executive's bonus, stock options, long-term incentive plan, and other noncash compensation. So, while many sites provide survey excerpts, it may be necessary to pay for the entire report to get the whole picture of the compensation package.

There are some excellent compensation resources that continue to publish information in print form and do not make their data available over the Internet. The National Institute of Business Management (NIBM) publishes an annual "Executive Compensation Survey" which covers salaries, bonuses, and perks offered by more than 500 small businesses to their highest-paid executives. Annual studies from 1989 to the present can be ordered on the NIBM Website at www.nibm.net. The "Officer Compensation Report," compiled by the Segal consulting firm, is a survey of executive compensation practices at small to medium-sized businesses, defined as companies with annual sales ranging from less than $2 million to more than $250 million. Ordering information is available at www.segalco.com/corporate/ocr.htm.

Compensation data is typically collected and published by consulting firms, governmental agencies, and trade associations. This chapter includes sites from all three sources. Data compiled by consulting firms is usually the most expensive of the three sources.

We have limited the sites in this chapter to those that have general national compensation data. There are a number of sites with excellent regional data as well as a myriad that focus on a single industry.

The sites are presented in alphabetical order. The sites listed in the "First and Foremost" section of this chapter are those that we have found to be reliable sources of statistics and analysis presented in easily accessible format. Sites offering all or part of the data for free will be rated higher than sites that offer similar data for a fee. "Best of the Rest" sites may focus on a niche area, be fee-only, or have limited navigation and output features.

FIRST AND FOREMOST

Abbott, Langer & Associates, Inc.

www.abbott-langer.com   (Exhibit 8.1)

Free and Fee-based site

Abbott, Langer & Associates, a human resources consulting firm, has been performing compensation surveys since 1967. The firm publishes current salary survey statistics for a number of industries. Abbott, Langer & Associates sells its detailed compensation reports from this site, but it also offers overview compensation data for free. For example, users can purchase the 495-page "Compensation in the Accounting/Financial Field," 20th Edition survey report of 40 benchmark jobs for $750.00. However, the six-page summary of the study is available for free and includes a listing of the median annual incomes for fourteen job titles (see Exhibit 8.1).

What can you expect to find?

- The "free summary data" link provides an overview of compensation trends by industry and a chart of median annual incomes for a range of positions, including president and chief financial officer
- A free compensation and benefits email newsletter that summarizes findings from new compensation surveys
- Detailed 100+ page compensation reports, for sale, by industry
- "Fun at Work," Abbott Langer's deep trove of human resource jokes
- News digest of articles on compensation and human resource management from a variety of industry journals

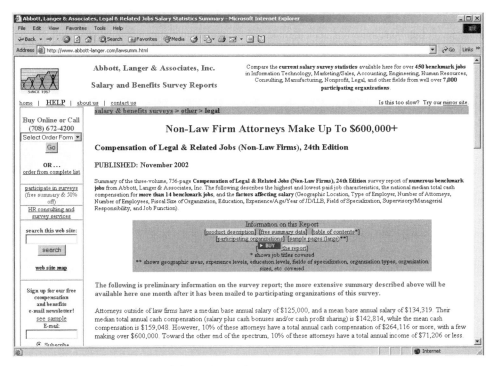

Exhibit 8.1   Abbott, Langer & Associates, Inc.

America's Career InfoNet (ACINet)

www.acinet.org/acinet   (Exhibit 8.2)

Free site

ACINet is part of the CareerOneStop portal, which operates as a federal-state partnership funded by grants to states. The OneStop portal includes three separate sites: America's Job Bank, America's Service Locator, and ACINet. ACINet covers information on wage and employment trends, on occupational requirements, and on state-by-state labor markets. It is sponsored by the U.S. Department of Labor and includes information pulled from a variety of state and federal government agencies, such as the U.S. Bureau of Labor Statistics (BLS) and various state Departments of Labor (see Exhibit 8.2).

Researchers can access salary and wage data either by a keyword or menu search. The menu search contains a list of general "job families" derived from the BLS Occupational Employment Statistics occupation list. Within each "job family" exists a more detailed list of occupational titles. It may be difficult to try to determine which category may contain the job title you need, so it may be more straightforward to simply use the keyword search feature. The search can then be defined by geographic area, such as state, district, or territory.

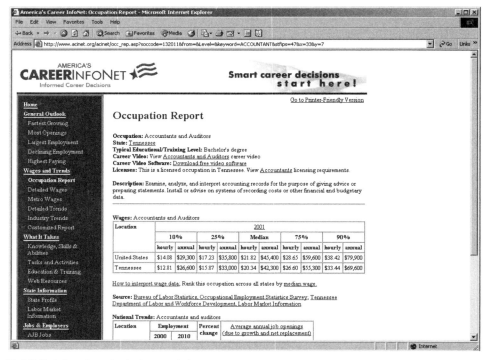

Exhibit 8.2 America's Career InfoNet

What can you expect to find?

- An array of occupational, demographic and labor market information at the local, state, and national levels
- Salary survey information by job type
- Links to career profiles in other publications, such as the *Princeton Review* and the *Occupational Outlook Handbook,* and local, state, and national career and labor market information sites

Best Jobs USA Salary Survey

www.bestjobsusa.com/sections/CAN-salsurvey/survey2002/index.asp

Free site

Best Jobs USA is a career information site operated by Recourse Communications Inc. The Best Jobs USA Salary Survey is a compilation of salary surveys from a variety of sources and publications, with each industry's information outlined in a separately downloadable .pdf file. For example, the file on public relations gives the salary range for 10 positions in that industry complied by Robert Half & Associates. The Sales & Marketing file includes salary data on 21 positions compiled by Abbott, Langer & Associates.

What can you expect to find?

- A summary of the findings from the most recent Employment Review's Annual Salary Survey
- Compilation of data by industry from a variety of published sources

Bureau of Labor Statistics

www.bls.gov   (Exhibit 8.3)

Free site

The Bureau's National Compensation Survey (NCS) provides data on occupational wages and employee benefits for localities, broad geographic regions, and the nation as a whole. Detailed wage and salary reports by metropolitan area can be downloaded from the NCS Website at www.bls.gov/ncs (see Exhibit 8.3).

The Bureau of Labor Statistics (BLS) collects and publishes a wealth of wage and salary data. The Occupational Employment Statistics (OES) program is an annual survey conducted by the U.S. Bureau of Labor Statistics to produce estimates of employment and wages for specific occupations. The OES program collects data on wage and salary workers in nonfarm establishments in more than 700 occupations. On the OES Website (www.bls.gov/oes) users can view salary reports by geographic area and by industry.

The *Occupational Outlook Handbook* is published annually by the BLS and is directed toward job seekers. Along with a discussion on the working conditions and necessary training and education for each occupation listed, the *Handbook* also provides data on earnings and expected job prospects. The site at http://stats.bls.gov/oco is searchable by occupation, and the sections on each position can be downloaded in .pdf format.

What can you expect to find?

- NCS reports in text or .pdf format showing wages by geographic area
- Data from the OES program showing number of employed people within each occupation title, median, mean, and annual hourly wage
- .pdf files of chapters from the *Occupational Outlook Handbook*

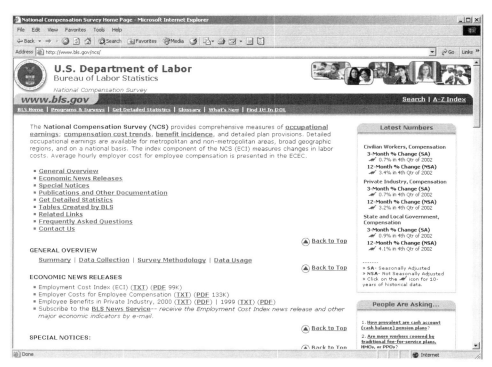

Exhibit 8.3   Bureau of Labor Statistics

CareerJournal

www.careerjournal.com   (Exhibit 8.4)

Free site

Published by the *Wall Street Journal*, *CareerJournal* is a portal of salary and job search-related information. The site provides wage and salary data organized by industry. The *Career Journal* staff maintains an article bank of salary surveys and trends from a number of trade and industry journals. For example, you can view a table of the average compensation for banking executives by position from the "Annual Compensation Survey" of the *Treasury Management Association Journal* or a "Study of Compensation in Public Internet Companies" by PricewaterhouseCoopers.

The site is directed primarily at job seekers and you will find the traditional job-hunting tools, including a resume database, job search discussion board, and job-hunting advice. The direct URL to the compensation page is www.careerjournal.com/salaries/index.html (see Exhibit 8.4).

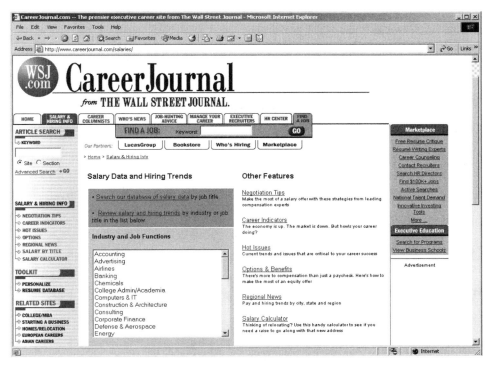

Exhibit 8.4   *CareerJournal*

What can you expect to find?

- Ability to generate customized salary reports by job title and geographic area
- Articles and salary tables for each industry sector
- Regional profiles containing news items that focus on labor issues in different regions of the country

eComp Executive Compensation Database

www.ecomponline.com

Free and fee-based site

The eComp site, operated by Aon Consulting, Inc., provides access to a database of compensation information on more than 50,000 executives from 12,000 U.S. publicly traded companies. The data is gathered from proxy statements, 10-Ks, and Registration Statements filed with the Securities and Exchange Commission.

Users can enter a company name or ticker symbol and get a table listing the company's top executives and their most recent annual salaries for free. Subscribers have access to more advanced search options and the ability to create custom reports by industry. Subscribers can also download retrieved information into an Excel spreadsheet and are provided free access to the 10k Wizard Website of public company filings.

What can you expect to find?

- Compensation data for the top five executives of each public company
- Total compensation including options and restricted stock
- Ability to create a peer group of companies to compare salary data

Economic Research Institute (ERI)

www.erieri.com

Fee-based site

ERI compiles and sells wage and salary surveys, executive compensation information, cost of living data, prevailing wage information, and employee benefit data and job employment data dealing with employee income and compensation and benefits training.

ERI's primary product is the Salary Assessor. The Salary Assessor is a database of compensation information for more than 4,750 positions in 300 U.S. and Canadian metropolitan areas. This product has attracted a following among business appraisers looking for data to support compensation adjustments in a valuation engagement because it is the same data used by the Internal Revenue Service. The Salary Assessor data is based upon an analysis of thousands of wage and salary surveys and sources.

Other products offered by ERI include the Geographic Assessor, a database of geographic pay and cost-of-living differentials by income level for more than 7,200 U.S. and Canadian cities, and the Executive Compensation Assessor, which covers management compensation data of 14,000 public companies.

Baker, Thomsen Associates, a privately held compensation and benefits consulting firm, owns ERI and also operates two other compensation sites reviewed in this chapter: SalaryExpert.com and SalariesReview.com.

What can you expect to find?

- A Dictionary of Occupational Titles containing more than 23,000 job descriptions.
- Detailed salary data by position in more than 2,000 industries. The reports include total direct compensation, sources, population estimates, and standard errors.

JobStar: California Job Search Guide

http://jobstar.org/tools/salary/index.cfm   (Exhibit 8.5)

Free site

This award-winning site is an excellent collection of salary surveys for more than 50 different industries. One section of the site covers general surveys, including cost-of-living studies, and a guide to printed surveys. Another section lists Profession-Specific Salary Surveys ranging from Accounting to Warehousing. While JobStar is a career database for California job seekers, the information it compiles on salaries and job hunting are useful to anyone looking for compensation data (see Exhibit 8.5).

The Bay Area Library & Information System operates JobStar. The involvement of this group of dedicated librarians along with corporate support from the *CareerJournal* site of the *Wall Street Journal* accounts for the high quality of this site.

What can you expect to find?

- Articles on job hunting and developing a resume, and a discussion forum.
- Links to over 300 general and industry-specific salary surveys. While the emphasis is on salaries in California, many of the links are to national surveys. Surveys run the gamut from wine producers to auto mechanics.

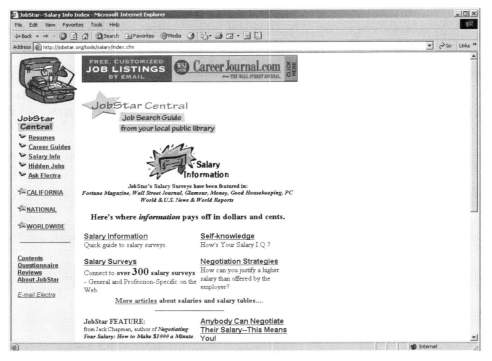

Exhibit 8.5   JobStar Central
JobStar: California Job Search Guide http://jobstar.org.

LIVEDGAR

www.gsionline.com

Fee-based site

The Securities and Exchange Commission mandates that publicly traded companies disclose the compensation of their chief executives, officers, and directors. Global Securities Inc. was one of the first companies to make searching the EDGAR database possible in an easy and cost-effective manner, with its LIVEDGAR database.

What can you expect to find?

- LIVEEDGAR's preformatted searches help researchers find examples of executive compensation tables, while drafting documents for their clients' use. These "canned" searches are found on the site's "Research Library." Examples of preformatted searches involving compensation include: Compensation Agreement and Compensation Committee Report.

- The Executive/Summary Compensation Table search allows users to search for compensation statistics by name, SIC codes, state, date, and keyword.
- Users can download the data directly into a spreadsheet.

SalariesReview.com and SalaryExpert.com

www.salariesreview.com

www.salaryexpert.com

Fee-based sites

Baker, Thomsen Associates, a privately held compensation and benefits consulting firm, operates these two sites, which offer general compensation data.

SalariesReview.com is a database of reports based upon consensus data from the Bureau of Labor Statistics and adjusted for online survey participation. Individual Wage & Salary Reports can be purchased and downloaded for any of more than 4,000 positions. Other available reports include Cost-of-Living and College Graduate Offers.

The SalaryExpert.com site has both a personal and a professional edition. The professional edition promotes the SalaryExpert Pro software product, which allows users to add the software to their desktop and access more than 30,000 positions for 44,455 zip and postal code areas within the United States and Canada.

What can you expect to find?

- Inexpensive reports on wages and salaries by position
- International salary reports by country
- Cost of living reports and detailed reports by position
- Software subscriptions that allow unlimited access to salary information

Salary.com

www.salary.com   (Exhibit 8.6)

Free and fee-based site

The Salary Wizard, available at salary.com is a free, "comprehensive salary tool enabling users to research salary ranges for thousands of job titles in a comprehensive set of career fields, sorted by occupation and region." The data is gathered from proprietary research and published reports. The salary.com site is a promotional tool for the firm's enterprise software products that include CompAnalyst, a compensation-benchmarking product. The Salary Wizard is a widely syndicated product used by a number of human resources sites (see Exhibit 8.6).

Salary.com offers two versions of the site, a Personal Edition targeted at job hunters and a second HR Edition aimed at corporate human resources departments. On the HR edition there are Compensation Market Studies and Job Valuation Reports available for purchase.

What can you expect to find?

- Salary data by job title and geographic location
- Compensation Market Studies
- News and feature articles on compensation and workplace trends and issues
- A collection of white papers on a variety of human resource topics

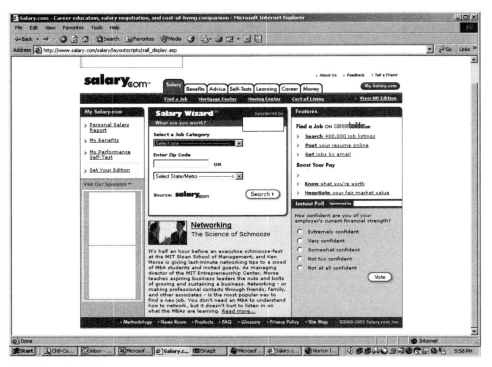

Exhibit 8.6   Salary.com

Trade Associations

http://info.asaenet.org/gateway/OnlineAssocSlist.html

Free and fee-based site

Trade associations often serve as clearinghouses of information for particular industries; therefore, it is worthwhile to check an association's Web page. Trade associations survey their members for compensation statistics, which they then compile, analyze, and sell to their members and often to the general public.

The American Society for Association Executives maintains a searchable Gateway to Associations on its Website, where users can either enter an association's name or choose from a list of industry categories to find an association.

Once you have located a Website for the trade association, use the site's keyword search tool or site map to locate the compensation data. While you may not find the survey available in its entirety for free on an association's Website, it is common to find portions of the study. If a trade association makes its salary surveys known to the public, it typically lists them under publications, research, or reports.

Similarly, a number of trade publications survey readers and publish salary guides. For example, *ComputerWorld* publishes an annual "Salary/Skills" survey each fall at www.computerworld.com/departments/surveys/skills.

Wageweb

www.wageweb.com

Free and fee-based site

Wageweb is an online "salary service which provides information on over 170 benchmark positions." Researchers can access national data free of charge, and subscribers can access the salary survey information, broken down by geography, number of employees, and industry, for a nominal fee. The Virginia consulting firm Human Resources Programs Development and Improvement maintains Wageweb.

What can you expect to find?

- The salary surveys are organized in eight broad industry topics. Each industry report covers anywhere from 9 to 30 benchmark positions and includes salary ranges and bonus information.

BEST OF THE REST

Business Magazine Special Issues

www.businessweek.com

www.forbes.com

Free sites

Business Weeks' annual compensation survey is available in its entirety from the magazine's Website. The compensation issue typically is published during the first quarter with an overview of public company executive salaries from the prior year.

The *Forbes* Website provides hundred of articles from current and past issues for free. Compensation-related articles include "Top paychecks at 50 big U.S. Companies," "The 25 highest-paid U.S. CEOs," and "Pitfalls of Stock Options."

What can you expect to find?

- The surveys typically focus on the highest paid executives in the country, rather than a detailed survey by industry.
- In addition to "Scoreboards" of the top compensated professionals, these special reports also contain related articles on the current trends in executive compensation as well as interviews with CEOs.

CompGeo Online

www.compgeo.net　　　(Exhibit 8.7)

Fee-based site

CompGeo provides detailed compensation information. The CompGeo database covers more than 1,000 job classifications across 297 survey locations in 23 surveyed occupation groups (see Exhibit 8.7). Products offered by Comp-Geo include:

- CompGeo Online, which is best suited for compensation research for a small number of jobs or job families within an occupation group.
- CompGeo Online Professional Reports is a special edition of CompGeo Online geared towards the needs of compensation professionals who need broad survey coverage for an entire occupation group across a geographic region or within a particular industry.
- The new CompGeo Online Professional Forecast Library covers all 23 occupational groups in the CompGeo Online database.

The site is detailed, and the pricing of reports is reasonable but the sight is cluttered and difficult to navigate.

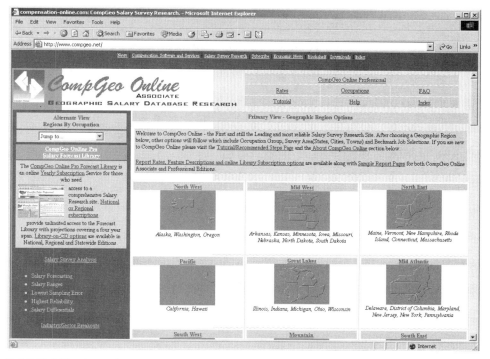

Exhibit 8.7 CompGeo Online

Executive Compensation Advisory Services

http://ecas.develements.com

Fee-based site

Executive Compensation Advisory Services publishes the "Executive Compensation Report" newsletter, along with a number of specialty reports such as the annual "Guide to Board Compensation" and "Top Executive Pay: Who's Making How Much in High Technology." All are available for purchase in print form or by online access.

Hewitt Compensation Center

https://was.hewitt.com/ebusiness/compensationcenter

Fee-based site

Hewitt Associates is a human resources consulting firm. Its Compensation Center Website has newsletters, articles, and current news stories covering compensation issues. Hewitt's many salary surveys can be purchased on the site. Hewitt surveys cover a number of industries and geographic areas such as: Catalog Industry Compensation Study, College and University Administrative Compensation Survey, and Dallas/Fort Worth Manufacturing Survey.

The Institute of Management and Administration (IOMA)

www.ioma.com

Fee-based site

IOMA publishes a number of newsletters dealing with management issues, including the "Report on Salary Surveys," which reports monthly on salary surveys from a variety of industries. Individual issues of the "Report on Salary Surveys" can be purchased online in .pdf format.

Risk Management Association (RMA) Annual Statement Studies

www.rmahq.com/Online_Prods/asstOL.html

Fee-based site

Risk Management Association (formerly Robert Morris Associates) publishes Annual Statement Studies, long a primary source of financial ratios used by business appraisers and other financial professionals. The data provided in RMA's Annual Statement Studies comes directly from the financial statements of more than 150,000 primarily small to medium-sized companies. Among the ratios calculated by RMA is the officers', directors', and owners' compensation as a percentage of sales. RMA's Annual Statement Studies are available online, by individual SIC Code. You can also order the entire Annual Statement Studies database that includes benchmarks for more than 600 industries.

William M. Mercer—Mercer Human Resource Consulting

www.imercer.com

Fee-based site

Mercer conducts more than 140 U.S. compensation and benefit surveys annually. Data is collected from 6,000 companies on over 5,000 jobs and 16 million employees. Mercer clients tend to be the human resources departments of both companies and nonprofit organizations. Reports can be purchased from the Mercer Website and typically cost several thousand dollars each. The MarketPricer Online feature is a tool that allows users to query, view, import, and export survey statistics.

WorldatWork

www.worldatwork.org

Fee-based site

WorldatWork, formerly the American Compensation Association and the Canadian Compensation Association, is a nonprofit association focusing on compensation, benefits, and related human resources issues. On the site, you will find news stories and articles available for purchase on these topics. Books available for purchase include the annual "Report on Total Salary," an 80-page report on compensation arranged by geographic area, industry group, employee category, and type of compensation.

CHAPTER 9

Websites for Conducting Merger and Acquisition Research

The Internet has revolutionized access to merger and acquisition (M&A) data. Before the advent of M&A databases on the Internet, researchers relied on print publications, which were often dated, or on electronic databases that were only available through a direct dial-up service with a difficult search procedure. M&A data providers have done well on the Internet, offering products that users are willing to pay for. Most of the M&A products on our recommended list are fee-based.

Financial professionals may seek out M&A data for a number of reasons:

- Business appraisers need to find transaction data for companies similar to subject company being valued.
- When looking for a possible buyer for a client's business, intermediaries need to identify the companies that have already made similar purchases.
- Journalists who follow the current M&A environment need to keep abreast of current M&A announcements and transactions on a daily basis.
- Lawyers need to review Securities and Exchange Commission (SEC) filings when drafting agreements between the two parties of a transaction.

Many of the online information services discussed in other chapters such as Dialog, Alacra, and LexisNexis offer access to merger and acquisition databases. For example, LexisNexis subscribers can access Investext Mergers and Acquisitions Reports, the IDD Mergers and Acquisition Database archive, the Mergerstat M&A Database, Mergerstat Review, and the SDC Mergers & Acquisitions Database.

The sites listed in the "First and Foremost" section of this chapter are those that we have found to be reliable sources of statistics and analysis presented in easily accessible format. Sites offering all or part of the data for free will be rated higher than sites that offer similar data for a fee. "Best of the Rest" sites may focus on a niche area, be fee-only, or have limited navigation and output features.

FIRST AND FOREMOST

Alacra

www.alacra.com

Fee-based site

Alacra, the data aggregator formerly known as XLS.com, is a leading global provider of business and financial information. Alacra builds online tools and services that allow users to find, analyze, package, and present business information.

Alacra provides access to dozens of databases containing quantitative business and investment information from a variety of content providers. One of the added-value elements to doing a search on a database provided through Alacra is the ability to download much of the content directly into a spreadsheet.

Alarca's content covers a wide range of business topics, including a number of M&A resources. Below is a listing of the premium M&A content providers accessible through Alacra.

What can you expect to find?

- M&A Monitor, a database of deal information on European transactions
- Mergerstat (discussed in a separate entry in this chapter), a database of detailed information on mergers, acquisitions, and divestitures that are publicly announced
- Thomson Financial Securities Data Worldwide M&A Database (discussed in a separate entry in this chapter), a database of public and private transactions involving at least a 5 percent ownership of a company

- In addition, the Thomson Carson Group and the Vickers Stock Research Corporation databases provide ownership information on public companies and databases such as Graham & Whiteside, Harris InfoSource, and CorpTech and are excellent sources for putting together buyers' and sellers' lists

Bizcomps

www.bizcomps.com (Product Information)

www.bvmarketdata.com (Data Access)

http://bizcomps.nvst.com (Data Access)   (Exhibit 9.1)

Fee-based sites

Bizcomps is a database of financial data on the sales of small businesses. Business intermediary Jack Sanders began the print version of the Bizcomps studies around 1979 because he saw the need for a centralized source of data for the sales of business valued under $1 million. Mr. Sanders gathers the data from full-time certified business brokers and intermediaries.

Bizcomps is a unique database in that it contains the multiples and terms of small business sales. Typically this data is difficult to find, since the buyer and seller in most cases are not required to disclose the data (see Exhibit 9.1).

Bizcomps contains up to 20 data fields on the sales of approximately 6,000 privately held companies. The average selling price of the companies in Bizcomps is approximately $308,000. The median selling price of the companies in Bizcomps is $135,000, which indicates that half of all sales are above this figure and half are below it.

What can you expect to find?

- Each transaction contains basic financial data on the acquired company and ratios such as seller's discretionary cash flow to gross sales, and rent to sales, as well as the value of inventory, the price of the sale, and the state where it occurred.

- Bizcomps is searchable by Standard Industrial Classification (SIC) code, North American Industry Classification System (NAICS), sales size, price, geographical area, and keyword.

- The name of the target and the acquiring company are *not* provided because neither the buyer nor the seller is required to disclose that information.

EXHIBIT #12 - ALL CENTRAL STATES PRINTING BUSINESSES

Sic #	NAISC#	Bus Type	Ask Price (000)	Ann Gross (000)	SDCF (000)	SDCF/ Gross Sales	Sale Date	Sale PR (000)	% Down	Terms	Sale/ Sales	Sale/ SDCF	Inv Amt	FF & E (000)	Rent/ Sales	Days on MKT	Fran Royalty	Area
2752	323114	Printer-Commercial	193	469	127	.27	12/31/99	187	26%	5 yrs. @ 10%	.40	1.5	7	226	10%	300		Texas
2752	323114	Printer-Laminating	1,500	2,136	267	.12	10/19/99	1,002	80%	8 yrs. @ a0%	.47	3.8	7.5	875	N/A	90		Central Kentucky
2752	323114	Printing Shop	480	707	194	.27	4/1/99	572	100%	N/A	.81	2.9	0	78	5.7%			Madison, WI
2752	323114	Printer-Commercial	325	1,358	145	.11	4/21/98	325	100%	N/A	.24	2.2	25	400	N/A	180		Central Iowa
2752	323114	Printer-Commercial	2,450	3,000	924	.31	1/31/98	2,180	90%	5 yrs @ 0%	.73	2.4	150	1M	N/A	210		Temple, TX
2752	323114	Printer-Commercial	1,525	3,500	750	.21	1/31/98	1,525	75%	3 yrs @ 10%	.44	2.0	75	1M	N/A	270		Texas
2752	323114	Print Shop-Franchise	435	386	121	.31	7/18/97	360	100%	N/A	.93	3.0	15	260	4%	98	5%	Louisville, KY
2752	323114	Printer-Commercial	147	262	34	.13	6/9/97	142	100%	10 yrs @ 8.5%	.54	4.2	3	100	6%	349		Grand Rapids, MI
2752	323114	Printing Shop	216	295	110	.37	5/8/97	178	15% SBA	7 yrs @ Pr.+2.5	.60	1.6	2	67	5.3%	28		North Texas
2752	323114	Printing Shop	54	92	33	.36	11/27/96	38	100%	N/A	.41	1.2	2	18	9%			Southern Iowa
2752	323114	Printer-Commercial	182	214	57	.27	11/15/96	148	47%	5 yrs @ 9%	.69	2.6	3	39	5.5%	50		Knoxville, TN
2752	323114	Printing Shop	218	296	110	.37	11/8/96	178	100%	N/A	.60	1.6	2	58	8.5%			Dallas/Ft. Worth
2752	323114	Printing Shop	220	200	50	.25	10/31/96	113	100%	N/A	.56	2.3	10	30	N/A			Austin, Texas
2752	323114	Printer-	160	164	60	.37	2/28/96	155	19%	7 yrs @	.95	2.6	2	100	7.6%			Cincinnati,

Exhibit 9.1   Bizcomps

Business Valuation Market Data

www.bvmarketdata.com   (Exhibit 9.2)

Fee-based site

Shannon Pratt, the well-known business valuation expert and newsletter editor, has established a Website of databases containing empirical data on guideline companies, guideline transactions, comparable sales data, business comparables, and market data directed primarily to business valuation professionals (see Exhibit 9.2).

The core database at BVMarketData is the Pratt's Stats Private Transaction Database. Pratt's Stats covers how deals are structured, including payment terms, employment agreements, and noncompete agreements. Users can download valuation multiples calculated for each transaction found in the database. Pratt's Stats offers detailed information on approximately 4,300 private and closely held business sales from 1991 to present, ranging in deal price from under $1,000,000 to $1,000,000,000. The data is collected primarily from business brokers and the actual companies involved in the deals. Pratt's Stats data is updated online monthly, with approximately 100 transactions added per month.

BVMarketData also hosts two other merger databases in addition to Pratt's Stats. These databases are Bizcomps (discussed earlier in this chapter) and the Pratt Public Companies Database. The Public Companies Database has detailed information on more than 500 public companies' business sales from 1995 to the present, ranging in deal price from under $1,000,000 to $1,000,000,000 in approximately 220 industries. Data for the Public Company Transaction Database comes from filings submitted to the Securities and Exchange Commission by the businesses' buyers.

In addition to detailed financial and transactional information relating to the sales of public and privately held companies, BVMarketData also provides data on control premiums, minority discounts, and marketability discounts. BVMarketData offers three databases on these topics, the Mergerstat/Shannon Pratt's Control Premium Study, the FMV Restricted Stock Study, and the Valuation Advisors' Lack of Marketability Discount Study.

Dr. Pratt is the author of two books that cover the use of data found at BVMarketData: *The Market Approach to Valuing Businesses*, (John Wiley & Sons, 2000) and *Business Valuation Discounts and Premiums* (John Wiley & Sons, 2000).

What can you expect to find?

- The Pratt's Stats database provides 70 data fields for each transaction, including summary balance sheets and income statements for the companies involved, as well as the terms of each transaction. Other data include SIC and NAICS codes, company location, employees, time in business, data and prices listed and sold, and noncompete and employment agreement terms and price allocation.

- Pratt's Stats is searchable by multiple criteria, and transactions may be downloaded or data exported to a spreadsheet for analysis.

- Mergerstat/Shannon Pratt's Control Premium studies compare the acquisition price for completed transactions of public companies with the former public market trading price.

- Data on marketability discounts.

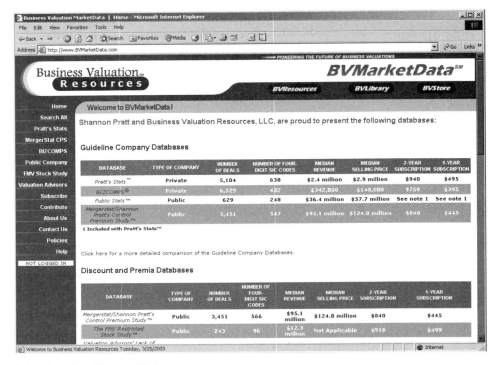

Exhibit 9.2   BVMarketData
Pratt's Stats™ is the official business-sales database of the International Business Brokers Association. Used with permission from Business Valuation Resources, LLC, 7412 SW Beaverton-Hillsdale Hwy, Suite 106, Portland, OR 97225; ph: (503) 291-7963; fax: (503) 291-7955. On-line (www.BVMarketData.com) and print/software subscriptions to Pratt's Stats™ are available.

Corporate Growth Deal Retriever

http://cgr.nvst.com/dealretriever/DealRetriever.asp

Fee-based site

The Corporate Growth Deal Retriever contains M&A transaction data derived from the *Corporate Growth Weekly Report.* The Deal Retriever is a searchable database of more than 3,000 transactions covering offers, takeover speculations, and market summaries of current mergers, acquisitions, divestitures, joint ventures, and initial public offerings within every SIC number.

What can you expect to find?

- All purchase price ratios, historical financial data, balance sheet information on buyer and seller and a description of each transaction. Valuation multiples include the following ratios: Price/Earnings, Price/Revenue, Price/Net Worth, Price/EBITDA, and Price/Assets.

- Key aggregate statistics and price multiple graphs for selected deals with robust search and sorting capabilities.

- Mid-market mergers and acquisitions of both publicly traded and privately held companies.

The Daily Deal at The Deal.com

www.thedeal.com   (Exhibit 9.3)

Free and fee-based site

The *Daily Deal* is a daily newspaper that focuses on mergers and acquisitions. Published Monday through Friday, researchers can find news of recent transactions, feature articles, and special reports five days a week. The publication gathers and compiles data from over a dozen financial information vendors.

The *Daily Deal* is one of a number of publications published by The Deal, LLC, a media company featuring original news reporting, financial data, and commentary on the deal-making community. Deal LLC products include TheDeal.com Website, e-newsletters, printed publications, and special reports.

Deal Focus is the year-in-review M&A database coving detailed information on the past year's deals, including reporting by *The Daily Deal*, *The Deal*, and TheDeal.com. Deal Focus provides unlimited access to this deal data on an annual subscription plan.

In addition to the *Daily Deal*, other publications from the Deal LLC are *The Deal*, a weekly magazine launched on November 4, 2002, and *Corporate Control Alert*, reporting on deals that are valued at $100 million or more and alter corporate control. The *Daily Deal* is available in print, in a digital format (this is an exact replica of *The Daily Deal* newspaper at www.TheDeal.com/tdddigital.html) and as a wireless channel on Avantgo for access on a handheld PDA device or Internet-enabled mobile phone (see Exhibit 9.3).

TheDeal.com offers a subscription that provides unlimited access to *The Deal's* commentary, statistics, special reports, and robust deal archives through its deal-specific and industry channels.

The Deal has more than 150 employees, including 80 full-time journalists. *The Deal's* editorial efforts are also supported by international correspondents in 15 countries, contributing columnists, and illustrators.

What can you expect to find?

- The *Daily Deal Scoreboard* contains useful charts, graphs, and tables. For example, the *Scoreboard* contains a daily roster of transactions, Multiples Day, and Pricing Day.
- Special reports such as compensation surveys of dealmakers.
- News about the industry "movers and shakers."

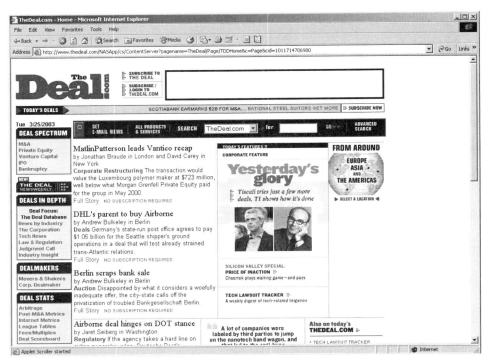

Exhibit 9.3   *The Daily Deal* at TheDeal.com

Done Deals

http://donedeals.nvst.com   (Exhibit 9.4)

Fee-based site

Done Deals' specialty is providing data on mid-market transactions, or those deals valued between $1 million and $250 million. The database adds hundreds of completed transactions each quarter and currently contains more that 5,000 transactions. Approximately half of the deals in the database are of companies under $14 million in value, the majority of which are privately owned. Data contained in the database is extracted from a variety of SEC filings, making the product an excellent source of information on the transactions where the acquiring company is public and the acquired company is private (see Exhibit 9.4).

The database is searchable by closing date, SIC code, price, buyer and/or seller name, keywords in the seller's business description, and type of target (private, public, subsidiary, and asset or stock sale, or both).

What can you expect to find?

- Purchase price ratios, such as price/earnings, price/cash flow from operations, price/revenue, price/assets and price/stockholders equity for each deal
- The ability to create regression and r-squared charts based on search results or user-designed criteria
- Company contacts provided (name of the executive handling the deal, address, phone)
- Price, terms, and sources of financing

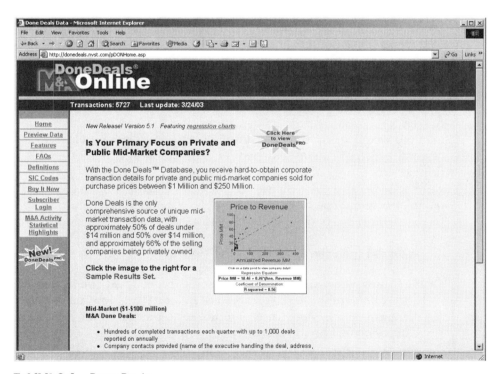

Exhibit 9.4 Done Deals

EDGAR Databases

***www.sec.gov (Securities and Exchange Commission,
free site)***   (Exhibit 9.5)

www.10kwizard.com (10k Wizard, fee-based site)   (Exhibit 9.6)

www.gsionline.com/online.htm (LivEdgar, fee-based site)

EDGAR filings are the disclosure documents that publicly traded companies are required to file with Securities and Exchange Commission (SEC). These required disclosure documents are called EDGAR filings (an acronym for Electronic Data Gathering, Analysis, and Retrieval), and they can be a great source of M&A information.

When a public company acquires another company, either public or private, and the transaction represents a particular amount of business in relation to the acquirer's current business, the acquiring company must disclose the terms of the deal to the SEC. Typically the particulars of the deal, including the acquired company's financial data, is included in a form 8-K filed at the time of the acquisition and is also usually reported in the company's annual 10-K filing. Note that the 8-K form is used to report the occurrence of any material events or corporate changes that are of importance to investors or security holders, not just acquisitions.

EDGAR documents are available directly from the SEC and from a variety of vendors. Information on resources for EDGAR documents is covered in more detail in Chapter 6, "Public Company Data." Below is a short list of databases that can be searched for acquisition information in 8-K and 10-K filings.

The M&A Filings database, accessible on Dialog, contains detailed abstracts of every original and amended merger and acquisition document released by the Securities and Exchange Commission since early 1985 through June 2000.

What can you expect to find?

- **SEC, www.sec.gov, free site.** The SEC redesigned the access to EDGAR documents on the SEC Website (see Exhibit 9.5). Now, users can search by company name, state, central index key, and SIC code. The SIC also has a Quick Forms Lookup feature.
- **10k Wizard, www.10Kwizard.com, fee-based site.** 10-K Wizard's database of EDGAR documents can be searched by keywords, phrases, company name, industry segment, SIC code, form group, form type, ticker, and date (see Exhibit 9.6). This search flexibility will allow users to search

by SIC code, while limiting the search to 8-K-related forms, and adding the keyword "acquisition."

- **LIVEDGAR, www.gsionline.com, fee-based site.** Global Securities Information Inc.'s (GSI) LIVEDGAR is a fee-based source of EDGAR documents; however, the fee is very reasonable and infrequent users can purchase individual documents without acquiring a monthly or annual subscription. LIVEDGAR offers users the ability to perform sophisticated searches across the EDGAR database. Once an 8-K is found that contains financial information on a target company, those financials can be downloaded directly into a spreadsheet. Another helpful feature is the ability to access preformatted searches created by the GSI staff in order to find similar documents, such as one of the many legal documents necessary between the buyer and the seller of a company. LIVEDGAR users can generate M&A league tables to rank transactions by counsel or financial advisor or look at the specific deals completed by a particular firm.

Exhibit 9.5　U.S. Securities and Exchange Commission

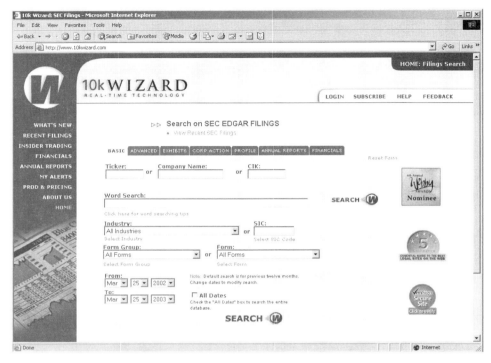

Exhibit 9.6 10k Wizard

Global Securities Information's Mergers & Acquisitions Database

www.gsionline.com/mna.html

Fee-based site

The Mergers & Acquisitions database contains transactions derived from the original SEC source documents. This database has an intuitive interface and is reasonably priced. The M&A database covers change in control transactions as well as any significant acquisition or sale of assets, equity, subsidiary, or business division.

What can you expect to find?

- Information on all public deals with a value of more than $1 million
- More than 70 types of transactions
- The ability to search by dozens of options, such as target financials, SIC codes, transaction value, and geographic region
- Concise summaries of each deal, including attorneys, financial advisors, and fees

Mergerstat

www.mergerstat.com

Fee-based site

Mergerstat products include the printed publications *Mergerstat Review*, *Mergerstat Transaction Roster*, and the *Mergerstat Control Premium Study*. The publications track mergers and acquisitions, unit divestitures, management buyouts, and certain asset sales and include industry analysis by size, premium, and transaction multiples.

Mergerstat analysts gather M&A information from SEC filings, investment banks, press releases, news sources, and professional contacts. Only those transactions valued at $1 million and over are included in the database, which is updated daily. Mergerstat has tracked the M&A market in print since 1963 and in online and electronic formats since 1992. The database contains deals involving both private and public companies.

In addition to the online M&A database, Mergerstat also publishes the *Corporate Acquisitions* newsletter, the *Mergerstat Review* (annual M&A trends), and the quarterly *Control Premium Study*.

Mergerstat, formerly a division of the investment bank and financial advisory firm Houlihan Lokey Howard & Zukin, was sold to FactSet Research Systems Inc. in January 2003. Mergerstat information is accessible through a variety of vendors, including Bloomberg, LexisNexis, and Alacra.

What can you expect to find?

- Data on deals dating back to 1992
- Data on cross-border transactions that involve U.S. companies
- The ability to create reports of deals based on a variety of data points, such as valuation multiples, premiums paid, seller financials, announcement and closing dates, and SIC code

NVST.com

www.nvst.com   (Exhibit 9.7)

Fee-based site

NVST.com is a Website that brings together investors, advisors, and entrepreneurs of privately held businesses. The content of the site is focused on all aspects of the life cycle of a business, from funding a business to selling a business. The NVST.com Website provides online access to professional journals, research databases, and educational resources for professional training (see Exhibit 9.7).

The site has links to M&A-related organizations, such as the Association for Corporate Growth and the International Merger and Acquisition Professionals, as well as a conference calendar. NVST.com also provides sample issues and subscriptions to publications such as *Fair Market Reporter, Buyouts, Mergers & Restructuring, M&A Today,* and *Merger & Acquisitions: The Dealmaker's Journal.*

What can you expect to find?

- Three M&A databases: Done Deals, Bizcomps, and the Corporate Growth Deal Retriever. Searches can be created by SIC code, transaction date, sale price, and/or revenue.
- NVST Research Reports covering industry-specific M&A data and statistics with details and analysis of the most significant transactions.

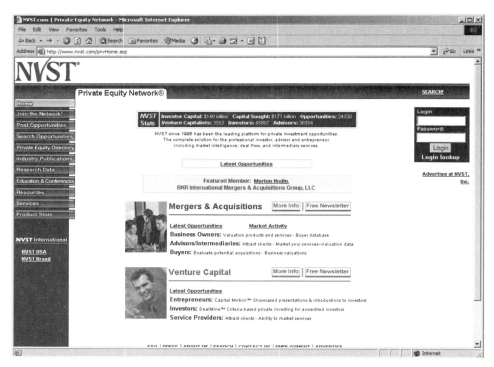

Exhibit 9.7 NVST.com

SNL Securities

www.snl.com   (Exhibit 9.8)

Fee-based site

SNL Securities is a banking research firm. The SNL DataSource database provides information on banks, thrifts, financial services companies, real estate investment companies, and insurance companies. SNL has corporate, financial, and trading data on individual banks, and maintains a database of over 10,000 bank mergers and acquisitions dating back to the late 1980s.

The SNL database covers historical transaction information for all deals and asset sales, including buyer/seller/target information, buyer and target financials, deal terms and considerations, pricing ratios specific to each industry type, advisers, deal analysis, and related news stories (see Exhibit 9.8).

SNL also publishes a number of banking industry newsletters, including the monthly *Bank Mergers & Acquisitions* and *Bank Mergers & Acquisitions Weekly*, a weekly email or fax newsletter that provides summaries and all the key financial data on the previous week's merger and acquisition activity.

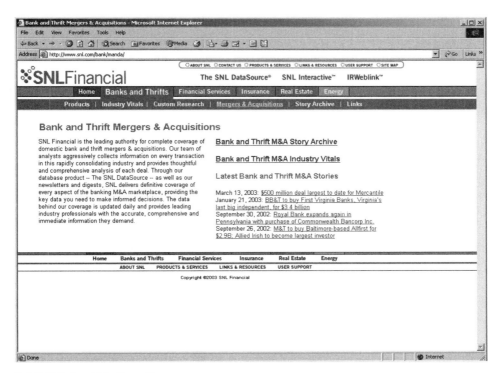

Exhibit 9.8   SNL Securities

What can you expect to find?

- Recent headlines from SNL publications *Specialty Lender Mergers & Acquisitions* and *Securities and Investments Mergers & Acquisitions*, as well as information about the company's M&A databases

- Historical financial data from the Federal Deposit Insurance Corporation, the Office of Thrift Supervision, the Federal Reserve, and credit union regulatory agency filings going back 10 years and 10 quarters for over 15,000 depository institutions in the United States.

- Detailed financial and market data on thousands of financial services companies

Thomson Financial Investment Banking/Capital Markets Group

Securities Data Company Worldwide M&A Database

www.tfibcm.com

Fee-based site

The Securities Data Company Worldwide M&A Database (SDC) from Thompson Financial provides extensive information on thousands of acquisitions, including name, address, deal terms, and amounts. Transactions reported include partial or completed mergers, divestitures, stock repurchases, self-tenders, spin-offs, and exchange offers. The SDC database is the most comprehensive source of M&A transaction data. It is the only publicly available source of deals dating back to 1979, although the database's true comprehensiveness begins with its coverage in the late 1980s and early 1990s. The database contains data on hundreds of thousands of transactions valued at over $1 million. The SDC database offers more information on non-U.S. deals than any other source.

Because the SDC database is so expensive, we recommend that users attend one of the training classes or place a call to the company's technical support line before initiating a search. This data is also accessible on Alacra.com and LexisNexis.

Thomson also maintains the Website for the publication Acquisitions Monthly at www.acquisitions-monthly.com which gives subscribers access to all the articles in the magazine. Acquisitions Monthly covers the mergers, acquisitions, and buyouts industry with statistics, analysis, and commentary on deals from Europe, the United States, and Asia. Approximately two thirds of the data on the Acquisitions Monthly Website is exclusive to the Web including Breaking news, Legal and Regulatory commentary, Company profiles, and an archive of all the print and Web articles published by Acquisitions Monthly since 1988.

What can you expect to find?

- A database that can be searched by approximately 1,200 different data items, such as target and acquirer business descriptions, deal terms, stock premiums paid, and financial and legal advisor fees
- The ability to create very specific searches, such as "all of the deals within SIC code 1711 between 2000 and 2002 that were for a majority interest, with a deal value of over $10 million and with EBIDTA multiples available"
- Other M&A products available from the Thomson Financial Investment Banking/Capital Markets Group include *Investment Dealers' Digest,* and *Mergers & Acquisitions: The Dealmaker's Journal*

BEST OF THE REST

American Society of Association Executives' (ASAE) Gateway to Associations

http://info.asaenet.org/gateway/OnlineAssocSlist.html

Free site

Trade associations often publish buyer's guides of and for their members. These guides can be excellent sources when putting together a buyer's or seller's list because they contain detailed descriptions of companies that participate within a particular industry. The ASAE site is a great place to start looking for an industry's trade association because it provides links to over 6,500 member associations.

Dealogic

www.dealogic.com

Fee-based site

Dealogic (formerly Commscan) is a research firm producing a number of M&A resources, including *M&A Desk* database with in-depth coverage of all U.S.-targeted M&A transactions from rumor stage to completion. M&A Desk includes information on fees, comparable transactions, multiples, premiums, and direct links to SEC filings. Dealogic also produces several publications, including *M&A Review*, a free publication delivered via email, *M&A Daily News Sheet*, which provides a daily recap of U.S. M&A news, and *M&A Fee Alert*, a daily publication highlighting disclosed fees on merger and acquisition advisory services.

Ingenta

www.ingenta.com

Free and fee-based site

Ingenta, formerly the Carl UnCover database, is an information service providing access to more than 25,000 journals in a variety of subjects. Researchers can use the database to find articles on topics relating to M&A, because journals such as *Mergers & Acquisitions, Harvard Business Review, Investment Dealers Digest,* and *Institutional Investor* are indexed. Most documents are available online but some older documents can be ordered online and then faxed to the user. Subscribers can also set up an alert service that informs the user of the table of contents of a new edition or articles on a defined subject. Ingenta is free to search and most articles are available for individual purchase.

Institute of Business Appraisers Market Database

www.go-iba.org

Fee-based site

The Institute of Business Appraisers (IBA) maintains a Market Database of guideline transactions for small businesses. The database includes information on 23,000+ sales of closely held businesses in more than 725 SIC codes. Access to the database is limited to IBA members.

International Business Brokers Association

www.ibba.org and www.masource.org

Free site

The IBBS set up a database of seller profiles on its Website, which is searchable by geographic region, revenue, and type of business. A profile is provided for each of the companies retrieved from the search results. Each profile contains a description of the business, geographic region, SIC code, revenues, adjusted profit, asking price, legal structure, and number of employees. Those interested in the business are asked to contact the IBBA for more information. Much of the data here is mirrored on the M&A Source site, a division of the IBBA directed at middle market intermediaries.

Investment Dealers Digest

www.IDDmagazine.com

Fee-based site

The Investment Dealers Digest covers newly registered securities and topics related to underwriting and mergers and acquisitions. At the IDD Website, subscribers can access news and feature stories, plus listings of newly registered securities, new issues, and more. Also available are quarterly rankings and Who's Who listings of the people involved in underwriting, M&A, private placement, and other specialized markets. The Investment Banking Database section contains weekly and year-to-date deals, league table, and fee information on investment banking sectors.

Kagan and Associates

www.kagan.com

Fee-based site

Fee-based site Kagan and Associates are industry experts on the media and telecommunications industries. Kagan publications, such as *CableWorld*, report on mergers and acquisitions in these industries. Kagan's *Media Money Newsletter* covers the leading media indicators, media merger and acquisition data, benchmarks and reference charts, and analysis of industry trends and issues. The Kagan On Demand feature allows users to search the Kagan subscriber databases free of charge and to purchase articles on a pay-per-item basis.

Mergers & Acquisitions Report

www.mareport.com

Fee-based site

Mergers & Acquisitions Report provides information on mergers, acquisitions, restructurings, and bankruptcies. It is available both online and in print. Each issue covers pending and ongoing deals as well as insights into industry trends, strategies, and the firms and people involved. Subscribers to the weekly publication have access to an M&A database, articles on industry trends, and news items.

Mergers & Acquisitions Report is part of the Thomson Media Group which publishes other M&A publications, including the monthly magazine *Mergers & Acquisitions, The Dealmaker's Journal*, which provides in-depth articles on the issues surrounding buying and selling businesses, and the *Directory of M&A Intermediaries*, a list of hundreds of dealmakers. Thomson Media Group also maintains the TakeoverStockReport.com site, which covers stocks involved in takeovers.

Merger Central

http://mergercentral.com

Fee-based site

MergerCentral offers a collection of M&A related news and publications, including a database of articles classified by industry. The site also has an M&A bookstore, job bank, and an M&A Directory. Subscribers have access to *MergerWeek*, a recap of the current week's deals plus analyses and articles.

Merger Market

www.mergermarket.com

Fee-based site

A London-based source of European deal data, Merger Market provides current and archived deal news stories, a database of European transactions valued over 10 million pounds, league tables, and lists of businesses for sale by company, sector, and/or geographic area.

MergerNetwork

www.mergernetwork.com

Fee-based site

MergerNetwork was the first online listing service for buyers and sellers of businesses. Today, MergerNetwork specializes in large businesses (over $5 million in sales) and is primarily a listing of companies for sale. Companies are listed by region, industry, and business size. A detailed business description is provided for each company listed. A subscription is required to search the MergerNetwork databases and obtain contact information for buyers and sellers.

Thomas Register of American Manufacturers

www.thomasregister.com

Free site

The *Thomas Register of American Manufacturers* is an established directory of manufacturers in the United States. Its online version, Thomas Register Online, is free but utilizes a registration and password program. The Register is an excellent site to use when putting together buyers' or sellers' lists of manufacturing companies. The database, currently containing information on over 170,000 companies, is searchable by company name, product, or service.

Webmergers.com

www.webmergers.com

Free and fee-based site

Webmergers, Inc. is a provider of M&A analysis, data, and advisory services to the high-technology sector. Webmergers offers users access to data, reports, and M&A commentary. An example is the 90+ page year-end report summarizing merger activity. This full report is available for purchase, and there is a lengthy summary along with eight sample pages available for free. Web-mergers core product is *Tech Deal Maker* (which has its own site at www .techdealmaker.com), a weekly M&A intelligence information service. Selected articles from *Tech Deal Maker* are available for free.

Webmergers sells a "Comparables Report" that lists mergers and acquisitions of properties that are similar to a subject property. The report includes: buyer, seller, date, price, summary of deal terms, and valuation metrics when available. Webmergers compiles these reports from its database of more than 2,500 Internet-related deals. Users can also sign up for the free weekly "Update of Web M&A News," which is delivered via email.

The Webmergers marketplace listing of buyers and sellers is now *TechDealNet: The Technology M&A Marketplace* at www.techdealnet.com and is no longer affiliated with Webmergers.com.

CHAPTER **10**

Websites for Intellectual Property Research

Financial professionals are increasingly finding intellectual property issues in the problems clients bring to them to solve. Business appraisers may need to identify and value intellectual property in the course of a business valuation engagement. Financial experts are asked to testify in litigation matters involving intellectual property. In this chapter, we feature a variety of sites designed to assist the financial profession in understanding, defining, and valuing intellectual property.

Traditional forms of intellectual property include patents, trademarks, and copyrights. The wide acceptance of the Internet has introduced a fox into the intellectual property henhouse and is driving much of what is happening in intellectual property legislation. Intellectual property issues such as domain name ownership rights, copyrighted materials used as Website content, and the patenting of business methods make front-page headlines.

The ability of the Internet to reach such a large group of people has radically changed the landscape of intellectual property information. Much of the information about intellectual properties such as patents and trademarks had been proprietary, controlled by a few specialty information providers.

After the U.S. Government Patent and Trademark Office's Website was launched in 1995, patent information was available free of charge through the Internet. Soon, patent offices in other countries begin making their databases available free on the Internet. Then commercial sites like the IBM Intellectual Property Network site (now Delphion) appeared with value-added services for a fee. Many options for patent research now exist, including information services such as LexisNexis with its comprehensive patent database, trademark information, and intellectual property regulations.

The purpose of this chapter is to give an overview of the sources for intellectual property information. This is not intented to be a how-to guide to patent or trademark searching nor a replacement for a legal search by an attorney.

FIRST AND FOREMOST

Delphion Intellectual Property Network

www.delphion.com

Free and fee-based site

The Intellectual Property Network began life as an internal IBM project to help their researchers, product developers, and intellectual property attorneys perform basic searches of patent data quickly and easily. IBM decided to allow public access to the site, and it has become one of the best-known and widely used patent search sites on the Internet. In 2000, IBM partnered with the Internet Capital Group to set up the IBM Intellectual Property Network as a separate company named Delphion. And in 2002, Thompson Corporation purchased Delphion for $22 million.

The Delphion Intellectual Property Network allows subscribers to search, view, and analyze patent documents. From the Delphion search page at www.delphion.com/research/, you can search the following collections of patent information:

- **United States Patents Applications.** The U.S. Patents Application collection contains complete text and images of all patents filed by the U.S. Patent and Trademark Office. This collection has bibliographic text, full text, and images of patent applications for U.S. patents filed from March 2001 to present.

- **United States Patents Granted.** This contains the complete text and images of all patents issued by the U.S. Patent and Trademark Office since 1974, and bibliographic text and some images since 1971. This collection also includes full images for Backfile patents dated 1790 to 1971.

- **Derwent World Patents Index.** The Derwent World Patents Index is a comprehensive database of value-added patent information that covers more than 10 million separate inventions from more than 20 million basic and equivalent patent documents.

- **European Patent Applications.** The European Patent Applications collection has bibliographic text and full-document images of applications for European patents issued from 1979 to present, and full text from 1987 to present. Data is published by the European Patent Office.

- **European Patents Granted.** The European Patents Granted collection contains European patents published by the European Patent Office. Coverage includes the bibliographic text and full-document images of European patents issued from 1980 to present, and full text from 1991 to present.

- **Patent Abstracts of Japan.** This collection contains unexamined patent applications in English for both Japanese and non-Japanese priorities.

- **Switzerland Images.** This collection contains images of more than 17,000 Swiss patents. For over 250,000 Swiss patents, bibliographic information from 1969 to present is searchable via the INPADOC collection.

- **WIPO Patent Cooperation Treaty (PCT) Publications.** PCT publications are abstracts, full-document images, and full text from over a hundred member countries including the United States.

In addition, the Delphion Intellectual Property Network allows searching of the INPADOC (International Patent Documentation Center) database that contains the bibliographic and family data of patent documents and utility models of 65 patent issuing organizations, including the European Patent Office and the World Intellectual Property Organization. Delphion's searchable database makes available patents and legal status actions dating back to 1968.

Summaries of IBM Technical Disclosure Bulletins, published from 1958 to 1998, are also available for searching and browsing on the Delphion Intellectual Property Network. The IBM Technical Disclosure Bulletin served as a forum for IBM employees to publish defensive disclosures of inventions that did not ultimately acquire patents. Over the years, these articles became one of the most often-cited references in patents. Over 48,000 references to IBM Technical Disclosure Bulletin articles are made in U.S. patents.

There are a number of options for searching the databases on the Delphion Intellectual Property Network. Searches can be conducted by keyword, patent number, inventor, or abstract, as well as by several other categories. Users can also browse categories of patent information. Searching and viewing the patent information is free. In most cases the information can be downloaded for a small fee.

Derwent, the patent specialist company within the Thomson Corporation, has its own Website at www.derwent.com. This Derwent Online site has an extensive collection of patent information including news, articles, and search help and access to the Derwent Patent Database.

In early 2003, Thomson announced plans to launch the Thomson Patent Store at www.thomsonpatentstore.com. Thomson claims this service will provide a comprehensive patent document delivery service, with fee-based Web access to current and historical patents from all over the world. Patents are available for immediate viewing, printing, or downloading in .pdf format.

Patents can be purchased on a pay-per-order basis. A free demo of the services is available which allows users to download up to 44 patents.

What can you expect to find?

- Detailed information on U.S. patents, including full images
- Patent information from Europe and Japan
- Links to other patent resources
- Gallery of unusual patents (bird diapers, pants separable at crotch for style mixing, Braille slot machine)

The Intellectual Property Mall

www.ipmall.fplc.edu   (Exhibit 10.1)

Free site

The Intellectual Property Mall is a collection of intellectual property resources assembled by the Franklin Pierce Law Center, an ABA-accredited law school located in Concord, New Hampshire. Despite its relatively small size, *U.S. News & World Report* consistently ranks the Franklin Pierce Law Center in the top five Intellectual Property (IP) law schools in the nation.

Franklin Pierce Law Center's IP Library is one of the premier intellectual property libraries in the country. Included in the Library's materials are unique collections of practitioner materials donated by intellectual property attorneys and corporate IP departments. The Library's user guides, listed on www.ipmall.info/about/userguid.asp, cover topics from the practical (How to locate IP Periodicals) to the amusing (Famous U.S. Patents). Unfortunately, little of the Library's extensive collection is accessible through the Website.

The Intellectual Property Mall has an extensive listing of intellectual property Web links organized by topic. The collection goes well beyond the obvious well-known links. If you want to find a list of links related to "Protecting Intellectual Property Within Horizontal Exchange Relationships" or "Insurance Coverage for Infringement Claims," this is the place to go.

What can you expect to find?

- Briefing papers on intellectual property topics
- Information about Franklin's top-rated intellectual property library
- Links to a variety of intellectual property sites

Exhibit 10.1　IP Mall

The Intellectual Property Transaction Database

www.fvginternational.com　　(Exhibit 10.2)

Fee-based site

The Financial Valuation Group, a business appraisal firm, has developed a proprietary database of empirical research on intellectual property. The searchable database of more than 3,000 transactions is accessible on the Financial Valuation Group Website. Information in the Intellectual Property Transaction Database includes data on payments made for royalties and licensing fees for the use of trademarks, patents, copyrights, and brand names.

This compilation of intellectual property transactions was gleaned from publicly available documents, primarily filings with the Securities and Exchange Commission. The transactions pertain to a wide range of industries, including Apparel, Chemicals, Computers, Electronics, Food Products, Medical, Pharmaceuticals, Restaurants, and Telecommunications.

The database is searchable by either Standard Industrial Classification (SIC) Codes or The North American Industry Classification System (NAICS). The detailed information on arm's length transactions in intellectual property is useful to expert witnesses, negotiators, and appraisers. Data from the Intellectual Property Database can be used to support claims for damages in intellectual property litigation cases, estimates of reasonable royalty percentage rates, and valuations of closely held companies and other intangible assets.

What can you expect to find?

- Royalty rate percentages paid in actual transactions
- Over 40 fields of data on each intellectual property transaction

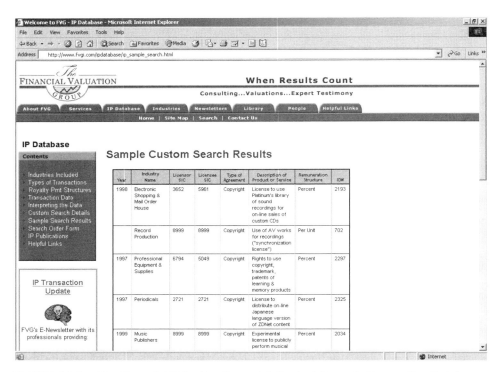

Exhibit 10.2   The Financial Valuation Group Intellectual Property Transaction Database

Law.com Intellectual Law Practice Center

www.law.com/professionals/iplaw.html (Exhibit 10.3)

Free and fee-based site

Law.com is a commercial site targeting attorneys and law students. The umbrella site, www.law.com is divided into five practice areas. In addition to the IP Center, there are practice areas for Corporate Law, Employment Law, Litigation, and Tech Law (see Exhibit 10.3).

All of the practice areas strive to offer one-stop shopping for the busy practitioner with coverage of breaking legal news, the latest case law, and practical information and legal analysis. The IP Center focuses on legal developments in the areas of patents, trademarks, copyrights, trade secrets, and unfair competition. Biotechnology, media, and entertainment law issues receive a lot of attention.

The IP News is well designed and content rich. The full text of current articles from publications such as the *American Lawyer* and the *National Law Journal* are displayed along with pictures, illustrations, and links to related articles. The IP News section also picks up intellectual property stories from daily and weekly legal newspapers in Washington, DC, New York, California, Texas, Pennsylvania, Florida, New Jersey, and Connecticut.

The Decisions section offers a summary of recent case decisions from all the federal circuits, the United States Supreme Court, and the appellate courts of most states. Detailed case analyses and the full citations of cases are available to subscribers who pay a small annual fee.

The site also features the full text of intellectual property articles from other publications such as *IP Law and Business* and practice tools such as sample agreements and other legal documents.

What can you expect to find?

- Articles from law journals on intellectual property topics
- Cases on intellectual property issues
- Practice papers that cover a topic in depth
- A law dictionary and links to state legal resources
- An online store where you can purchase books and software

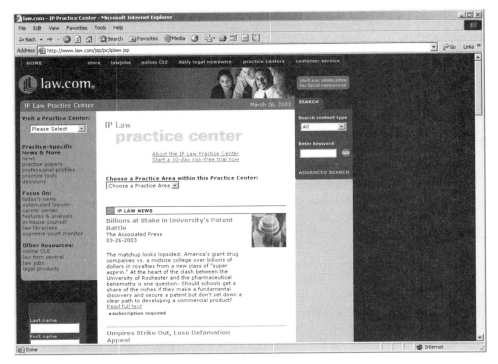

Exhibit 10.3   Law.com

MicroPatent

www.micropat.com

Fee-based site

Founded in 1989, MicroPatent was the first company to provide patent document delivery services. MicroPatent provides a database for searching and displaying the full text and images in .pdf format of United States patents (from 1836), European Patents (from 1988), Patent Cooperation Treaties (from 1978), British patents (from 1979), and German patents (from 1989) as well as the front page of Japanese patents (from 1976).

Users can search the digital archive of more than 33 million documents and then purchase just the patent documents needed and pay per document. You can download patent documents to your computer or printer.

MicroPatent and its related companies (Master Data Center, Faxpat/ Optipat, and Trademark.com) provide services for researching, managing, and licensing patents, trademarks, and other types of intellectual capital services on a global basis.

What can you expect to find?

- Access to extensive libraries of patent information from around the world

Patent Café Intellectual Property Network

www.patentcafe.com   (Exhibit 10.4)

Free and fee-based site

Patent Café is an intellectual property portal with a collection of news, advice, software, books, legal, financial products, intellectual asset management tools, patent analytics management tools, and educational support materials (see Exhibit 10.4). Patent Café actually comprises a number of separate properties with unique URLs under common ownership. PatentCafe.com's Internet Properties include:

- www.PatentCafe.com IP Directory
- www.IPSearchEngine.com Enterprise ASP
- www.2XFR.com Technology Exchange
- www.CafeZine.com Online IP Magazine
- www.PatentCafe.com/Directory Web Listings
- www.CafeForums.com IP Community
- www.IPBookstore.com IP Book Store
- www.LockMyDoc.com Digital Rights Mgt. Portal
- Kids.PatentCafe.com Kid Inventors Portal

If you are looking for basic intellectual property information, start your visit to Patent Café at the FAQ page www.patentcafe.com/faq. Here you will find dozens of questions and answers on intellectual property topics. There are FAQ sections on patents, trademarks, international patents, trade secrets, and copyrights.

The Patent Café makes an effort to address a concern common to most sites targeting inventors—fraud. There is an entire section on the site devoted to fraud issues at www.patentcafe.com/inventors_cafe/fraud.html. Here, inventors can learn how to avoid scams and report fraudulent activities.

The Patent Café IP Search Engine at www.IPSearchEngine.com allows users searchable access to over 600 patent, nonpatent art, trademark, and domain databases, and more than 100 million searchable data records from over 70 separate Websites. The site overlays a search page over databases from patent-issuing entities like the U.S. Patent Office and the European Patent Office.

The Patent Café Mall sells books, software, and desk sculpture. If you fall in love with the site, you can also get your official Patent Café hat or mouse pad here.

What can you expect to find?

- Lots of "how-to's" for inventors, how to patent/sell/market/exploit your invention
- Articles on a variety of intellectual property issues
- Extensive searchable database of patent information
- Bookstore of intellectual property resources

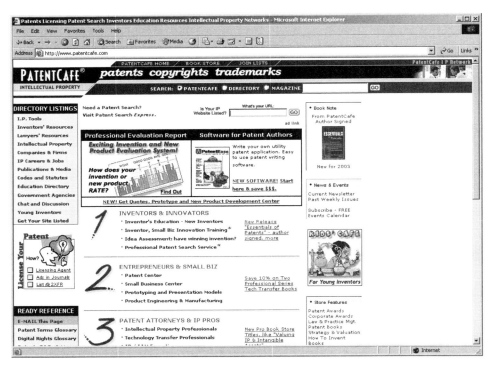

Exhibit 10.4   Patent Café
Printed by Permission © 1996-2003, PatentCafe.com, Inc.

Thomson & Thomson

www.thomson-thomson.com

Free and fee-based site

Thomson & Thomson is a well-respected trademark, copyright, title, and domain name research company. The IP Resources section of the Thomson & Thomson Website contains a selection of recent articles and cases and issues of in-house newsletters including Client Times, Bytes in Brief, and the Thomson & Thomson news service. There is also an IP Fundamentals section that does an excellent job of covering the basic issues involved in trademark, copyright, and domain name research.

Thomson & Thomason's primary database is Trademarkscan. The Trademarkscan database provides information on all active registered trademarks, service marks, and applications for registration filed at the U.S. Patent and Trademark Office. The database also covers trademark applications filed with a number of foreign trademark registration agencies. Thomson & Thomson has a proprietary online service—SAEGIS—that can be used to access Trademarkscan at this Website, but Trademarkscan is also accessible through other information vendors such as Dialog and WestLaw.

What can you expect to find?

- Articles on trademark, copyright, and domain name issues
- Ability to search for service marks and trademarks
- Information on other Thomson & Thomson products including document filing and retrieval services and music media searching

The United States Copyright Office

http://lcweb.loc.gov/copyright   (Exhibit 10. 5)

Free site

The Website for the United States Copyright Office is part of the Library of Congress site. This should be your first stop for learning about copyright information. The copyright basics page at www.loc.gov/copyright/circs/circ1.html provides detailed information on the practical aspects of copyright use and law (see Exhibit 10.5).

The Copyright Basic information is from the "Copyright Information Circulars and Form Letters" series. These circulars cover a wide variety of copyright topics and can be downloaded in .pdf format from the www .copyright.gov/circs/ page. There are dozens of fact sheets, letters, and opinions here on topics including "Copyright Registration for Online Work," "Reproductions of Copyrighted Works by Educators and Librarians," and "How to Investigate the Copyright Status of a Work."

The Law & Policy section on the site covers current legislation, reports and studies, and congressional testimony. Here you will also find the Copyright Office summary of the 1998 Digital Millennium Copyright Act and guidelines for fair use of copyrighted material.

What can you expect to find?

- Frequently asked questions about copyright issues
- Summary of copyright legislation
- News bulletins at www.copyright.gov/newsnet/

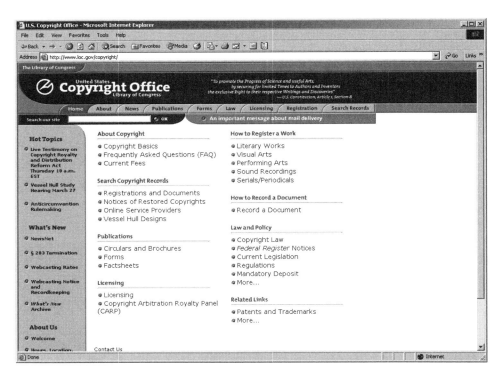

Exhibit 10.5   United States Copyright Office

United States Patent and Trademark Office

www.uspto.gov   (Exhibit 10.6)

Free site

The United States Patent and Trademark Office (PTO) is the base for intellectual property rights information in the United States. The primary services provided by the PTO include processing patents and trademarks and disseminating patent and trademark information. Since 1991, the PTO has operated in much the same way as a private business, providing products and services to customers in exchange for fees, which are used to fully fund operations (see Exhibit 10.6).

The centerpiece of the PTO site is the huge searchable database of patents and trademarks. Users can search text and images of patents dating back to 1976 and registered and full-page images of patents dating back to 1790. The Patent Applications database covers patent applications published since March 2001 and is searchable by multiple fields. The PTO has accepted trademark applications electronically since October 1998.

The Electronic Business Center (EBC) on the PTO site at www.uspto.gov/ebc/indexebc.html is the e-commerce portal, linking users to the systems that enable them to do business with the USPTO electronically. From the EBC you can submit a patent application, check the status of a patent application, and register to conduct business with the PTO.

If you are looking for patent information, start with the Patent home page at www.uspto.gov/main/patents.htm. On this page, you will find guides and reference resources covering patent information. Documents range from independent inventor resources to rosters of patent attorneys to a white paper on business methods patents. If you are looking for basic patent information, go to the General Information Concerning Patents page at www.uspto.gov/web/offices/pac/doc/general/index.html. Here you will find answers to questions such as, "What can be patented?" and "Who may apply for a patent?"

Similarly, the Trademark home page at www.uspto.gov/main/trademarks.htm gives access to trademark resources such as the U.S. Trademark Electronic Search System (TESS), online trademark applications, and legal resources such as guidelines for the trademark registration of Internet domain names. The Trademark Electronic Business Center section of the site at www.uspto.gov/web/menu/tmebc/index.html is the PTO's attempt to provide a single place to locate all the different electronic search systems and methods of doing trademark business. From here you can access the TESS search system, file a trademark application, or check on the status of existing applications.

The USPTO Information Dissemination Service has created an online products and services catalog at www.uspto.gov/web/offices/ac/ido/oeip/catalog/index.html. The products include such items as a print version of the "Code of Federal Regulations, Title 37 Patents, Trademarks, and Copyrights" and a video on how to conduct a patent search.

Libraries that participate in the Patent and Trademark Depository Library Program (www.uspto.gov/go/ptdl) of the USPTO have historical patents, some as old as two hundred years. A list of the participating libraries is available at www.uspto.gov/go/ptdl/ptdlib_1.html.

What can you expect to find?

- Trademarks and patents definitions and basic information
- Searchable database of patents and trademarks
- U. S. Trademark law rules of practice and federal statutes
- Online applications for patents and trademarks

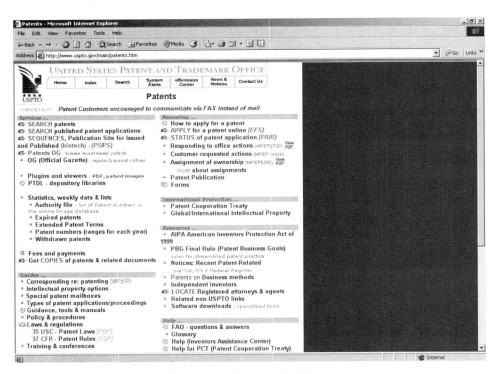

Exhibit 10.6   United States Patent and Trademark Office

University of Texas Copyright Crash Course

www.utsystem.edu/OGC/IntellectualProperty/cprtindx.htm   (Exhibit 10.7)

Free site

The Copyright Crash Course is an excellent introductory resource to copyright law for the layperson. The site was designed for faculty and students at the University of Texas who are using copyrighted materials in the development of new courses, as supplemental materials, and as part of student projects. Some of the materials will only be of interest to those in academia (like the excellent discussion paper on "Ownership of Lectures—Commercial Notetaking in University Courses." But most of the information has a much broader appeal (see Exhibit 10.7).

The Fair Use section of the site is a lengthy discourse that includes a section on individual liability for infringement, a walk through the four factor fair use test, and rules of thumb for fair use of various types of copyrighted materials. If the material cannot be used under the fair use exception, users are directed to the "Getting Permission" section of the site, which covers in detail how to identify copyright owners and obtain permissions to use copyrighted works.

There are also sections on the site that cover the rules for using materials available on the Internet. There are more than two dozen presentations (some in PowerPoint format and some in HTML) covering various copyright issues available for viewing on the site.

There is also a tutorial on the site that takes visitors through a series of scenarios about copyright use and then tests them on their knowledge.

What can you expect to find?

- Insightful commentary on copyright issues by the general counsel of the University of Texas
- Guidelines for fair use and for acquiring copyright permissions
- Presentations on a variety of copyright related topics

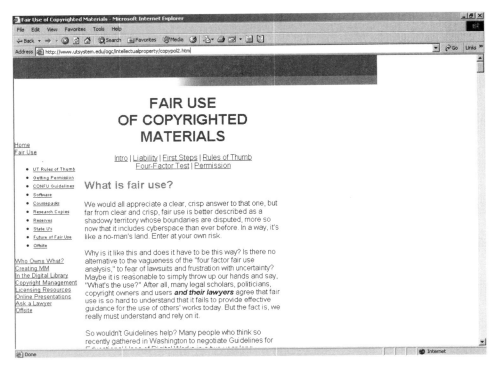

Exhibit 10.7 UT Copyright Crash Course
Georgia Harper, University of Texas System.

World Intellectual Property Organization

www.wipo.org (Exhibit 10.8)

Free site

The World Intellectual Property Organization (WIPO) is an international organization dedicated to helping ensure that the rights of creators and owners of intellectual property are protected worldwide. The WIPO operates as a specialized agency of the United Nations. Currently 179 counties are WIPO members, including the United States. WIPO has assumed a leading role in drafting agreements and legislation dealing with intellectual property issues related to the Internet. The WIPO site includes copies of treaties, statistical information, and articles on the latest developments in this focus area (see Exhibit 10.8).

The WIPO site is divided into four sections: (1) About WIPO, (2) About Intellectual Property, (3) News and Information Resources, and (4) Activities and Services. In the first section, you will find background on the WIPO and information on the treaties administered by the WIPO in the field of intellectual property. These treaties cover internationally agreed-upon standards of intellectual property protection in each country, registrations and filings, and classification systems.

The About Intellectual Property section contains a brief general discussion about patents, trademarks, and copyrights. This section also contains a discussion on a topic unique to the WIPO site: "geographical indications." Geographical indications refer to the use of place names to add value to the product or service associated with them. The World Intellectual Property Organization site lists the following examples "Champagne," "Cognac," "Roquefort," "Chianti," "Pilsen," "Porto," "Sheffield," "Havana," "Tequila," and "Darjeeling." (Apparently the World Intellectual Property Organization doesn't recognize any geographical indications within the United States.)

The News and Information Resources section is where you will find the "meat" of the useful information on the site. Here, you will find downloadable copies of the WIPO magazine in .pdf format and access to the WIPO Electronic Bookshop offering dozens of publications for purchase.

This section also contains a link to the Intellectual Property Digital Library hosted by the WIPO at http://ipdl.wipo.int. It is here that you will find searchable databases housing patent and trademark information from various countries. Also in this section is the Collection of Laws for Electronic Access (CLEA) database, an electronic archive of intellectual property legislation. CLEA contains the full text of intellectual property legislation of a number of countries and the European Community, as well as the full text of all treaties administered by WIPO.

The fourth section of the site, Activities and Services, covers the programs administered by the WIPO.

WIPO has published a report, "Intellectual Property on the Internet: A Survey of Issues," (http://ecommerce.wipo.int/survey/index.html) that addresses the far-reaching impact that digital technologies—the Internet in particular—have had on the international intellectual property system.

What can you expect to find?

- Databases of patent information
- Articles from the WIPO magazine and other WIPO publications
- Text of intellectual property treaties from around the world

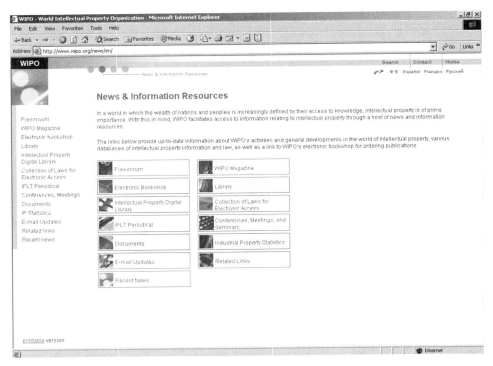

Exhibit 10.8   World Intellectual Property Organization
Screenshot of a webpage of the World Intellectual Property Organization (WIPO), the owner of the copyright. Website address: www.wipo.int.

BEST OF THE REST

ABA Intellectual Property Law Section

www.abanet.org/intelprop

Free site

The Intellectual Property Law section (formerly the Section of Patent, Trademark, and Copyright Law) of the American Bar Association (ABA) is the largest intellectual property organization in the United States. Membership in the section is limited to members of the bar association, but the section's Website has a number of resources available to the public.

For those interested in developments in intellectual property law, the section tracks relevant legislation and reports the status on current bills in Congress. The site also provides free access to some ABA IP publications such as the Bulletin and the E-Blast.

Association of Research Libraries Copyright and IP Center

http://arl.cni.org/info/frn/copy/copytoc.html

Free site

No one is surprised that libraries have a great interest in copyright developments and trends. The Association of Research Libraries (ARL) has put together a collection of copyright resources as part of their Federal Relations and Information Policy Program.

The site has information on current legislation, including Congressional testimony on various pieces of copyright legislation. You will also find information on international developments in copyright law, copies of articles from the ARL newsletter, and a historical timeline that traces the development of copyright law since its enactment into U.S. Federal law in 1790.

BizFindLaw Intellectual Property Center

http://biz.findlaw.com/intellectual_property/

Free site

The respected FindLaw site has added an Intellectual Property section directed at the business community. In addition to directories of intellectual property attorneys, there are articles about copyright issues, frequently asked questions, and forms that small business owners can use to document inventions. There are also sample licensing agreements and state-by-state information.

Copyright Clearance Center

www.copyright.com

Fee-based site

The Copyright Clearance Center (CCC) is a nonprofit licensing agent for text reproduction rights. The Center facilitates compliance with U.S. copyright law by "licensing systems for the reproduction and distribution of copyrighted materials in print and electronic formats."

The CCC manages rights for thousands of publishers and authors. Users of CCC include corporations, government agencies, trade associations, law firms, document suppliers, libraries, academic institutions, copy shops, and bookstores.

On this site, the CCC hosts an extensive database of permissions for purchase. Want to make copies of an article from the Business Valuation Review? Click on the database search button and search by title to find it and purchase the right to copy. Note that the database contains only citations for the materials, not the text of the materials.

Copyright Website

www.benedict.com

Free site

> The Copyright Website is the Website of intellectual property attorney Benedict O'Mahoney who has created an excellent resource that explains the basics of copyright law and the registration process. Additionally, Mr. O'Mahoney has included a fascinating collection of examples of copyright infringement in the motion picture and music recording industries.
>
> The Copyright Website is also home of the Copyright Wizard, a Web-based copyright registration service. The Wizard process completes the appropriate copyright application form, burns a copy of the digital assets to a compact disc for deposit, and submits the completed application to the United States Copyright Office.

Department of Energy Patent Database

www.osti.gov/dublincore/gencncl/

Free site

> Department of Energy (DOE) owns title to approximately 1,500 unexpired U.S. patented inventions and, in some cases, their foreign counterparts. Generally, these patents are available for license to applicants for commercial use of the invention. Users can use the search interface on this site to search the cumulative database that covers DOE patents developed since 1978.

European Patent Organization ESP@CENET

http://ep.espacenet.com

Free site

> ESP@CENET is a free patent search service provided by the European Patent Organization. This site allows users to search the patents registered with the European Patent Office and the World Intellectual Property Organization Patent Cooperation Treaties (PCT).

Get the Patent

www.getthepatent.com

Fee-based site

> Cartesian Products, Inc., a research and development company based in Newton, Massachusetts, owns GetthePatent.com. The site gives users access

to complete patent images for all USPTO, EPO, and WIPO (PCT) patents, as well as the national publications of France, Germany, Great Britain, Japan, and Switzerland. The GetthePatent archive contains the full text and bibliographic information for every USPTO patent issued since 1976, as well as all published USPTO patent applications. GetthePatent allows users to download multipage patent files in a compressed file format. Depending on volume, patents can be purchased for as little as $0.50 each.

The Intellectual Property Law Server

www.intelproplaw.com

Free site

The Intellectual Property Law Server is a service of the Technology Law Group at Bennett Jones LLP Calgary, Alberta. The Intellectual Property Law Server provides information about intellectual property laws including patent, trademark, and copyright. Resources include comprehensive links, general information, and space for professionals to publish articles and forums for discussing related issues. The site's distinguishing feature is the Intellectual Property news which includes a search matrix of current news in five intellectual property categories using eight major search engines and summaries and links to major IP news stories archived by week.

Intellectual Property Rights Helpdesk

www.ipr-helpdesk.org

Free site

The Intellectual Property Rights Helpdesk is a service supporting creativity and innovation in Europe. The site is a repository for briefing papers, questions-and-answers, glossaries, and in-depth information on European intellectual property issues. The site houses the text of legislation and treaty agreements concerning copyrights and other intellectual property rights.

IP Menu

www.ipmenu.com

Free site

IP Menu is a product of Phillips Ormonde & Fitzpatrick, an international intellectual property law firm located in Australia. The IP Menu is a great collection of intellectual property links, product descriptions, and news stories.

Intellectual Property Owners Association

www.ipo.org

Free site

> The Intellectual Property Owners Association (IPO) focuses exclusively on protecting rights of intellectual property owners. The IPO shines with its news service and legislative and judicial updates. The *IPO Daily News* announces intellectual property developments, including court cases, current legislation, and alerts to intellectual property stories in the news. The "IP in the Courts" section of the site has summaries of precedential opinions of the U.S. Court of Appeals for the Federal Circuit. The IPO site also maintains an annual list of the top patent holders based upon filings with the U.S. Patent & Trademark Office.

International Trademark Association

www.inta.org

Free site

> The International Trademark Association (INTA), a group of more than 4,200 trademark holders in more than 160 countries, works to promote trademarks in international commerce. INTA publishes a wide range of authoritative materials, including books and a trademark law journal that are available for purchase on the site. The Association's Website includes information on a variety of topics including Brand Valuation, Trademark Licensing, Trademark Infringements and Statutory Redress, and European Community Trademarks.

Questel

www.questel.orbit.com

Fee-based site

> Questel-Orbit is a provider of patent, trademark, and domain name information. It's primary product is Qpat database covering U.S. Patents from 1971, U.S. Patent Applications from March 2001, European Patents from 1991, European Applications from 1978, PCT Applications from 1978, and French Patents from 1966. Questel-Orbit provides users with access to the Derwent World Patents Index Database covering bibliographic data relating to patent specifications issued by a number of international patent offices.

RoyaltySource

www.royaltysource.com

Fee-based site

RoyaltySource is a Website operated by AUS Consultants to sell subscriptions to the Licensing Economics Review and data from their royalty rate database. RoyaltySource has a searchable database of technology and trademark sale and licensing transactions. The RoyaltySource transaction database includes:

- Licensee and Licensor, including industry description or code
- Description of the property licensed or sold
- Royalty rate details
- Other compensation, such as upfront payments or equity positions
- Transaction terms, such as exclusivity, geographical restrictions, or grant-backs
- Source of Information

RoyaltyStat

www.royaltystat.com

Fee-based site

RoyaltyStat is a subscription database of royalty rates and license agreements compiled from the filings of U.S. publicly traded companies with the Securities and Exchange Commission. RoyaltyStat can be searched by Standard Industrial Classification code or by full-text queries. Subscribers can access the full text of a license agreement along with a spreadsheet with information about the licensor, licensee, property description, royalty rate, exclusivity, duration, and territory covered by the license. Subscribers can purchase information for a single license agreement or an annual subscription that allows downloading of up to 150 agreements.

SurfIP

www.surfip.gov.sg

Free and fee-based site

The SurfIP Portal, a special project of the Intellectual Property Office of Singapore (IPOS) was developed to serve the IP community as a one-stop portal for intellectual property information. SurfIP offers access to databases of the

European Patent Office, the United Kingdom Patent Office, United States Patent Office, and the World Intellectual Property Organization. The search channel feature allows users to search all these databases simultaneously.

In addition to the SurfIP portal, the IPOS also operates the ePatents Website (www.epatents.gov.sg/), which enables online patent filing, and the e-Trademarks Website (www.ipos.gov.sg/service/etrademarks.html), for electronic filing of trademarks.

Trademark.com

www.trademark.com

Fee-based site

Trademark.com is a division of MicroPatent and one of many intellectual property offerings from Information Holdings Inc. Trademark.com has a searchable database of Federal, State, and Common Law trademarks. The database also includes domain names and international trademarks.

The WATCH File at the University of Texas

http://tyler.hrc.utexas.edu/

Free site

If you are only going to do one thing, do it well. The WATCH File (Writers, Artists, and Their Copyright Holders) has a very specific mission, which it accomplishes admirably.

The WATCH File is a database containing the names and addresses of copyright holders. There is also information for those in charge of the archives of authors and artists housed in libraries in North America and in the United Kingdom. WATCH is a joint project of the Harry Ransom Humanities Research Center at the University of Texas at Austin and the University of Reading Library, Reading, England.

The WATCH File was established to provide scholars with information about whom to contact for permission to publish text and images under copyright, but can be useful to anyone who seeks to use copyrighted material. The site contains an excellent discourse on locating copyright holders in the United States and the United Kingdom.

CHAPTER **11**

Tax and Accounting Sites

Death and taxes and childbirth. There's never a convenient time for any of them.

—Margaret Mitchell

Accountants have realized the value of the Internet and are now looking to it as a primary resource for research, news, downloading software, and purchasing business products. A survey conducted by the Electronic Accountant in mid-2002 revealed that 61 percent of all accountants surveyed plan to increase their use of the Internet for tax research over the next year. The survey also found that the use of CD-ROM and print products by accountants had declined precipitously over the past three years as users turned to the Internet.

There are now an abundance of accounting and tax resources on the Internet. These range from tax research services to accounting news sites to sites offering continuing education. The Internet has also become an important source of training and support for financial software products such as Quickbooks, Inacct, NetLedger, and bCentral Small Business Manager.

The accounting portal concept continues to evolve. Users gravitated toward the sites offering industry news, discussion forums, continuing education resources, accounting-related links, and tools like financial calculators. Increasingly, the portals are charging for access to special features and premium content. Be aware that several of the accounting portals use the same news feeds, so in many cases the news sections are not a distinguishing feature unless they include original reporting.

The most ambitious and controversial Internet undertaking by a major accounting organization was the CPA2Biz portal launched by the American Institute of CPAs in June 2001. CPA2Biz was a major departure for the AICPA in a number of ways. Rather than focus on delivering member services for the nonprofit AICPA, the CPA2Biz portal actively marketed services to the clients of members and solicited investment from a number of partners, including Microsoft, Aon, and Thomson Financial. Organized as a commercial corporation, CPA2Biz was positioned for an initial public offering, but the decline in the stock market in 2001 and 2002 postponed it. In 2002, AICPA President Barry Melancon divested his personal interest in CPA2Biz amid conflict-of-interest concerns.

Internet portals were not the only controversial issues facing accountants in 2002. Massive accounting scandals at firms like Enron and Worldcom made arcane accounting issues front-page news. The accounting news Websites were filled with stories of accounting industry change and reform. The collapse of Arthur Andersen reduced the Big Five to the Big Four, and the demise of the www.arthurandersen.com site removed an excellent source of accounting content from the Web.

The first stop on the Internet for financial professionals doing tax work should be one of the major tax research services such as Research Institute of America (RIA) or Commerce Clearing House (CCH). All the major tax research services have now replaced or supplemented their printed services with Web-based access. LexisNexis, the legal research service, has a Tax & Accounting Suite of Research Services as well, giving users access to tax codes, regulations, IRS interpretive materials, and journals. In addition to these powerhouse sites, we will also cover other free and low-cost options for tax research for practitioners who do not need such a robust service.

Many of the sites profiled here are so full of content that a short review cannot begin to cover all the material that you might find. Some of the large accounting firm sites listed in this chapter have hundreds of pages that cover the various industry and practice areas, each with their own publications and research papers. We encourage you to explore these sites using their internal search aids, such as search engines and site maps, to locate information of interest to you.

The sites listed in the "First and Foremost" section of this chapter are those that we have found to be reliable sources of statistics and analysis presented in an easily accessible format. Sites offering all or part of the data for free will be rated higher than sites that offer similar data for a fee. "Best of the Rest" sites may focus on a niche area, be fee-only, or have limited navigation and output features.

FIRST AND FOREMOST

American Institute of Certified Public Accountants

www.aicpa.org

www.cpa2biz.com

Free and fee-based sites

When the AICPA announced plans in 2000 for CPA2Biz, a collaborative small business portal site in partnership with state CPA societies, there was some uncertainty as to what this would mean for AICPA.org. Although some of its content did shift to CPA2Biz, AICPA.org came back in 2002 with a redesign and a renewed focus on providing current information on important issues facing the profession.

The AICPA.org site provides detailed information on the Institute's operations and programs, including legislative and regulatory developments affecting the accounting profession. There are also career resources, including a job bank and information on hiring trends in the industry. The AICPA published *Journal of Accountancy* is available online. Selected articles are available for free from each issue beginning in 1997. An online index covers stories since 1996. There are no products available for purchase on AICPA.org. All product sales are handled by www.cpa2biz.com.

In its short life, the CPA2Biz site has been redesigned twice. The site offers a generous amount of content but the organization and design leave something to be desired. The resource center of the site contains 11 modules, each devoted to a different practice area such as Tax or Business Valuation. Content in the modules includes articles and publications, news, and tools. CPA2Biz has built a strong presence with online educational programs. The AICPA CPE program, InfoBytes, is hosted here as well as other CPE offerings from Micro-Mash and Microsoft. Information for AICPA conferences is now hosted on CPA2Biz, so users can register online and download brochures.

Subscribers can also access online services such as the *AICPA Resource: Accounting & Auditing Literature* product on CPA2Biz. Also, CPA2Biz has automated some of the membership services so that dues can be paid online.

The AICPA maintains a list of links to the Websites of State CPA Societies at www.aicpa.org/states/stmap.htm. The quality of information available at State CPA Society Websites varies considerably, but if you are lucky enough to be in one of the states with a vibrant Web community for CPAs, be sure to take advantage of it.

What can you expect to find?

- Online publications, including the *Journal of Accountancy*, the *CPA Letter*, and the *Practicing CPA*
- Exposure drafts of proposed statements of position
- Ethics and standards information
- AICPA publications for sale
- Resource centers with in-depth information by practice area

Big Four Major Accounting Firm Sites

Deloitte & Touche—www.deloitte.com   (Exhibit 11.1)

Ernst & Young—www.ey.com   (Exhibit 11.2)

KPMG—www.kpmg.com

PricewaterhouseCoopers—www.pwcglobal.com

Free and fee-based sites

The largest accounting firms all have multiple Websites with varying amounts of information. Count on finding interesting newsletters, many on niche industries and topics, and articles written by staffers. Many of the publications available for download are .pdf files preserving the graphics and design of the original print publications. Most of the data is free, but some firms sell studies and books published by employees.

Deloitte & Touche also makes publications from the firm's different practice areas available on the Web, such as the 129-page *"Business Succession Planning Guidebook,"* and *Healthcare Review*, a monthly newsletter providing interviews and commentaries from leading health care executives and policy makers on current health industry issues (see Exhibit 11.1).

To find publications and newsletters on the Ernst & Young site, go to the Issues & Perspectives section and click on the Library link. This will take you to publications like *CrossCurrents*, the slick monthly magazine for the financial services industry, and *Risks That Matter*, a study that looks at the underlying causes of increases and decreases in shareholder value (see Exhibit 11.2).

The primary KPMG site at www.kpmg.com has a limited amount of free information, such as short articles about industry practice areas. Use the search engine on the KPMG site to search for white papers, articles, and newsletters. An example of what you will find there is the 28-page white paper "Strategic Management of Intellectual Property: Enhancing Organizational Success by Unlocking the Value of Ideas." There is a greater selection of information at the new Bearing Point (formerly KPMG Consulting) site at www.bearingpoint .com. Here you will find case studies, articles, white papers, and research reports by clicking on the library link. The sites for individual countries, like the U.S. site at www.us.kpmg.com, also have publications by industry sectors (such as the 12-page research report "KPMG's Auto Executive Survey 2002").

The PricewaterhouseCoopers site also has a number of publications available for download, ranging from "The Impact of Electronic Records in Litigation and Criminal Investigations" to the "Executive Perspective Newsletter." PwC also maintains the Lodging Research site (www .lodgingresearch.com), offering industry reports and research on the lodging industry.

What can you expect to find?

- Newsletters on industry trends and practice areas
- Articles, case studies, and working papers
- Tax information and information about working globally

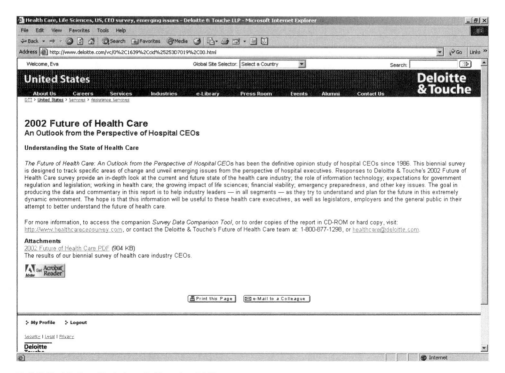

Exhibit 11.1   Deloitte & Touche LLP

Exhibit 11.2   Ernst & Young

Bureau of National Affairs

www.bna.com   (Exhibit 11.3)

Fee-based site

The Bureau of National Affairs (BNA) is a leading publisher of print and electronic news and information, reporting on developments in health care, business, labor relations, law, economics, taxation, environmental protection, safety, and other public policy and regulatory issues. BNA produces more than 200 news and information services (see Exhibit 11.3). Among their Web-based products, those of interest to tax and accounting professionals are:

- **TaxCore.** Full-text tax regulation and IRS documents updated daily.
- **Tax Management Portfolios on the Web.** Working papers and bibliographies. Portfolios cover Limited Liability Companies, International Pension Planning, Estate Planning, and more.

- **Tax Management State Tax Library on the Web.** A library of information on state tax issues.
- **Tax Management Tax Practice Library.** A tax research database, including all major primary tax resources, tax analysis, practice tools, and news.

BNA maintains a separate Website for Tax Management products at www.bnatax.com.

What can you expect to find?

- Tax research service
- Quality portfolios and analysis of major tax issues
- Practice tools

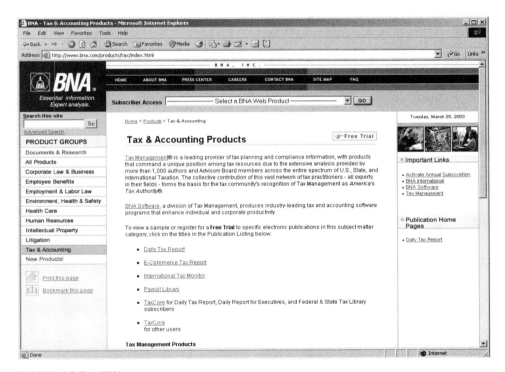

Exhibit 11.3   BNA

Commerce Clearing House (CCH)

www.cch.com

Free and fee-based site

Commerce Clearing House (CCH), is a major provider of tax and business law information and software. CCH produces approximately 700 publications in print and electronic form for not only the accounting profession but also for legal, human resources, banking, securities, insurance, government, and health care professionals. The main CCH site at www.cch.com is an umbrella for the company's six Websites:

- **Federal and State Tax Group.** http://tax.cch.com
- **The Business and Finance Site.** http://business.cch.com
- **Health, Medical and Entitlements.** http://health.cch.com
- **Human Resources.** http://hr.cch.com
- **Business Owner's Toolkit.** www.toolkit.cch.com
- **ProSystemfx.** www.prosystemfx.com

Accounting professionals will be most interested in the FAST site (Federal And State Tax). The FAST site has some free information, but the primary focus is access to CCH's online fee-based tax research products. The extent of the tax data available is mind-boggling. Suffice it to say that virtually every aspect of taxation, tax law, and tax regulation is covered by a CCH database.

The Business Owner's Toolkit site provides a wealth of free data for those running a small business. The extensive online SOHO guidebook has thousands of pages of information on starting, financing, managing, and marketing a small business. The Business Tools section has free downloadable sample business documents, financial spreadsheet templates, and checklists. There is a small business advice column, Ask Alice, where you can submit your questions about running a business.

The other CCH sites offer primarily product information and database access corresponding to each site's focus area, along with a selection of free news and articles.

What can you expect to find?

- Every conceivable item related to taxes

CPA Journal

www.cpajournal.com   (Exhibit 11.4)

Free site

> The New York Society of CPAs publishes the monthly *CPA Journal*, a technical-reviewed publication aimed at public practitioners, management, educators, and other accounting professionals. The *CPA Journal* is a long-established and well-respected publication. An editorial review board composed of CPAs, attorneys, and other professionals helps to keep the quality of the articles high. On the Website, you will find subscription information and the table of contents for the current issue. While there is no access to articles in the current issue, the site has a great archive where you can access most of the *CPA Journal's* excellent articles published since 1989. There is a one-month delay in posting the current month's articles to the archive (see Exhibit 11.4).

> *What can you expect to find?*

> • Great articles from one of the accounting profession's most respected publications on topics ranging from auditing to consulting

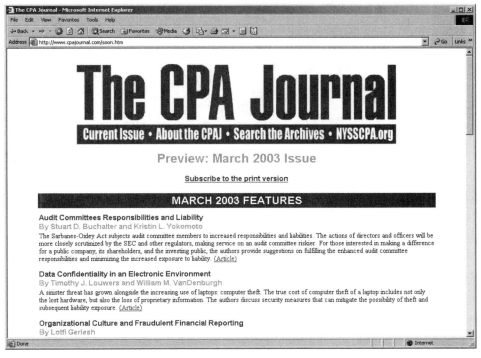

Exhibit 11.4   The *CPA Journal*
The CPA Journal, www.cpajournal.com.

Electronic Accountant

www.electronicaccountant.com   (Exhibit 11.5)

Free site

The site features accounting news stories from "Newswire," a daily news feature written by accounting editors, and a selection of feature articles on the accounting industry from the magazines published by the Accounts Media Group (AMG) including *Accounting Today*, *Practical Accountant,* and *Accounting Technology*.

The Electronic Accountant site is a product of the AMG (formerly Faulkner and Gray) that is now owned by Thomson Financial. Also on the site are special reports like the Tax Research Survey, interviews with leaders in the accounting profession, and the top 100 links, along with product information and discussion forums (see Exhibit 11.5).

Go to the Electronic Accountant for the excellent "Newswire" and to read stories from the current issues of AMG publications. These features set this site apart from the other accounting sites.

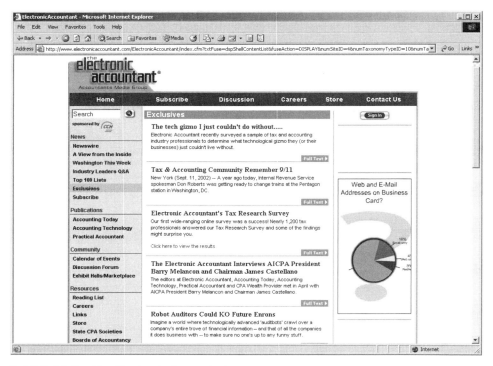

Exhibit 11.5   The Electronic Accountant

What can you expect to find?

- The cover stories from the current issues of *Practical Accountant, Accounting Today*, and *Accounting Technology*
- Well-written news stories on the hot topics in accounting
- Discussion forums on accounting and auditing topics

Internal Revenue Service

www.irs.gov (Exhibit 11.6)

Free site

The IRS has done a much better job than many other federal government agencies when it comes to organizing large amounts of information. The IRS has a number of resources targeted to tax professionals, including the *Digital Dispatch Mailing List*, which covers information on important upcoming tax dates, tax forms, and publications recently posted to the IRS Website, and IRS news releases and special announcements. There is also an email newsletter, the *IRS e-News for Tax Professionals*, designed to provide localized information for tax professionals by geographic area (see Exhibit 11.6). The IRS posts current news stories in the Newsroom at www.irs.gov/newsroom.

Bypass the consumer information on the main IRS site and go directly to the IRS Tax Professionals site at www.irs.gov/taxpros/index.html. Here you can access a variety of forms, instructions, and regulations.

Note that the Web address for the IRS is www.irs.gov *not* www.irs.com. The IRS.com address does have some consumer-oriented tax information, but it is not affiliated with the IRS. It is operated by the DotCom Corporation, which identifies itself as a firm that "obtains Website addresses that are currently being underutilized."

What can you expect to find?

- Information on every aspect of tax filing
- Tax forms
- IRS regulations
- Aggregate statistics compiled for tax returns
- IRS publications

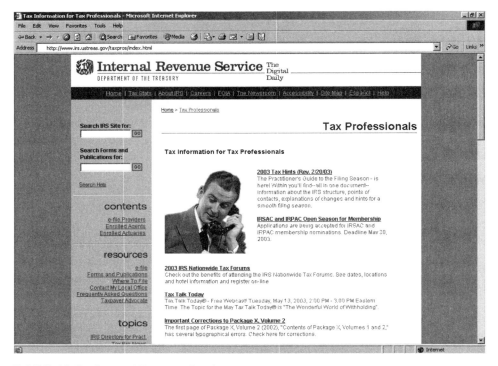

Exhibit 11.6   Internal Revenue Service

Kleinrock's Tax Expert Online

www.kleinrock.com

Fee-based site

Kleinrock's has long had a reputation as a low-cost provider of tax research data on CD-ROM. Now that data is available to subscribers online. The TaxExpert Online's Research area contains more than 180,000 full-text documents of federal tax material. This collection includes the complete Code and Treasury regulations, Tax Court and other federal cases, and a wealth of IRS materials. Kleinrock's also includes the much-needed plain-English explanations of federal tax law linked to the primary source documents. The Tax Expert Online also includes access to Kleinrock's Daily Tax Bulletin, with daily news stories from the IRS, Treasury, Congress, and the federal courts.

What can you expect to find?

- Analysis and explanation of federal tax law and its application
- Collection of tax planning and practice articles and election statements
- IRS regulations, rulings, and procedures

RIA and RIA Checkpoint

www.riahome.com

http://riacheckpoint.com

Fee-based sites

RIA (formerly Research Institute of America) is a subsidiary of Thomson Corporation and the world's largest provider of tax research.

RIA's primary tax research product is Checkpoint. Checkpoint covers a vast amount of data including federal editorial materials, state and local tax information, estate planning materials, IRS rulings and releases, federal court decisions, and pending and enacted tax legislation. Checkpoint also integrates *BNA's Daily Tax Report* for current information on key legislative, regulatory, and legal tax developments.

In addition to tax research, Checkpoint gives users access to estate planning resources, financial journals, and payroll/pension information.

Check the main RIA site for free current tax news from *Tax Watch* and free excerpts from selected RIA publications. There are also handy tools like a program to download tax rates to your personal digital assistant.

What can you expect to find?

• Exhaustive tax research and articles on a variety of financial topics

SmartPros

www.smartpros.com   (Exhibit 11.7)

Free and fee-based site

SmartPros.com (formerly Accounting Pro2Net) operates an accounting portal with an emphasis on continuing education. Here, you will find an extensive bank of news stories, original articles, and links to a wide range of resources for research, networking, and career development. SmartPros, which also operates an Engineering portal, has divided the accounting portal into the following focus areas: General Accounting, Accounting & Auditing, Financial Planning, Human Resources, International, Legal, Corporate Finance, Students, Tax, and Technology (see Exhibit 11.7).

The original material on the site in the form of news and analysis, commentary, research materials, articles, and educational material is the primary reason to visit this site.

SmartPros has a strong educational focus and has developed a Professional Education Center (http://education.smartpros.com). As part of this center, SmartPros has teamed with the AICPA to offer the CPA Report (CPAR), an annual CPE subscription program for public accountants. The online courses feature streaming video, course outlines, online transcripts, and links to related content.

All of the information on the site is free with the exception of the continuing education classes and items for sale in the marketplace area.

What can you expect to find?

- Original articles on a variety of accounting topics, glossary of audit terms, and accounting career center
- Continuing education courses on general accounting topics, and governmental and not-for-profit issues as well
- Free email newsletter subscriptions and "coffee break" work distraction page

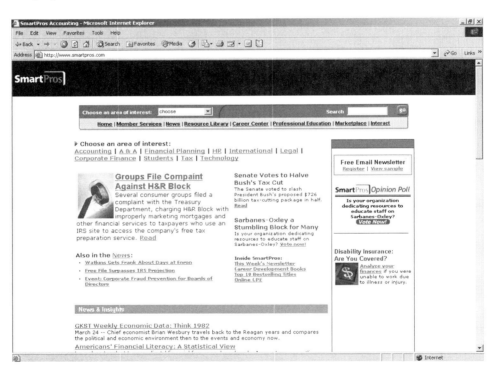

Exhibit 11.7   SmartPros

Tax Analysts

www.tax.org   (Exhibit 11.8)

Free and fee-based site

Tax Analysts products are a great value for tax research on or off the Internet. As the only nonprofit tax research vendor, Tax Analysts' primary product is *TaxBase*. Subscribers to *TaxBase* on the Web at www.taxbase.tax.org get access to current awareness products like *Tax Notes Today* as well as the *Federal Research Library*, which has an extensive collection of full-text documents including statutes, regulations, rulings, and court decisions and the *State Tax Library*. Other products accessible on the Tax Analysts site include state and international tax databases and specialty publications such as the *Insurance Tax Review*. Tax Analysts supplies tax information to a number of other vendors including LexisNexis, Dialog, and Westlaw (see Exhibit 11.8).

The Tax Analysts' site also has a significant amount of free content. The daily Tax Wire (www.tax.org/TaxWire/taxwiref.htm) covers current tax stories and an archive of articles from the *National Tax Journal* is available. "Readings in Tax Policy" is a compilation of some of the best articles published by Tax Analysts. Organized by subject into a collection of Briefing Books, the articles illuminate key issues in tax policy and administration. Feature stories cover international, state, and e-commerce issues. And finally, don't miss the Tax Quotes page (source of the Margaret Mitchell quote at the beginning of this chapter).

What can you expect to find?

- Voluminous amounts of tax information—regulations, forms, news stories, rates, court cases
- Current stories from *Tax Notes*, the federal tax journal of record
- Quotes from the famous and not-so-famous about the vagaries of taxation

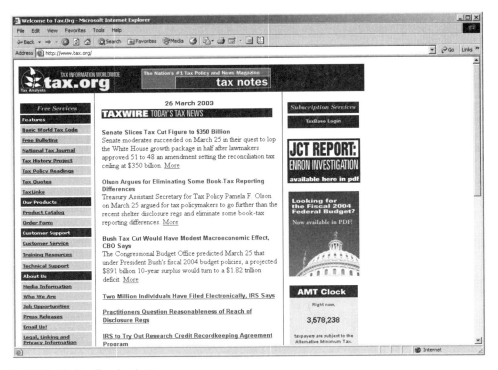

Exhibit 11.8   Tax Analysts

BEST OF THE REST

Accounting Research Network

www.ssrn.com/arn/index.html

Free site

Accounting Research Network (ARN) is a collection of scholarly works on a multitude of accounting topics. ARN publishes abstracts of top-quality research papers dealing with empirical, experimental, and theoretical research in financial and managerial accounting, auditing, and tax strategy.

Accounting & Tax Database

www.proquest.com

www.dialog.com

Fee-based sites

The Accounting & Tax Database combines abstracts of articles published in nearly 300 accounting and tax publications with official releases from the

AICPA and FASB and selective indexing of tax-related information in thousands of business journals. Also included are citations to relevant articles from over 800 newspapers, business journals, dissertations, and news magazines. The Accounting & Tax database is only accessible with subscriptions to information services such as Dialog or Proquest.

AccountingWeb

www.accountingweb.com

Free and fee-based site

AccountingWeb is an online community for accountants following the portal model. AccountingWeb offers news, original articles, email newsletters, and a discussion forum.

In the first edition of *Best Websites*, we recommended AccountingWeb for its excellent workshops, expert guides, and partnership with Brainwave. While the news content is still excellent, AccountingWeb has dropped these distinguishing features and now charges for its more in-depth articles and features, which are now classified as premium content.

AuditNet

www.auditnet.org

Free site

Audit information is not plentiful on the Internet, but AuditNet pulls together a collection of resources that auditors will find helpful. AuditNet has dozens of audit programs available for downloading from the site. Auditors will also find job postings and other career resources along with information on audit training programs.

CFO.com

www.cfo.com/channel/1,5357,1,00.html

Free site

CFO magazine has an excellent Website filled with free articles from current and past issues of the magazine. CFO.com has an Accounting Channel which pulls together content, both magazine articles and online-only features, on accounting industry issues. The Accounting Channel features current news stories, tools such as a Black-Scholes model for valuing put and call options, and special reports such as a buyers' guide for accounting software.

Comperio

www.pwcglobal.com/gx/eng/about/svcs/comperio/

Fee-based site

Comperio is an online library of financial reporting and assurance literature from PricewaterhouseCoopers. Comperio includes access to global financial reporting and assurance literature as well as a variety of Pricewaterhouse-Coopers guidance. Content is gathered from the AICPA, Financial Accounting Standards Board (FASB), and Securities and Exchange Commission (SEC).

Federal Tax Law

www.taxsites.com/federal.html

Free site

Federal tax law resources are a key part of tax research. Many of the resources are available from the government agencies that publish them. So, you will find the U.S. tax code at the House of Representatives Website and the Code of Federal Regulations on the Government Printing Office site. The Tax Sites page on Federal Tax law provides links to these and other federal tax resources from a single page. There are also links to commercial sites that offer or comment on federal tax regulations.

Tax Sites has more than just links to federal tax information. Dennis Schmidt, a professor of accounting at the University of Northern Iowa, designed this comprehensive index as a "starting point" for most tax and accounting subject searches. Professor Schmidt does the two basic things necessary to make a link site work—he lists high-quality sites and updates them frequently. While this seems obvious, it is rare to find a well-maintained link site. Check the Tax Sites home page at www.taxsites.com for links to more tax resources.

FTA State Tax Rates

www.taxadmin.org/fta/rate/tax_stru.html

Free site

The membership of the Federation of Tax Administrators includes the principal tax collection agencies of all 50 states. On their Website you can find current information on income tax rates by state. There is also information on sales and excise taxes and surveys of tax practices by state.

PPCnet

www.ppcnet.com

Free and fee-based site

On PPCnet, the Website of tax and accounting industry publisher Practitioners Publishing Company (PPC), now owned by Thomson Corporation, subscribers can access a variety of products, including Tax Action Bulletins, Tax and Business Alerts, the Audit Compliance Program Creator, and the Quarterly National Economic Analyses. The online store at PPCnet sells PPC's print and CD-ROM products, including the popular *Guide to Business Valuations*, coauthored by Jay Fishman and Shannon Pratt, and the *Guide to Divorce Engagements.*

Regulations and Standards

www.fasb.org (Financial Accounting Standards Board)   (Exhibit 11.9)

http://accounting.rutgers.edu/raw/gasb (Governmental Accounting Standards Board)

www.iasc.org.uk/cmt/0001.asp (International Accounting Standards Board)

Free and fee-based sites

These organizations are all part of the regulatory environment of the accounting industry. The Financial Accounting Standards Board (FASB) is the primary standard-setting organization in the accounting field. FASB posts proposed changes to current and/or future standards for comment on this site. A listing of financial accounting standards, including a summary of the pronouncement and information on the status of the standard is available on the site (see Exhibit 11.9). Use the FASB Publications Ordering System at http://store.yahoo.com/fasbpubs to purchase standards.

The Government Accounting Standards Board (GASB) is the primary standard-setting organization in the government accounting field. Summaries and status of GASB standards are available on this Website. Standards can be purchased online at http://store.yahoo.com/gasbpubs/info.html.

The International Accounting Standards Board (IASB) is an organization of experts from nine countries who set global accounting standards. New reports and summaries of IAS standards are available on the site and can be purchased here using British pounds.

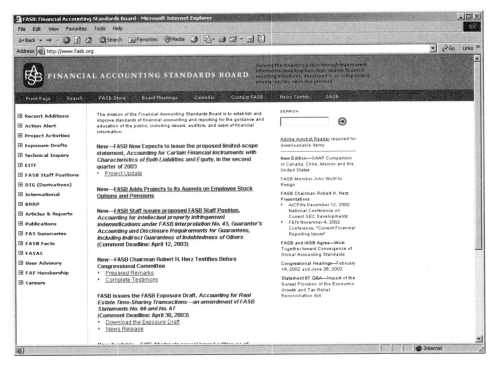

Exhibit 11.9 Financial Accounting Standards Board
The home/front page of the FASB, copyright by the Financial Accounting Standards Board, 401 Merritt 7, Norwalk, CT 06856, is reproduced by permission.

Writing Skills for the Tax Professional

www.gsu.edu/~accerl

Free site

According to a 1999 article in the *CPA Journal*, recruiters identified writing skills as one of the most important characteristics used to screen accounting applicants, ranking it higher than technical skills, work experience, or the reputation of the university the applicant had attended. Recognizing that many financial professionals are deficient in this area, the University of Georgia funded a site to assist grammatically challenged accountants. The site is filled with helpful advice, exercises, and tools. Take the wordiness self-test at your own risk.

CHAPTER 12

Websites for International Business Research

The Internet has made the world a smaller place. Now data that was once only available in a foreign country can be accessed from your desktop. However, it would be a mistake to think that locating international data is as easy as checking the U.S. Census Bureau. Creating a comprehensive list of Websites for international business research is a monumental task. Each country is unique, as are its information sources. In addition, many countries do not share the United States's democratic attitude toward sharing information, and many governments have not compiled and archived data, let alone made it available to the public. Needless to say, researching a foreign company, country, or industry may be difficult, and the research process will probably take longer than usual. But the task is easing, as more and more information-rich sites from countries around the world are made available. As you might expect, many of the sites you find will not be in English, so if you don't speak the language in question, start with a good dictionary or a bilingual friend.

Fortunately, many librarians, information specialists, and businesspeople have recognized the difficulty of researching a foreign country or industry and have created metasites, or portals, that can serve as great starting places for your research. Take advantage of the efforts of these individuals who have already scoured the Web, selected and reviewed the best Websites, and organized them.

Be aware that many U.S. business information sites also have versions that operate in other countries. For example, the respected information provider Hoovers, Inc. (www.hoovers.com) has corporate and financial information on thousands of U.S. companies. Hoovers also operates a site in the United Kingdom at www.hoovers.com/uk that covers news and financial information on British companies. The accounting information portal AccountingWeb (www.accountingweb.com) has a site in the United Kingdom at www.accountingweb.co.uk.

Don't overlook county-specific general search engines like Google as a resource for tracking down business information. Google offers international researchers a suite of language tools (access them by clicking on the *language tools* link on the Google home page www.google.com). The language tools include a translation program for the translation of text on Web pages and an option to set the Google interface to a selected language. (There are over 80 language choices, including pig latin.) The language tools page also includes a link to the 45 country-specific Google sites like Google U.K. at www.google.co.uk and Google Liechtenstein at www.google.li.

Information services such as LexisNexis and Dialog, discussed earlier in this book, are also great sources for international information. These services have hundreds of global news sources, economic analyses, and international company data.

Given the number of good sites for international research, this chapter can only touch on a small percentage. Financial professionals who have a need for in-depth international information should consider looking at more detailed search guides such as Sheri Lanza's excellent book, *International Business Information on the Web* (CyberAge Books, 2001) or *Super Searchers Cover the World: The Online Secrets of Global Business Researchers* by Mary Ellen Bates (CyberAge Books, 2001).

The sites listed in the "First and Foremost" section of this chapter are those that we have found to be reliable sources of statistics and analysis presented in easily accessible format. Sites offering all or part of the data for free will be rated higher than sites that offer similar data for a fee. "Best of the Rest" sites may focus on a niche area, be fee-only, or have limited navigation and output features.

FIRST AND FOREMOST

American Chambers of Commerce Abroad

www.uschamber.org/chambers/international/international_directory.asp

Free site

American Chambers of Commerce Abroad (AmChams) are voluntary associations of U.S. businesses and individuals doing business in a particular country and firms and individuals of countries who operate in the United States. AmChams pursue trade policy initiatives, make available publications and services, and sponsor a variety of business development programs. There are AmChams in 82 countries promoting U.S. business interests abroad.

What can you expect to find?

- A directory of AmChams and their Websites. Each site provides business-related publications and services for the country in which it is located.

- Typical AmCham services include: export-import trade leads; business and government contacts; luncheon and dinner meetings featuring U.S. and foreign business leaders and officials; periodic news bulletins and other publications; an information clearinghouse on trade, investment, and commerce; an information center for customs duties, tariffs, and regulations; and library and reference facilities for member use.

Bureau van Dijk

www.bvdep.com   (Exhibit 12.1)

Fee-based site

Bureau van Dijk is an aggregator of business information on European companies. The Website of this Belgium-based company provides an excellent tool for targeting companies within a particular industry or accessing detailed financial data. Researchers can target their companies of interest by using the free directory.

The amount of data available from Bureau van Dijk is vast. The service offers detailed company reports on more than 7 million European companies and profiles on the largest 1.5 million U.S. companies (see Exhibit 12.1).

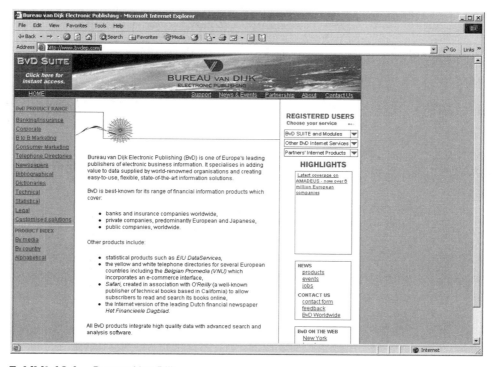

Exhibit 12.1   Bureau Van Dijk

What can you expect to find?

- Detailed company reports on European companies
- Statistical databases
- Directories, technical, legal and bibliographical databases

Commercial Service—U.S. Department of Commerce

www.usatrade.gov   (Exhibit 12.2)

Free site

The Commercial Service, founded in 1980, is the global business unit of the Department of Commerce. The Commercial Service maintains 151 international offices in 83 countries with a mission to increase the number of U.S. firms that benefit from international trade.

The Commercial Service offers a wealth of information that focuses on international trade. The Country and Industry Market Research section (www.export.gov/cntryind.html) contains hundreds of reports, including Country Commercial Guides (prepared annually by U.S. Embassy Staff and containing information on the business and economic situation of foreign countries), Industry Sector Analyses (in-depth analysis of specific industry sectors and subsectors within a given market), and International Market Insight (brief updates highlighting specific market opportunities, trade events, or changes in market conditions) (see Exhibit 12.2).

At the main export page (www.export.gov), users will find detailed information of all aspects of exporting. There is a section on exporting news and press releases, market reports, and trade missions and delegations. There is an *Export Quick Reference Guide* and information on Export Promotion Programs & Services.

What can you expect to find?

- Multilateral Development Bank Reports
- Trade counseling and contact services as well as trade leads
- Customized market research
- A wide variety of informative newsletters of interest to the exporting public

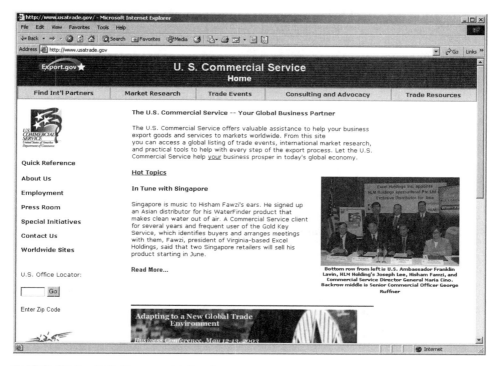

Exhibit 12.2 U.S. Commercial Service

CorporateInformation

www.corporateinformation.com (Exhibit 12.3)

Free site

CorporateInformation, owned by Wright Investors' service, is a resource for international research on companies and industries. From the home page researchers can search by industry, country, or company name. Using the "research a company" selection on the home page will take users to a list of free company profiles on major companies located in that country along with links to country-specific data.

Users can also use the Research a Country's Industry feature to find information about a specific industry in a designated country. For example, entering "Automotive" in the industry box and "Argentina" in the country box, generated a list of sources relating to the automotive industry in Argentina. The search results not only contained links to a market research report, but also an industry update from Mercosul, and a profile of automotive firms in the country and links to their Websites (see Exhibit 12.3).

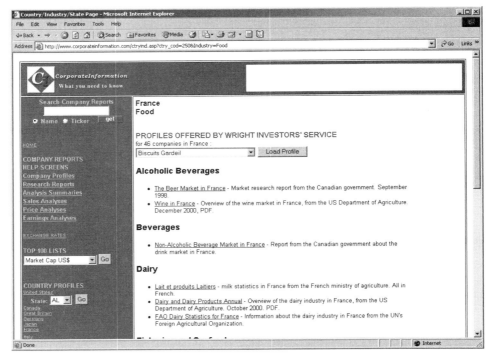

Exhibit 12.3   CorporateInformation

What can you expect to find?

- Links to hundreds of sites relating to industries and companies around the world
- Country-specific background information, exchange rates, stock exchange quotes, and economic indicators

Datamonitor

www.datamonitor.com

Fee-based site

Datamonitor is a market research firm based in London. Datamonitor publishes reports covering primarily the U.K., France, Italy, Germany, Spain,

Europe, and the United States. A specialized team of industry experts produces Datamonitor reports which discuss products, the competitive environment, pricing, market share, and other key issues affecting industries.

Datamonitor's extensive array of products includes Premium Analysis Services which involve customized research, Dashboard Services (country, industry, and company profiles from previously published data), and free services including business directories and news stories.

What can you expect to find?

- Market, company, and issue reports
- Interactive databases
- Country profiles

DataStar

www.datastarweb.com

Fee-based site

DataStar is a leading European information service allowing subscribers to access more than 350 databases of worldwide business and technical information. DataStar is known as a premier provider of European company information and news on East & West Europe. The DataStar databases offer a variety of business information, including news, industry analysis, and market research.

The databases on DataStar contain information ranging from a directory-type listing of companies or associations, to an in-depth financial statement for a particular company, to a citation with bibliographic information and an abstract referencing a journal, conference paper, or other original source, to the complete text of a journal article.

What can you expect to find?

- Current news articles on international issues
- Financial statements for foreign companies
- Industry overviews

Economist/Economist Intelligence Unit

www.economist.com

www.eiu.com

Free and fee-based sites

The London-based *Economist* magazine is one of the world's most respected sources for independent global economic and political news. If the Economist .com Website did nothing more than reproduce a portion of the content of the print magazine, it would still be a "First and Foremost" site, but the Economist .com goes well beyond being an electronic version of the magazine.

The core of the Website is the wealth of current news stories, many of which are free. Articles are arranged in the sections including Opinion, World, Business, Finance & Economics, Science & Technology, and Diversions.

In addition to the articles, Economist.com has a large collection of reference materials including:

- **Country Briefings (www.economist.com/countries).** News, country profiles, forecasts, and statistics available for 60+ nations.
- **Business Encyclopedia (www.economist.com/encyclopedia).** Contains a business dictionary covering over 6,000 related terms; practical guides explaining finance, marketing, personnel, and e-commerce; and 144 biographies of important business minds.
- **Backgrounders (www.economist.com/research/backgrounders).** Concise summaries of complex issues in politics, finance, business, science, and technology.
- **Surveys (www.economist.com/surveys).** A series of articles covering a country, industry, financial topic, or technology issue.

Print subscribers get access to all of the content of the *Economist* prior to publication and access to an archive of all articles published in the *Economist* since 1997. Visitors to the site can purchase articles on a pay-per-view basis or subscribe to online access only.

The *Economist* also owns Economist Intelligence Unit (EIU), one of the world's leading producers of country analysis, at www.eiu.com. Over the 50+ years that the EIU has been producing international research and analysis, they have built a global network of more than 500 analysts, editors, and correspondents. EIU.com is a virtual library offering all of the Economist Intelligence Unit's publications on a subscription or pay-as-you-go basis. EIU produces more than 3,000 publications and provides economic and political analysis and forecasts for 200 countries and regions.

One of EIU's primary publications is the *Country Report. Country Reports* analyze political and economic trends with a focus on how national, regional, and global events will affect businesses. Each report examines and explains the political scene, economic policy, the domestic economy, and foreign trade in a country and provides concise 18- to 24-month forecasts.

What can you expect to find?

- In-depth news and commentary
- Detailed information by country
- Background on current international issues

ELDIS Country Profiles

nt1.ids.ac.uk/eldis/newcountry.htm

Free site

ELDIS is a development resource directory of Websites, databases, library catalogues, and email discussion lists. ELDIS receives funding from several organizations, including the U.K. Department for International Development and the World Bank.

What can you expect to find?

- Country profiles containing a county overview and descriptions of local business culture and customs, expatriate tax guide, customs and import duty regulations, and medical and security reports
- A database of links to more than 200 other useful Websites for each country

Euromonitor

www.euromonitor.com

Fee-based site

Euromonitor International is a global market research firm. Founded in 1972, Euromonitor publishes market research reports, business reference books, and online information systems. Euromonitor products are classified into three research divisions: Market Analysis, Business Reference, and Consultancy. The Market Analysis division produces consumer industry market reports and online databases. The Business Reference division publishes reference books and databases covering background country statistics and lifestyle statistics, market data and forecasts for products, profiles of leading companies, and strategies for success. The Consultancy division conducts customized research.

What can you expect to find?

- Industry reports
- Country profiles
- Statistical compilations

European Union Business Resources

www.eurunion.org/infores/business/business.htm

http://europa.eu.int/business/en/index.html

Free sites

These two sites provide information on doing business in the European Union. Overviews of relevant legislation, business advice, and information about the euro are provided. The key issues section covers the following topics: public procurement, intellectual property rights, funding opportunities, the euro, and the environment. There is also a free European business directory.

What can you expect to find?

- Business directories
- European trade associations
- Investment opportunities in Europe
- Links to the Chambers of Commerce of the EU members in the United States, U.S. government services for exporters, and U.S. private sector organizations

globalEDGE

http://globaledge.msu.edu/ibrd/ibrd.asp   (Exhibit 12.4)

Free site

The globalEDGE site, maintained by Michigan State University, has developed into an extensive knowledge base of international business data.

The resource desk section includes Country Insights, which are outlines of the business climate, political structure, history, and statistical data for more than 190 countries. This section includes regional and country-specific links, in addition to a general overview of each geographic area.

Users can also access the "Market Potential Indicators" study conducted by Michigan State University to compare emerging markets on several dimensions. This study ranks 24 countries identified as "Emerging Markets" by *Economist* magazine (see Exhibit 12.4).

What can you expect to find?

- Links to U.S. and international news, periodicals, journals, articles, and research papers
- Links to regional and country-specific statistical and information sources
- International trade information and trade leads, along with a glossary of terms and acronyms used for international business
- Company directories and yellow pages

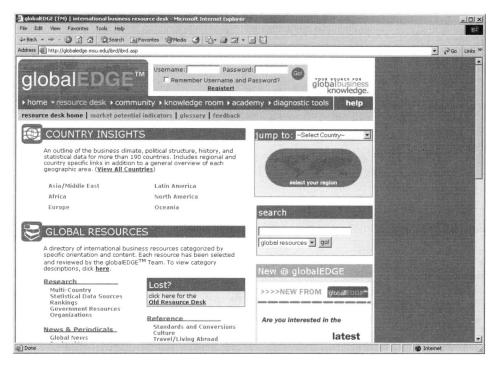

Exhibit 12.4   globalEDGE

Global Business Opportunities (GLOBUS) and the National Trade Data Bank (NTDB)

www.stat-usa.gov/tradtest.nsf

Free and fee-based site

The Global Business Opportunities (GLOBUS) and National Trade Data Bank (NTDB) site is part of STAT-USA/Internet, a service of the U.S. Department of Commerce, providing authoritative information from the federal government of the United States to the business, economic, and trade community.

GLOBUS/NTDB is a must-stop site for those interested in doing business overseas or finding out about a particular market or industry. Users have access to the NTDB Global Trade Directory, a searchable database of manufacturers, resellers, and buyers around the world, and to EuroTrade Online for current trade data for the 15 European Union member nations.

The Market and Industry Research section has the following types of reports: International Marketing Insight, Multilateral Development Bank, Industry Sector Analysis, Foreign Agricultural Market, and Country Commercial Guides.

What can you expect to find?

- Extensive country and market research
- Up-to-date and historical "global business opportunity leads"
- International trade statistics, such as U.S. exports and imports by commodity and country
- Current exchange rates
- Current press releases regarding U.S. import and export price indexes, USDA export sales, and U.S. international trade in goods and services

Global EDGAR

www.globaledgar.com

Fee-based site

Global EDGAR provides access to company information and SEC filings for more than 30,000 companies in 90+ countries. Users can search the database using company name or ticker symbol or browse by country or exchange listing. Global EDGAR also has an advanced search feature that allows for free text searching.

The information available varies by company, but for many companies the documents include government filings, annual reports, and news items. Users can sign up for an annual subscription for unlimited access to the database or use the pay-per-document plan. The pricing is very reasonable when compared to other global financial databases. Subscriptions start at $9.95 per month and individual documents are $5.00 each.

Global EDGAR offers an alert service to notify subscribers when documents on their selected companies become available.

What can you expect to find?

- Full-color annual reports in .pdf format
- Equity, bond, and other prospectuses for North American companies. International prospectuses are available from Global EDGAR partner Europrospectus
- Financial statements

Global Insight

www.globalinsight.com

Fee-based site

Global Insight, Inc. was formed by combining two of the most well-known economic data and forecasting entities in the United States, Data Resources (DRI), and WEFA (formerly known as Wharton Economic Forecasting Associates). Global Insight provides the comprehensive economic coverage of countries, regions, and industries.

The Countries and Regions section of the Website includes country analysis, forecasts, and economic data. In this section, subscribers can access current economic analysis for more than 200 countries, global risk evaluations for 117 countries, global market sizing for over 66 industry sectors in 70 countries, and coverage of oil, coal, gas, and electricity markets for over 70 countries.

The economic and financial data available from Global Insights are impressive. There are more than 90 historical databases covering global financial markets, international economies, and U.S. national, regional, and industrial markets.

What can you expect to find?

- Detailed economic and financial data for global markets
- Brief collection of free articles and sample reports to those who register as a guest on the site
- Webcasts by industry experts on current international issues

International Business Resource Connection

www.ibrc.bschool.ukans.edu   (Exhibit 12.5)

Free site

The International Business Resource Connection (IBRC) is a business outreach program within the School of Business at the University of Kansas. The IBRC helps small and medium-sized companies broaden their international business skills and explore available international trade opportunities. The IBRC has assembled a collection of international trade and business resources on the Internet that is organized by country and includes original reporting like that found in the Cultural Perspective Reports (CPRs). The CPRs are designed to provide a U.S. businessperson with a cultural overview of a foreign country, with particular emphasis on business customs and practices (see Exhibit 12.5).

What can you expect to find?

- Trade Databases
- Detailed information on every country's business, government, and travel resources
- International trade statistics

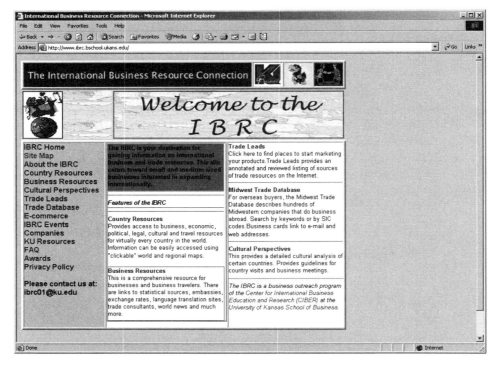

Exhibit 12.5   The International Business Resource Connection

International Trade Center

www.intracen.org

Free and fee-based site

The International Trade Center is an executing agency of the United Nations Development Programme, and through its Website provides a set of tools for monitoring national and sectoral trade performance. ITC produces and disseminates market research and trade analysis for exporters, importers, and trade support institutions in developing countries and transitional economies. These Market Analysis Portals benchmark the national trade performance of 184 countries by sectors and specific products.

What can you expect to find?

- Country-specific export profiles based on trade statistics derived from COMTRADE of the United Nations Statistics Division, the world's largest trade database
- Concise "market brief" reports on export products of interest to developing countries

Kompass

www.kompass.com

Free and fee-based site

Kompass provides product, contact, and other information for 1.7 million companies worldwide. Researchers can search in a variety of languages by product or service, and by company or trade name. The search can also be limited by geographic area. A user may access kompass.com for free and have access to the database using limited search criteria, view limited company lists, and be able to download a selection of full company profiles.

Subscribers have access to unlimited company lists (with telephone and fax numbers), an unlimited number of full company profiles, the company list sorting feature, and financial data where available. This directory is an excellent source for finding basic information about a company or pulling together a list of a company's competitors.

What can you expect to find?

- Directory of international companies including the company contact information, number of employees, information on executives, key figures, and products and services

U.S. Department of State Business Center

www.state.gov/business/

Free site

> The U.S. Department of State Business Center offers a wealth of information for conducting business internationally. The Department of State's Office of Commercial and Business Affairs supports U.S. firms doing business overseas by offering problem-solving assistance in opening markets, leveling the playing field, and resolving trade and investment disputes.

> Firms who want to work with the U.S. Department of State will find this site invaluable. The site has a lengthy and detailed "Guide to Doing Business With the Department of State." The Guide covers information about obtaining federal contracts, trade promotion activities, and subcontracting opportunities.

> The site contains Background Notes on dozens of countries. Background Notes provides information about a country's geography, people, government, economy, history, politics, travel, and business. These typically are 5 to 10 page overviews. Organized by region, then by country, a Background Note is available for just about every country in the world.

> The main U.S. State Department Website at www.state.gov is host to the Department of State Foreign Affairs Network (DOSFAN) which provides global access to official U.S. foreign policy information, including Dispatch and Background Notes on countries and international organizations; congressional reports on trade practices; human rights, terrorism, narcotics control, and other subjects; directories of key officers at foreign service posts; travel information; and more.

> *What can you expect to find?*

> - Information on working with the U.S. Department of State
> - Foreign Per Diem Rates
> - Doing Business Abroad Guide

Wall Street Journal Online

www.wsj.com   (Exhibit 12.6)

Fee-based site

> The *Wall Street Journal* is known for its extensive coverage of world business news. Subscribers to the *Wall Street Journal Online* can access the "World News" home page with dozens of news reports and feature stories on international

business issues. From the "World News" page, readers can select an individual country's news page for a menu to find dozens of country-specific stories from Dow Jones newswires and the *Wall Street Journal*.

Unlike subscribers to the print edition of the *Wall Street Journal*, who must choose only one geographic edition of the paper to receive, online subscribers can view the editions from Asia, Europe, and the Americas.

The *Wall Street Journal* provides free access to the Special Reports section of the Website at http://interactive.wsj.com/public/resources/documents/special.htm, which does include international reports such as the *Central European Economic Review, European Mutual Funds Quarterly Review, Asian Economic Survey, World Business Report*, and *World Economic Forum* (see Exhibit 12.6).

What can you expect to find?

- In-depth original reporting on major international business topics

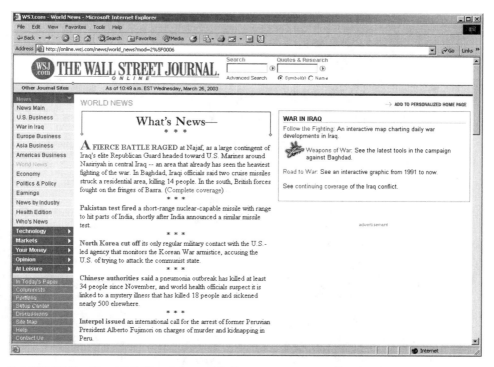

Exhibit 12.6 The *Wall Street Journal* Online

World Factbook

www.odci.gov/cia/publications/factbook/index.html   (Exhibit 12.7)

Free site

Published by the Central Intelligence Agency (CIA), the *Factbook* has been a long-standing source of background information on countries. Each chapter includes data on the country's economy, government, communications, geography, people, transportation, and military. Appendices include detailed information on international organizations and groups and international environmental agreements. The *Factbook* can be downloaded in its entirety from the Website for free (see Exhibit 12.7).

What can you expect to find?

*   Detailed information by country covering governmental, political, and economic issues

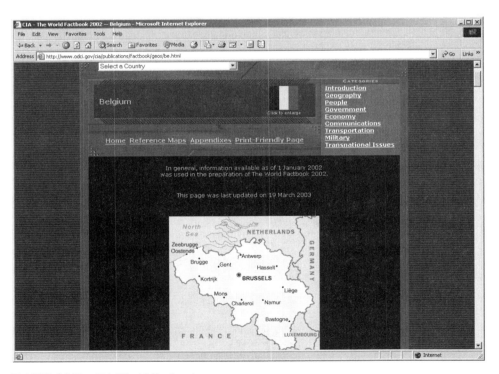

Exhibit 12.7   CIA *World Factbook*

BEST OF THE REST

allAfrica

http://allafrica.com

Free site

> AllAfrica.com is a news aggregator offering more than 500 daily news stories from around the continent. From this leading provider of African news world-wide, there are even country-specific pages, from Algeria to Zimbabwe. The "Sustainable Africa" section covers environmental and developmental issues across the continent and offers resource documents.

Bank Hapoalim

www.bankhapoalim.co.il

Free site

> Israeli Bank Hapoalim's Website provides reports on the Israeli capital market. There is also information and analyst's reports for leading Israeli companies. Also included are daily stock and bonds prices, and updated economic forecasts. The site can be viewed in four languages: Hebrew, Russian, Spanish, and English.

Basic Guide to Exporting

www.unzco.com/basicguide/index.html

Free site

> *A Basic Guide to Exporting* is a publication of the U.S. Department of Commerce in Cooperation with Unz & Co., Inc. The full-text of *A Basic Guide to Exporting* is available on this Website. The Guide covers topics such as Determining Your Products' Export Potential, Developing a Market Plan, Preparing Your Product for Export, and Conducing Business Abroad.

BolagsFakta

www.bolagsfakta.se

Free site

> BolagsFakta is a database of Swedish company annual reports and other financial information.

Business Europe

www.businesseurope.com/cmn/index.jsp

Free site

> Business Europe focuses on European small- and medium-sized enterprises (SMEs). The site offers original news analysis, expert advice, online forums, a business directory, and marketplace. The Resources section contains How-to Guides to assist SME owners in complying with government regulations, and establishing good management practices. Business Europe has gathered information on popular topics into "zones." For example, there is a Start Up Zone with information on opening a new business and an Import/Export Zone showing companies how to enter foreign markets.

China Big

www.chinabig.com

Free site

> This metasite offers links to a variety of Chinese business information. The site has both a domestic and a global trade directory. There is information on business travel in China and a section on Chinese laws and regulations, including intellectual property laws.

China Online

www.chinaonline.com

Free and fee-based site

> China Online provides access to more than 100 sources of economic and business information about China. The content includes general interest business stories, news and analysis relevant to specific industries, maps, and background information on Chinese political and business leaders. Europe Brief industry outlooks and current news items are free to access. Reports such as the *China Economic Quarterly* are available for purchase on the site.

Company Records On-Line (CAROL)

www.carol.co.uk

Free site

> Company Records On-Line (CAROL) is an online service offering direct links to the financial pages of listed companies in Europe and the United States. The database is searchable by company name, region, sector, or stock exchange.

Consensus Economics

www.consensuseconomics.com

Fee-based site

Consensus Economics is an international economic survey organization. Each month Consensus Economics polls more than 600 economists to obtain their forecasts and views. These surveys cover estimates for the principal macro-economic variables (including growth, inflation, interest rates, and exchange rates) in over 70 countries. Publications include the Asia Pacific Consensus Forecasts, the Latin American Consensus Forecasts, the Eastern Europe Consensus Forecasts, G-7 Countries and Western Europe Consensus Forecasts, and USA Consensus Forecasts. Free sample publications are available along with current data articles.

DATAINTAL

http://estadisticas.sieca.org.gt/dataintalweb/

Free site

DATAINTAL offers trade statistical information on imports and exports from 29 countries in North and South America. The information dates from 1980 and is searchable by country.

EDGAR Online Global Reports

www.edgar-online.com/global_reports.asp

Fee-based site

The EDGAR Online service offers access to a library of financial reports for international companies. Subscribers can browse by Company, Country, Exchange, or Index or do targeted searches. Annual and interim financial reports can be downloaded in Adobe .pdf format.

EUbusiness

www.eubusiness.com

Free site

EUbusiness is a business portal of information about the European Union. Here you will find information on EU law and EU business developments, and information on how to do business in European countries.

EUROPAGES: The European Business Directory

www.europages.com

Free site

> EUROPAGES is a yellow pages type directory of 500,000 companies in 30 European countries. The site is searchable by product, service, and company name. Researchers can also search through a list of business categories, such as Fruits & Vegetables or Building Materials.

Europrospectus

www.europrospectus.com

Fee-based site

> The europrospectus.com site offers users access to a database of debt, equity, and warrant prospectuses, SEC filings, mergers & acquisition documents, and annual reports. The database has more than 100,000 prospectuses of debt, equity, warrant and M&A deals, and adds about 400 new ones every week. Europrospectus offers full text searching of the database which is a significant feature, as many sources for prospectuses offer only scanned images that are not text searchable.

Federation of International Trade Organizations
International Trade/Import-Export Portal

www.fita.org

Free site

> The Federation of International Trade Associations (FITA) is a network of 300,000 companies belonging to more than 350 international trade associations in the U.S.A, Canada, and Mexico. The International Trade/Import-Export Portal offers links to: international trade leads, trade news, trade events, Web resources, and job postings.

Forbes International 500

www.forbes.com/2002/07/03/internationals.html

Free site

> *Forbes* publishes an annual list of the 500 largest companies based outside the United States. The listing is based on a composite ranking for sales, profits, assets, and market value. Users can view the list by Rank, Company, Country, Industry, Revenues, or Enterprise Multiple.

Global Business Centre

www.glreach.com/gbc

Free site

The Global Business Centre is a directory of links to international Websites. The center specializes in linking users to non-English-language sites. The site is organized by subject within each language: business, culture, online publications, and e-zines, leisure, jobs, shopping, and travel.

HierosGamos: The Comprehensive Law and Government Portal

www.hg.org/1table.html

Free site

HierosGamos was one of the first legal and governmental sites on the Internet, and, despite its cluttered home page, is a comprehensive starting point for law-related information. The "Law and Government Resources" page has information arranged by country. For each country, Hieros provides links to the main government site, the CIA *World Factbook* report, the section pertaining to that country from the Law Library of Congress, and the country-specific sites from the Internet *Legal Resource Guide*.

Hoover's

www.hoovers.com

www.hoovers.com/uk

Free and fee-based sites

While Hoover's is known for its in-depth profiles of U.S. public companies, the site also provides quite a bit of information on selected international companies; in fact, the Hoover's database covers 65,000 companies around the world. You can search the database by company name to find foreign companies or check the Hoover's Non-U.S. Company Directory. Additionally, Hoover's maintains a site in the United Kingdom.

International Finance Corporation

www.ifc.org

Free site

The International Finance Corporation (IFC) promotes sustainable private sector investment in developing countries as a way to reduce poverty. IFC is the largest multilateral source of loan and equity financing for private sector projects in the developing world. IFC provides advice and technical assistance to private businesses and governments in developing countries. The Research Desk section of the site offers access to numerous reports including *Corporate Governance in China, Doing Better Business through Effective Public Consultation and Disclosure*, and technical papers such as *The Effects of Hyper-Inflation on Accounting Ratios: Financing Corporate Growth in Industrial Economies*.

International Statistical Agencies

www.census.gov/main/www/stat_int.html

Free site

Compiled by the U.S. Census Bureau, this site provides a link to the national statistical agencies for dozens of countries.

Latin American Network Information Center

lanic.utexas.edu

Free site

The Latin American Network Information Center (LANIC) is a part of the Institute of Latin American Studies at the University of Texas at Austin. LANIC is a metasite of information on Latin America. There are more than 12,000 unique links in the LANIC collection of sites relating to Latin America. The University does an excellent job keeping these links updated and accurate.

In addition to LANIC, the University of Texas is also home to the Asian Network Information Center (ASNIC), the Middle East Network Information Center (MENIC), and the Russian and East European Network Information Center (REENIC).

Latin Focus

www.latin-focus.com

Free and fee-based site

The Latin Focus Website collects data from government sources, economic forecasts, market analysis covering economic performance, political risk assessments, and financial market developments. Users can access free news stories, economic indicators, and business opportunity information.

Latin Focus publishes the *The Latin Focus Consensus Forecast,* a monthly country-specific and regional publication focusing on the current state of affairs and the future developments in the seven largest markets in Latin America. Subscribers have access to more than 100 country forecasts.

Lex Africa Business Guides

http://mbendi.co.za/werksmns/lexaf/

Free site

Lex Africa is a network of African law firms. The Lex Africa site features business guides prepared by member law firms for 12 African countries. Each business guide features investment information, forms of business organizations, taxation, exchange control, tariffs, intellectual property issues, and privatization issues.

Mbendi: Africa's Leading Website

www.mbendi.co.za

Free and fee-based site

Consulting firm Mbendi Information Services Ltd.'s Website provides country, company, and business-related information for every country in Africa. Users can purchase subscriptions to more than 50 different e-newsletters on topics such as media and technology, and business opportunities. Mbendi works to help the business community identify African business opportunities.

MenaBusiness

www.menabusiness.com

Free site

The MenaBusiness site is a resource for companies and individuals considering doing business in the MENA (Middle East and North Africa) region. The site includes detailed country information for Algeria, Egypt, Morocco, Saudi Arabia, and the United Arab Emirates.

New Zealand Companies Office Database

www.companies.govt.nz

Fee-based site

> Detailed financial data on registered New Zealand companies. Incorporation records are available and data includes information on directors and shareholders.

Planet Business

www.planetbiz.com

Free site

> Planet Business provides links to the yellow pages of just about every country in the world, organized by country.

System for Electronic Document Analysis and Retrieval (SEDAR)

www.sedar.com

Free site

> SEDAR, the System for Electronic Document Analysis and Retrieval, is the electronic filing system for public companies and mutual funds in Canada. The SEDAR Website contains copies of the disclosure documents filed in the system, as well as profiles containing basic information about each company or mutual fund group.

Thomas Register of European Manufacturers

www.tipcoeurope.be

Free and fee-based site

> The European counterpart to the Thomas Register of American Manufactures, this directory contains listings for more than 207,000 industrial suppliers, organized by 10,500 industrial product classifications, in six languages, and from 17 European countries. Researchers can search by company name in one of six languages, or work down a list of 10,000 industrial product descriptions. The site is free to search but registration is required. Each listing contains company contact information and a link to the company's Website and catalog if available.

Webstat

http://seitti.funet.fi:5000/etusivu_en.html

Free site

WebStat is a database of official statistical sources from all over the world. The material is classified by subject field and by country. The database is free text searchable or users can search by country or subject. The search result contains a description of the source (which can be a table, a document, an entire publication, or a database) and a direct hyperlink to it. The database is compiled and maintained by the Library of Statistics Finland.

Another useful database of international information from the Library of Statistics Finland is the *World in Figures* at www.stat.fi/tk/tp/maailmanumeroina/index_en.html. This site allows users to access 28 Excel tables of country-specific structural data on all the countries of the world.

CHAPTER 13

Public Records

Public records are documents that are gathered by various public offices and agencies with the purpose of making them available to the general public. Public records include, but are not limited to, lawsuit data and court dockets, death records, business entity filings, real estate records, and lien filings. However, just because information is by law considered "public," does not mean that it is easily obtainable. Furthermore, the type and quantity of public records available on the Internet varies greatly from state to state, and to further complicate the issue, what is and is not considered "public" varies from state to state.

If you are interested in additional information on public records, read Carole Levitt's "How Public Are Public Records?" located at www.netforlawyers.com/ article_public_records.htm. For a more in-depth explanation of public records research, consult *Naked in Cyberspace: How to Find Personal Information Online*, by Carole A. Lane (Cyber Age Books, 2002).

Many governments have put public records online, however these records may exist in databases that are part of the Invisible Web, that is, Web pages that cannot be found by search engines. Therefore, it is necessary to check sites such as The Search Systems Public Records Locator. In addition, some public records are just too difficult to obtain on your own because of logistical or time constraints. A service like KnowX collects public records from dozens of jurisdictions, indexes them, and provides them to the public for a fee.

The sites listed in this chapter are great starting points for public records research. You may find just the data you need, or you may find a site that charges a fee to obtain the record for you.

FIRST AND FOREMOST

Choicepoint

www.choicepointonline.com   (Exhibit 13.1)

Fee-based site

ChoicePoint is a public company and a respected provider of identification and credential verification services. Much of the data on this site was previously available only in commercial public records databases offered by subscription. ChoicePoint is a great service for those willing to pay for "locating a claimant or witness, identifying or verifying assets, investigating fraud, or in need of a public record searched at a courthouse."

Search costs vary depending on the records searched, but are generally reasonable. An application for an account is required and can take up to 10 days for approval (see Exhibit 13.1).

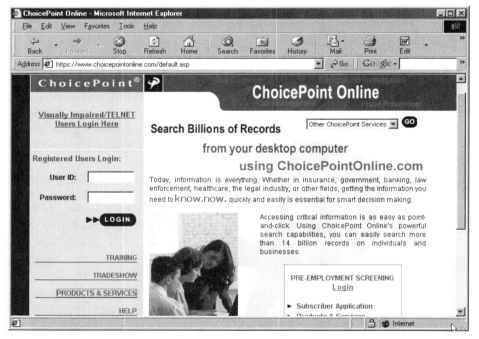

Exhibit 13.1 ChoicePoint
ChoicePoint and the ChoicePoint logo are registered trademarks of ChoicePoint Asset Company.

What can you expect to find?

- A database of 14 billion public records on individuals and businesses, concerning bankruptcies, liens, judgments, corporation and limited partnership records, motor vehicle and property ownership, and credit reports.

KnowX

www.KnowX.com

Fee-based site

KnowX allows users access to public record data on a pay-as-you-go basis. Information available includes real estate records, liens, death records, asset ownership, and professional license information. The source for this information is the commercial public records service called Information America, which is also available on Westlaw.

KnowX does not charge a monthly, subscription, or registration fee, but charges by the search or record. Some searches are free, others run from $1.50 to $9.95. Records are available for purchase on a per item basis with costs as low as $3.95, depending on the record.

What can you expect to find?

- A search form that allows researchers to locate businesses, locate people, run background checks, evaluate assets, verify professional licenses, research business reports such as those from Dun & Bradstreet, and locate "other" records such as marriage and divorce documents.

NETROnline: Real Estate Information and Public Records Research

www.netronline.com (Exhibit 13.2)

Free site

NETROnline is a portal for property information, deeds & mortgage copies, tax records, parcel maps, assessment records, and public records nationwide. As a portal, the site provides links to the sources of the data, not the data itself (see Exhibit 13.2).

What can you expect to find?

• The site's Public Records database provides links to official state Websites, and tax assessors' and recorders' offices' Websites that are designed for online public access of their jurisdiction's public records. The database is organized by state and then country. Links are provided to the appropriate office's Website, or contact information is given if no Website is available.

• The Property Data Store sells parcel maps, property comparable reports, property detail reports, transfer detail reports, and recorders' index searches.

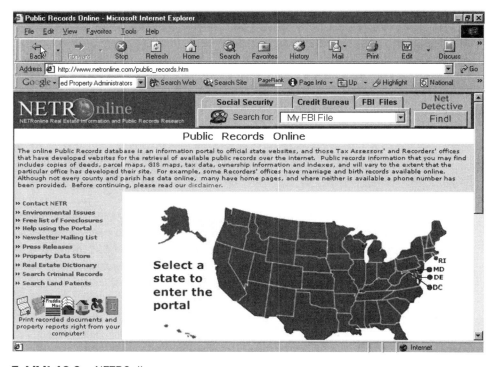

Exhibit 13.2   NETROnline

Public Record Sources

www.publicrecordsources.com

Free and fee-based site

This site is sponsored by The Public Record Retrieval Network (PRRN), the largest trade organization representing professionals in the public record industry, consisting of more than 660 members in 50 states that retrieve documents from local government agencies in over 2,000 counties nationwide.

What can you expect to find?

- Links to over 1,330 state, county, city, and federal (court) Websites that provide free access to public record information.
- The ability to search by state or county for a "Local Document Retriever." This person or firm is a member of the Public Record Retriever Network and is in the business of obtaining state or local government public records for a fee.
- The Public Record Research System, which is a subscription-based public record locator that provides public record access procedures and contact information to more than 26,000 government agencies that house public records. The system "provides you with the information you need to access public records directly from the the agency that houses them." Subscriptions begin at $39.00.

search systems Public Record Locator

www.searchsystems.net

Free and fee-based site

This site is one of the largest and most comprehensive collection of links to free public record databases on the Internet. This site provides links to over 10,000 free public records databases. Depending on the state, there are licensing records, court records, unclaimed property, sex offender registries, and so on, as well as some county-level databases. While most databases listed are free, there are some that are fee-based.

What can you expect to find?

- The ability to search by state, city, or county level, and then by category, such as foreclosures.
- The site's Premium Services provide fee-based access to statement criminal records in more than 35 states.

USSearch

www.1800ussearch.com

Fee-based site

USSearch.com is a publicly traded company that specializes in location and verification services, such as identity verification, individual location, criminal record checks, employment and education verifications, professional reference checks, credit and motor vehicle record checks, drug screening, and pre-employment verification services. Prices range from $19.95 to $295.00.

What can you expect to find?

- Access to public records on bankruptcy, judgments, death records, address location for asset verification, people and business locating, fraud prevention, and employment screening. Databases available for searching include U.S. Military Personnel, Boat Registrations, Business Affiliations, FAA Aircraft Registrations, FAA Pilot Licenses, Federal Firearms and Explosives Licenses, National DEA Controlled Substance Licenses, National Deeds, National Marine Radio Licenses, National Trademarks/Service Marks, and ABI Business Directory. Pricing varies if different database combinations are searched, but fees are reasonable.

BEST OF THE REST

Discreet Research

www.public-records.net

Fee-based site

Discreet Research gathers public records from electronic public record filings, databases, public record vendors, court records, and state repository databases.

Users can search for criminal records and outstanding warrants as well as credit reports, motor vehicle records, and professional licenses.

National Association of Unclaimed Property Administrators (NAUPA)

www.unclaimed.org

Free site

The National Association of Unclaimed Property Administrators consists of state officials that have the responsibility of "collecting and reuniting lost owners with their unclaimed property." According to the NAUPA, unclaimed property consists of "various types of intangible personal property. Savings and checking accounts, uncashed checks, securities, dividends, insurance refunds or claims, oil royalties, wages, utility refunds/deposits, bail bonds, and child support payments." As an owner of lost assets, you can use the Find Property link and search by state.

Merlin Information Services

www.merlindata.com

Fee-based site

Merlin Data was created by a former California private investigator. Most of the databases are specific to California. However, there are several that contain national data, including Banko, a national bankruptcy listing. Merlin allows access to a variety of records, including criminal records, marriage licenses, and professional licenses. Charges vary according to database but are generally reasonable.

National Criminal Justice Reference System (NCJRS)

www.ncjrs.org/courwww.html

Free site

NCJRS is a federally funded service sponsored by the U.S. Department of Justice and the Executive Office of the President. The NCJRS site provides justice and substance abuse data "to anyone interested in crime and public safety including policymakers, practitioners, researchers, educators, community leaders, and the general public." The site provides links to the court-related sites throughout the United States. In addition, the NCJRS Abstracts Database contains summaries of more than 170,000 criminal justice publications.

National Public Records Research Association (NPRRA)

www.nprra.org

Free site

NPRRA is a trade association for those individuals and firms that provide public records research. The association's Website provides a directory, organized by state, of members who can be hired to research public records.

U.S. Death Records

www.llrx.com/columns/reference14.htm

Free site

This article discusses and provides links to various Internet sites that provide death records.

Index

ABA Intellectual Property Law section, 168
Abbott, Langer & Associates, Inc., 112–113, 115
ABI/INFORM database, 59
About.com, 22–23
Accounting, *See* Taxes and accounting
Accounting Pro2Net, *see* SmartPros
Accounting Research Network, 190
Accounting & Tax Database, 190–191
AccountingWeb, 23, 61, 191, 195
Accounts Media Group, 184
ACINet, *see* America's Career InfoNet
Acquisitions Monthly, 144
Advanced search features, 12–15
Advertising:
    on AltaVista, 9
    as "featured" listings, xxi
    through vortals, 32
Africa:
    AllAfrica, 213
    Lex Africa Business Guides, 219
    Mbendi, 219
    MenaBusiness, 219
AICPA, *see* American Institute of Certified
    Public Accountants
Alacra, xxii, 17–18
    for betas, 75–76
    earnings estimates, 79
    merger and acquisition data, 130–131
AllAfrica, 213

Alltheweb, 5–6
    customization with, 5
    .pdf files indexed by, 12
    as top search engine, 2
AltaVista, xxi, 6
    ads on, 9
    .pdf files indexed by, 11
    PostScript files indexed by, 11
    sponsored sites with, 9
    as top search engine, 2
A.M. Best Insurance Company Directory and
    Reports, 107
American Bar Association (ABA), 168
American Chambers of Commerce Abroad,
    196–197
American Compensation Association, 127
American Demographics, xx
American Economic Association, 55
American FactFinder, 49
American Institute of Certified Public
    Accountants (AICPA), 176–178
American Lawyer, 157
American Society of Association Executives'
    (ASAE) Gateway to Associations, 66–68,
    123, 145
America's Career InfoNet (ACINet), 114–115
AOL, paid placement with, 8
Aon Consulting, Inc., 118, 176
Applied Reasoning Inc., 54
Arthur Andersen, 176

ASAE, *see* American Society of Association Executives' Gateway to Associations
Asian Network Information Center (ASNIC), 218
Asia Pacific Consensus Forecasts, 215
ASNIC (Asian Network Information Center), 218
Association of Research Libraries Copyright and IP Center, 169
Associations on the Net, 67
AuditNet, 191
Audit Techniques Guides, 70
AUS Consultants, 173

Baker, Thomsen Associates, 119, 121
Bank Hapoalim, 213
Banko, 229
Bank One Corporate Economics Group (CEG), 50
A Basic Guide to Exporting, 213
Bates, Mary Ellen, xxi, 196
Baur, York, 16
Bay Area Library & Information System, 119
BEA (Bureau of Economic Analysis), 51
BEARFACTS, 51
Beige Book, 43
Bennett Jones LLP, 171
Best Jobs USA Salary Survey, 115
Betas, 75–77
    Alacra, 75–76
    Multex Investor, 76
    Wall Street Research Net, 77
Beta Books for Companies, 75
Beta Books for Industries, 76
Biehl, Kathy, 99–100
Big Four major accounting firm sites, 178–180
Bizcomps, 131–133, 142
BizFindLaw Intellectual Property Center, 169
Bizminer, 68
Bloomberg, xxii
BLS, *see* Bureau of Labor Statistics
BNA, *see* Bureau of National Affairs
BolagsFakta, 213
Bonds, 77–78
    Bondtrac, 77
    Federal Reserve Board, 77
    T-Bills, Notes & Bonds Online, 78
    Yahoo Bond Center, 77–78
Bondtrac, 77
Bonuses, 111. *See also* Salary and executive compensation surveys
Boolean searching, 12–13
BrightPlanet, 10
British patents, 158
Broad and shallow searches, 16

B2B, *see* Business-to-business
Bureau of Economic Analysis (BEA), 51
Bureau of Labor Statistics (BLS), 38–39, 115–116
Bureau of National Affairs (BNA), 180–181
Bureau van Dijk, 197–198
The Business and Finance Site, 182
Business.com, 23–24, 34
Business CreditUSA.com, 107
Business Cycle Indicators (Conference Board), 51
Business entity filings, 223. *See also* Public records
Business Europe, 214
Business Filings Databases, 99–100
Business journals, 37
Business magazine special issues, 124
Business methods, patenting of, 151
Business Newspapers, 37
Business Owner's Toolkit, 182
Business press, 57
Business-to-business (B2B):
    publications, 58
    vortals, 32–35
Business Valuation Market Data, 132–134
"The Business Web," 17
Business Week Online, 68
BusinessWeek salary and executive compensation surveys, 124
Buyer's lists, 34

Cached links (Google), 3
California:
    JobStar: California Job Search Guide, 119–120
    Merlin Information Services, 229
Canadian Compensation Association, 127
Canadian Securities Administrators, 94
CareerJournal, 117–118
CareerOneStop portal, 114
Carl UnCover, 146
CAROL (Company Records On-Line), 214
Cartesian Products, Inc., 170
CBS Marketwatch, 79–80
CCC (Copyright Clearance Center), 169
CCH, *see* Commerce Clearing House
CEG (Bank One Corporate Economics Group), 50
Census of Governments, 49
Center for Economic Studies (CES), 49
Center for the Study of Rural America, 45
Central Intelligence Agency (CIA) *World Factbook*, 212
CES (Center for Economic Studies), 49
CFO.com, 191
Chambers of Commerce, 37–38, 67, 196–197
Chem-Etrade.com, 34

China Big, 214
China Online, 214
ChoicePoint, 224–225
ChooseEnergy.com, 34
CIA *World Factbook,* 212
CI Strategies and Tools (Fuld & Company), 33
CLEA (Collection of Laws for Electronic Access), 167
Closed-end mutual funds, 79–81
Collection of Laws for Electronic Access (CLEA), 167
Commerce Clearing House (CCH), 176, 182
Commercial Service — U.S. Department of Commerce, 198–199
Commscan, 145
Company Records On-Line (CAROL), 214
Compensation, *see* Salary and executive compensation surveys
Comperio, 192
CompGeo Online, 124–125
Conference Board Business Cycle Indicators, 51
Congressional Budget Office Projections, 51–52
Consensus Economics, 52, 215
Construction industry, 23
Consulting, xix
Consumer spending (for online content), xx
Copyrights, 151, 169, 170, 174. *See also* Intellectual property research
Copyright Clearance Center (CCC), 169
Copyright Crash Course, 165
Copyright Website, 170
Corporate Control Alert, 135
Corporate Growth Deal Retriever, 134–135, 142
CorporateInformation, 24, 25
    international business research, 199–200
    private company data, 100
    public company data, 84–85
    stock quotes, 81
CorpTech, 100–101
Council of Economic Advisers, 40
Country data, *see* International business research
Country Reports, 203
Court dockets, 223. *See also* Public records
CPA2Biz, 176, 177
CPA Journal, 182, 183
CPA Letter, 178
Crawlers, 11
Credit reporting agencies, 99
Criminal data, *see* Public records

The Daily Deal at TheDeal.com, 135–136
Databases, 12
Data Buffet (Economy.com), 42, 43

DATAINTAL, 215
Datamonitor, 200–201
Data Resources (DRI), 46, 47, 207
Datastar, 201
The Deal, 135
Dealogic, 145
Death records, 223. *See also* Public records
Deloitte & Touche, 178, 179
Delphion, 151, 152
Delphion Intellectual Property Network, 152–154
Derwent World Patents Index, 152, 153, 172
Dialog, xxi, xxii, 17, 196
Dialog Open Access, 59–60
Digital Dispatch Mailing List (IRS), 185
DirectHit, 3
Directories. *See also* Portals
    About.com, 22–23
    Europages, 216
    Global business Centre, 217
    The Invisible Web Directory, 12
    Kompass, 209
    periodical, 58
    for private company data, 99
    search engines vs., 1
    Thomas Register of American Manufacturers, 106, 149
    Thomas Register of European Manufacturers, 220
Discreet Research, 228–229
DismalMarket.com, 42
The Dismal Scientist, 24, 25, 42
Dogpile, 15, 16
Domain codes, 14
Domain name ownership rights, 151
Done Deals, xx, 136–137, 142
DotCom Corporation, 185
Dow Jones Publication Library, 95
Dow Jones & Reuters Company, 18
DRI, *see* Data Resources
DRI-WEFA, 47, 207
Dun & Bradstreet, 101–102, 109

Earnings estimates, 79
Eastern Europe Consensus Forecasts, 215
ECNext Knowledge Center, 60–61
E-commerce portal, 163
EComp Executive Compensation Database, 118
EconBase, 52
EconData, 52
Econdata.net, 52
Economagic, 39–40
Econometrics Laboratory (Berkeley), 53
Economic Censuses, 49

Economic Information Systems, 53
Economic Insight Report, 53
Economic Policy Institute (EPI), 53
Economic Report of the President, 40–41
Economic research, 37–56
    Bank One Corporate Economics Group, 50
    Bureau of Economic Analysis, 51
    Bureau of Labor Statistics, 38–39
    Conference Board Business Cycle
        Indicators, 51
    Congressional Budget Office Projections,
        51–52
    Consensus Economics, 52
    EconBase, 52
    EconData, 52
    Economagic, 39–40
    Econometrics Laboratory (Berkeley), 53
    Economic Information Systems, 53
    Economic Policy Institute, 53
    Economic Report of the President, 40–41
    Economics Research Network, 53–54
    The Economist, 54
    Economy.com, 41–43
    Federal Reserve System, 43–46
    Fedstats, 36
    The Financial Forecast Center, 54
    Global Insight, 46–47
    Government Information Sharing Project,
        54–55
    Haver Analytics, 55
    IDEAS, 55
    on local conditions, 37–38
    National Bureau of Economic Research,
        47–48
    Resources for Economists on the Internet, 55
    STAT-USA, 56
    U.S. Census Bureau, 49–50
    Wachovia, 56
    Yardeni's Economics Network, 56
Economics Briefing Room, 49
Economics Research Network, 53–54
Economist, 54, 202–203
Economist Intelligence Unit (EIU), 202–203
Economy.com, 25, 41–43, 69
EDGAR (Electronic Data Gathering, Analysis,
    and Retrieval), xx, 83
    EDGAR-Online, 86
    EDGAR Online Global Reports, 215
    EDGARScan, 86–87
    FreeEDGAR, 88
    Global EDGAR, 206–207
    LIVEDGAR, 90–91, 120–121, 139
    merger and acquisition data, 138–140

    private company data, 107–108
    SEC Info, 94–95
    10k Wizard, 84, 138–140
EDGAR Online, 86
    FreeEDGAR, 88
    Global Reports, 215
EDGARScan, 86–87
EIU, *see* Economist Intelligence Unit
ELDIS Country Profiles, 203
Electronic Accountant, 175, 184–185
Electronic Business Center, 163
Electronic Data Gathering, Analysis, and
    Retrieval, *see* EDGAR
ELibrary, 96, 108
Employment statistics, 38
Encyclopedia of Associations, 67
Enron, 176
Entrepreneur Magazine, 108
EPatents Website, 174
EPI DataZone, 53
EPI (Economic Policy Institute), 53
ERI (Economic Research Institute), 118–119
Ernst & Young, 178, 180
EUbusiness, 215
Euromonitor, 203–204
Europages, 216
Europe:
    Bureau van Dijk, 197–198
    Business Europe, 215
    Company Records On-Line, 214
    Consensus Forecasts, 215
    Datamonitor, 200–201
    Datastar, 201
    EUbusiness, 215
    Euromonitor, 203–204
    Europages, 216
    European Union business resources, 204
    Europrospectus, 216
    patents, 152, 153, 158, 170, 172
    Thomas Register of European Manufacturers,
        220
European Patent Organization esp@cenet, 170
European Union business resources, 204
Europrospectus, 216
Excel spreadsheets, downloads to, 38, 42
Executive compensation, *see* Salary and execu-
    tive compensation surveys
Executive Compensation Advisory Services, 125
Executive Compensation Survey (NIBM), 112
Ex-Exec Tracker, 108
Experian, 102–103
*The Extreme Searcher's Guide to Web Search
    Engines* (Randolph Hock), 7

Factiva, xxi, xxii, 17–19
Factset, xxii
FASB, *see* Financial Accounting Standards Board
FAST (Federal and State Tax), 182
Faxpat/Optipat, 158
Featured sites, xxi, 8
Federal and State Tax (FAST), 182
Federal Research Library, 189
Federal Reserve Economic Data (FRED), 45
Federal Reserve System, 43–46
 Federal Reserve Banks, 43–45
 Selected Interest Rates, 77
Federal Tax Law, 192
Federation of International Trade Associations
 (FITA) International Trade/Import-Export
 Portal, 216
Fedstats, 36
Fee-based Websites, xx–xxii, 17–19
Financial Accounting Standards Board (FASB),
 193, 194
Financial Economics Network, 53–54
The Financial Forecast Center, 54
Financial software, 175
Financial Times Surveys, 69
Financial Valuation Group, 155
FindLaw, 26–27, 169
FirstGov, 27
First Research Industry Reports/Profiles, 57,
 61–62
FITA (Federation of International Trade
 Associations), 216
Food Industry portal, 69
Forbes Magazine, 103
 International 500, 216
 Private 500, 103
 salary and executive compensation
  surveys, 124
Foreign companies/countries/industries, *see*
 International business research
Franchise 500, 108
Franklin Pierce Law Center, 154
FRED (Federal Reserve Economic Data), 45
FreeEDGAR, 88
FreeLunch.com, 42
Free Websites, xx, 10
French patents, 172
Frost & Sullivan Research Publications, 69
FTA State Tax Rates, 192
Fuld & Company, 33

Gale Group Trade and Industry Database, 59
GASB (Government Accounting Standards
 Board), 193

German patents, 158
Get the Patent, 170–171
Global Business Center, 217
Global Business Opportunities and National
 Trade Data Bank (GLOBUS/NTDB), 206
Global EDGAR, 206–207
GlobalEDGE, 204–205
Global Insight, 46–47, 207
Global Securities Information Inc. (GSI), 120
 LIVEDGAR, 90, 120–121, 139
 Mergers & Acquisitions Database, 140
 144A/Private Placement Database, 96
Goffe, Bill, 55
Goldman Sachs Research on Demand, 96
Google:
 Advanced Search features, 13, 15, 17
 cached pages in, 3
 extent of, 1
 for international business information, 196
 .pdf files indexed by, 11, 12
 PostScript files indexed by, 11
 site rankings in, 5
 sponsored sites with, xxi, 9
 on tool bar, 16–17
 as top search engine, 2
Google News, 28
Government(s). *See also under* United States...
 Census of, 49
 FirstGov, 27
 HierosGamos, 217
Government Accounting Standards Board
 (GASB), 193
Government Information Sharing Project,
 54–55
Government Printing Office, 40
G-7 Countries and Western Europe Consensus
 Forecasts, 215
GSI, *see* Global Securities Information Inc.

Harris InfoSource, 70, 109
Harvard Business Review, 146
Haver Analytics, 55
Health Medical and Entitlements, 182
Heating, Ventilation, and Air Conditioning
 (HVAC) industry, 58
Hewitt Compensation Center, 125–126
HierosGamos, 217
Hock, Randolph, 7
Hoovers.com, 21, 29, 83
 earnings estimates, 79
 Industry Snapshots, 70
 international business information, 195, 217
 private company data, 103–104

Hoovers.com (*continued*)
    public company data, 88–89
    stock quotes, 81
Hotbot, 3
"How Public Are Public Records?" (Carole
    Levitt), 223
Human Resources (CCH Website), 182
Human Resources Programs Development and
    Improvement, 123
HVAC industry, 58

IASB (International Accounting Standards
    Board), 193
IBA (Institute of Business) Appraisers Market
    Database, 146
IBBA (International Business Brokers
    Association), 146
IBISWorld, 70
IBM Intellectual Property Network, 151, 152
IBM Technical Disclosure Bulletin, 153
IBRC (International Business Resource
    Connection), 208
IDC, xx
IDEAS, 55
IFC, *see* International Finance Corporation
Inc. 500, 104
Inc. Magazine, 104
Industry analysis, 34
Industryclick.com, 34–35
Industry information, 57–73
    About.com, 23
    Bizminer, 68
    Dialog Open Access, 59–60
    ECNext Knowledge Center, 60–61
    Economy.com Industry Reports, 69
    Financial Times Surveys, 69
    First Research Industry Profiles, 61–62
    Frost & Sullivan Research Publications, 69
    Global Insight, 46–47
    Harris InfoSource, 70
    Hoover's Industry Snapshots, 70
    IBISWorld, 70
    Industryclick.com, 34–35
    Integra Industry Reports, 62–63
    IRS Market Segment Specialization
        Program, 70
    ITA Basic Industries, 71
    from libraries, 58
    Manufacturing.net, 71
    MarketResearch.com, 64–65
    MindBranch, 71–72
    MoBDN Industry-at-a-Glance Reports, 72
    plan of research for, 57

Plunkett Research Online, 72
    portals for, 58
    Teoma, 4
    Thomson Research, 65–66
    Trade Association Directories, 66–68
    trade publications, 58
    U.S. Census Bureau: Industry Resources,
        72–73
    ValuationResources, 31, 32
    ValuationResources Industry Resources
        Report, 73
    vortals for, 32–35
    WetFeet.com, 73
Industry Insider database, 66
Information America, 225
Information Holdings Inc., 174
InfoSpace, 15
Ingenta, 146
Institute of Business (IBA) Appraisers Market
    Database, 146
The Institute of Management and Administra-
    tion (IOMA), 126
Institutional Investor, 146
Insurance industry, 107
INTA (International Trademark Association), 172
Integra Industry Reports, 62–63
Integra Information, 105
Intellectual Property Digital Library, 167
The Intellectual Property Law Server, 171
The Intellectual Property Mall, 154–155
Intellectual Property Office of Singapore
    (IPOS), 173–174
Intellectual Property Owners Association, 172
Intellectual property research, 151–174
    ABA Intellectual Property Law section, 168
    Association of Research Libraries Copyright
        and IP Center, 169
    BizFindLaw Intellectual Property Center, 169
    Copyright Clearance Center, 169
    Copyright Website, 170
    Delphion Intellectual Property Network,
        152–154
    Department of Energy Patent Database, 170
    European Patent Organization esp@cenet, 170
    Get the Patent, 170–171
    The Intellectual Property Law Server, 171
    The Intellectual Property Mall, 154–155
    Intellectual Property Owners Association, 172
    Intellectual Property Rights Helpdesk, 171
    The Intellectual Property Transaction Data-
        base, 155–156
International Trademark Association, 172
IP Menu, 171

Law.com Intellectual Law Practice Center, 157–158
  MicroPatent, 158–159
  Patent Café Intellectual Property Network, 159–160
  Questel, 172
  Royalty Source, 173
  Royalty Stat, 173
  SurfIP, 173–174
  Thomson & Thomson, 161
  Trademark.com, 174
  United States Copyright Office, 161–162
  United States Patent and Trademark Office, 163–164
  University of Texas Copyright Crash Course, 165–166
  The Watch File at the University of Texas, 174
  World Intellectual Property Organization, 166–168
Intellectual Property Rights Helpdesk, 171
The Intellectual Property Transaction Database, 155–156
Interest rates, 77–78
  Bondtrac, 77
  Federal Reserve Board, 77
  The Financial Forecast Center, 54
  T-Bills, Notes & Bonds Online, 78
  Yahoo Bond Center, 77–78
Internal Revenue Service (IRS), 70, 185–186
International Accounting Standards Board (IASB), 193
International Business Brokers Association (IBBA), 146
International Business Information on the Web (Sheri Lanza), 196
International business research, 195–221
  AllAfrica, 213
  American Chambers of Commerce Abroad, 196–197
  Bank Hapoalim, 213
  Basic Guide to Exporting, 213
  BolagsFakta, 213
  Bureau van Dijk, 197–198
  Business Europe, 214
  China Big, 214
  China Online, 214
  Commercial Service — U.S. Department of Commerce, 198–199
  Company Records On-Line, 214
  Consensus Economics, 215
  CorporateInformation, 199–200
  CorporateInformation.com, 24–25
  DATAINTAL, 215
  Datamonitor, 200–201
  Datastar, 201
  ECNext Knowledge Center, 60–61
  Economist, 202–203
  Economy.com, 41
  EDGAR Online Global Reports, 215
  ELDIS Country Profiles, 203
  EUbusiness, 215
  Euromonitor, 203–204
  Europages, 216
  European Union business resources, 204
  Europrospectus, 216
  FITA International Trade/Import-Export Portal, 216
  Forbes International 500, 216
  Global Business Center, 217
  Global Business Opportunities and National Trade Data Bank, 206
  Global EDGAR, 206–207
  globalEDGE, 204–205
  Global Insight, 46–47, 207
  HierosGamos, 217
  Hoover's, 217
  International Business Resource Connection, 208
  International Finance Corporation, 217–218
  International Statistical Agencies, 218
  International Trade Center, 209
  Kompass, 209
  Latin American Network Information Center, 218
  Latin Focus, 218–219
  Lex Africa Business Guides, 219
  Mbendi, 219
  MenaBusiness, 219
  New Zealand Companies Office Database, 220
  Planet Business, 220
  SEDAR, 220
  Thomas Register of European Manufacturers, 220
  U.S. Department of State Business Center, 210
  Wall Street Journal Online, 210–211
  Webstat, 221
  World Factbook, 212
International Business Resource Connection (IBRC), 208
International Finance Corporation (IFC), 217–218
International Patent Documentation Center, 153
International Statistical Agencies, 218
International Trade Center, 209
International Trademark Association (INTA), 172
Internet research, trends in, xix–xxii

Investext database, 65

Investment Dealers Digest, 146, 147

Invisible Web, xix, 10–12, 223

The Invisible Web (Chris Sherman and Gary
  Price), 12

The Invisible Web Directory, 12

IOMA (The Institute of Management and
  Administration), 126

IP Law and Business, 157

IP Menu, 171

IPO.com, 97

IPOS, *see* Intellectual Property Office of
  Singapore

IProspect, 9

IRS, *see* Internal Revenue Service

I/S Analyzer, 21

Israel, 213

ITA Basic Industries, 71

IWon, 3

Japanese patents, 153, 158

JobStar: California Job Search Guide, 119–120

Journal of Accountancy, 177

Jupiter, 12

Kagan and Associates, 147

Keywords, 16

Kleinrock's Tax Expert Online, 186

KnowX, 223, 225

Kompass, 209

KPMG, 178–179

Lane, Carole A., 223

Language tools, 196

LANIC (Latin American Network Information
  Center), 218

Lanza, Sheri, 196

Latin American Consensus Forecasts, 215

Latin American Network Information Center
  (LANIC), 218

Latin Focus, 218–219

Law.com Intellectual Law Practice Center,
  157–158

Law Crawler, 26

Lawsuit data, 223. *See also* Public records

Legal resources. *See also specific topics*
  BizFindLaw Intellectual Property Center, 169
  Collection of Laws for Electronic Access, 167
  federal tax law, 192
  FindLaw, 26–27
  HierosGamos, 217
  Intellectual Property Law Server, 171
  Kleinrock's Tax Expert Online, 186

Law.com Intellectual Law Practice Center,
  157–158
  LIVEDGAR, 90
  RIA Checkpoint, 187

Levitt, Carole, 223

Lex Africa Business Guides, 219

LexisNexis, xxii, 17, 18
  intellectual property information, 151
  international information, 196
  M&A data, 129
  Tax & Accounting Suite of Research
    Services, 176
  as value-added information service, xxi

Librarian's Index to the Internet, 12, 29

Libraries:
  ARL Copyright and IP Center, 169
  industry information in, 58
  Intellectual Property Digital Library, 167
  in Patent and Trademark Depository
    Library Program, 164

Library of California, 29

Library of Statistics Finland, 221

Lien filings, 223. *See also* Public records

LIVEDGAR, 90–91
  M&A data, 139
  salary and executive compensation
    surveys, 120–121

Local economic information, 37–38

Long-term incentive plans, 111. *See also* Salary
  and executive compensation surveys

M&A data, *see* Merger and acquisition data

M&A Desk database, 156

Magazines, private company data from, 99

Main Street Economist, 45

Manufacturing industries, 70

Manufacturing.net, 71

Market data, 75–82
  Alacra, 75–76, 79
  betas, 75–77
  bonds and interest rates, 77–78
  Bondtrac, 77
  CBS Marketwatch, 79–80
  earnings estimates, 79
  Economy.com, 41–43
  Euromonitor, 203–204
  Federal Reserve Board, 77
  International Trade Center, 209
  Morningstar, 80
  Multex Investor, 76
  open- and closed-end mutual funds, 79–81
  stock quotes, 81–82
  T-Bills, Notes & Bonds Online, 78

Wall Street Research Net, 77, 82
Yahoo! Bond Center, 77–78
Yahoo! Finance, 81
Yahoo! Finance Mutual Funds Center, 80–81
MarketResearch.com, 64–65
Market research firms, 57
Market Segment Specialization Program
    (MSSP), 70
MarkIntel reports, 66
Master Data Center, 158
Mbendi, 219
McLaughlin, Laurianne, 8, 9
Media. *See also* Publications
    elibrary, 108
    industry information in, 57, 58
    lists of, 37
Media Finder, 58
Media General Financial Services, 76
Melancon, Barry, 176
MenaBusiness, 219
MENIC (Middle East Network Information
    Center), 218
Mercer Human Resource Consulting, 126
Mergent Online, 83, 93
Merger and acquisition (M&A) data, xx, 129–149
    Alacra, 130–131
    ASAE Gateway to Associations, 145
    Bizcomps, 131–132
    Business Valuation Market Data, 132–134
    Corporate Growth Deal Retriever, 134–135
    The Daily Deal at The Deal.com, 135–136
    Dealogic, 145
    Done Deals, 136–137
    EDGAR databases, 138–140
    Global Securities Information's M & A
        Database, 140
    Ingenta, 146
    Institute of Business Appraisers Market
        Database, 146
    International Business Brokers
        Association, 146
    Investment Dealers Digest, 147
    Kagan and Associates, 147
    Merger Central, 148
    Merger Market, 148
    MergerNetwork, 148
    Mergers & Acquisitions Report, 147–148
    Mergerstat, 141
    NVST.com, 141–142
    SNL Securities, 143–144
    Thomas Register of American Manufacturers,
        149

Thomson Financial Securities Data Com-
        pany Worldwide M&A Database,
        144–145
    Webmergers.com, 149
Merger Central, 148
Merger Market, 148
MergerNetwork, 148
Mergers & Acquisitions Report, 147–148
Mergers and Acquisitions, 146
Mergerstat, xx, 133, 141
Merlin Information Services, 229
Metacrawler, 15, 16
Metals Industry, 23
Meta search engines, 15–16
Michigan State University, 204, 205
MicroPatent, 158–159, 174
Microsoft, 176
Middle East:
    MenaBusiness, 219
    Network Information Center (MENIC), 218
MindBranch, 71–72
Missouri Business Development Network
    (MoBDN) Industry-at-a-Glance Reports, 72
Mitchell, Margaret, 175
Moody's Financial Information Services,
    see Mergent Online
Morningstar, 80
MSN:
    Money Central, 81, 93
    paid placement with, 8
    .pdf files ignored by, 11–12
MSN Search, 3
MSSP (Market Segment Specialization
    Program), 70
Multex, 57
Multex Investor, 76, 92
Mutual funds, 79–81
    CBS Marketwatch, 79–80
    Morningstar, 80
    SEDAR, 97
    Yahoo! Finance Mutual Funds Center, 80–81

Naked in Cyberspace (Carole A. Lane), 223
National Association of State Chief Informa-
    tion Officers, 29
National Association of Unclaimed Property
    Administrators (NAUPA), 229
National Bureau of Economic Research
    (NBER), 47–48
National Compensation Survey (NCS), 115, 116
National Criminal Justice Reference System
    (NCJRS), 229

National Institute of Business Management
    (NIBM), 112
National Law Journal, 157
National Public Records Research Association
    (NPRRA), 230
National Tax Journal, 189
National Trade Data Bank (NTDB), 206
NAUPA (National Association of Unclaimed
    Property Administrators), 229
NBER, *see* National Bureau of Economic
    Research
NBER Digest, 47, 48
NBER Reporter, 47, 48
NCJRS (National Criminal Justice Reference
    System), 229
NCS, *see* National Compensation Survey
NETROnline, 225–226
Newslink, 37
Newspapers. *See also specific papers*
    local, listing of, 37
    private company data from, 99
News Websites, 176. *See also specific sites*
New Zealand Companies Office Database, 220
NIBM (National Institute of Business
    Management), 112
Noncash compensation, 111. *See also* Salary and
    executive compensation surveys
Notess, Greg, 2
NPRRA (National Public Records Research
    Association), 230
NTDB (National Trade Data Bank), 206
NVST.com, 141–142

Occupational Employment Statistics (OES),
    115–116
Occupational Outlook Handbook, 116
OES, *see* Occupational Employment Statistics
"Officer Compensation Report" (Segal), 112
144A/Private Placement Database, 96
OneSource, xxii
One Source Business Browser, 94
Online Publishers Association, xx
Open-end mutual funds, 79–81
Oregon State University, 54

Paid search placement, 8–10
Passworded sites, 12
Patents, 151, 163, 170–172. *See also* Intellectual
    property research
Patent and Trademark Depository Library
    Program, 164
Patent Café Intellectual Property Network,
    159–160

Patent Café IP Search Engine, 159–160
Patent Cooperation Treaties (PCT), 153, 158, 172
Pay-as-you-go pricing plans, xxii
PCT, *see* Patent Cooperation Treaties
.pdf files, 11–12
Periodicals:
    directories of, 58
    trade, 57
Peters, Jerry, 21, 31
Phillips Ormonde & Fitzpatrick, 171
Planet Business, 220
Plunkett Research Online, 72
Pop-up/pop-down ads, 9
Portals, xxii, 1, 21–33
    About.com, 22–23
    accounting, 175–176, 187, 195
    AccountingWeb, 23
    Business.com, 23–24
    CareerOneStop, 114
    CorporateInformation.com, 24, 25
    The Dismal Scientist, 24, 25
    e-commerce, 163
    Economy.com, 25
    FindLaw, 26–27
    FirstGov, 27
    Google News, 28
    Hoover's.com, 21, 29, 83
    HVAC, 58
    industry, 58, 69
    for intellectual property information,
        173–174
    for international business research, 195
    International Trade/Import-Export, 216
    invisible Web access via, 12
    Librarian's Index to the Internet, 29
    NETROnline, 225–226
    Patent Café, 159–160
    Publist.com, 30
    State Search, 29
    Statistical Resources on the Web, 30–31
    for stock quotes, 81
    subject-specific, 21
    Tobacco Industry, 58
    ValuationResources.com, 31, 32
    Yahoo!, 21
    Yahoo! Finance, 31, 33
Portal B- (Alacra), 17
PPCnet, 193
Practicing CPA, 178
Practitioners Publishing Company, 193
Pratt, Shannon, 132, 133
Pratt Public Companies Database, 133
Pratt's Stats, xx, 132–133

Précis (Economy.com), 43, 69
Price, Gary, 11, 12
PriceWaterhouseCoopers, 86, 178, 179, 192
Primedia publications, 34, 35
Private company data, 99–110
    A.M. Best Insurance Company Directory
        and Reports, 107
    Business CreditUSA.com, 107
    Business Filings Databases, 99–100
    CompaniesOnline, 107–108
    CorporateInformation, 100
    CorpTech, 100–101
    Dun & Bradstreet, 101–102
    EDGAR, 108
    eLibrary, 108
    Ex-Exec Tracker, 108
    Experian, 102–103
    Forbes Magazine and Forbes Private 500, 103
    Franchise 500, 109
    Hoover's.com, 29, 103–104
    Inc. Magazine and Inc. 500, 104
    Integra Information, 105
    TechSavvy, 109
    Thomas Register of American Manufacturers,
        106
    Vault Reports, 109
    zapdata, 109–110
Product identification, 34
ProSystemfx, 182
PRRN (The Public Record Retrieval
    Network), 227
Prudential Securities Incorporated, 56
PTO, *see* United States Patent and
    Trademark Office
Publications. *See also specific publications*
    Accounting Research Network, 190
    Accounting & Tax Database, 190–191
    AICPA Website, 177–178
    on Big Four accounting Websites, 178–179
    Commerce Clearing House, 182
    elibrary, 96
    MarketResearch.com, 64
    Patent Cooperation Treaty publications, 153
    Publist.com, 30
Public company data, 83–97
    Business.com, 24
    CorporateInformation, 84–85
    EDGAR-Online, 86
    EDGARScan, 86–87
    eLibrary, 96
    FreeEDGAR, 88
    Goldman Sachs Research on Demand, 96
    Hoover's.com, 29, 88–89

IPO.com, 97
    LIVEDGAR, 90–91
    Mergent Online, 93
    MSN Money Central, 93
    Multex Investor, 92
    144A/Private Placement Database, 96
    One Source Business Browser, 94
    SEC Info, 94–95
    SEDAR, 97
    10k Wizard, 84
    Value Line, 97
    Wall Street City, 97
    Wall Street Journal Briefing Books, 95
    Wall Street Research Network, 95–96
Public libraries, 58
The Public Record Retrieval Network
    (PRRN), 227
Public records, 223–230
    ChoicePoint, 224–225
    Discreet Research, 228–229
    KnowX, 223, 225
    Merlin Information Services, 229
    National Association of Unclaimed
        Property Administrators, 229
    National Criminal Justice Reference
        System, 229
    NETROnline, 225–226
    NPRRA, 230
    Public Records Sources, 227
    Search Systems Public Records Locator, 223,
        227–228
    U.S. Death Records, 230
    USSearch, 228
Public Records Sources, 227
Publist.com, 30

Questel, 172
Quick and dirty searches, 16

Rappoport, Avi, 11
Real estate records, 223. *See also* Public records
Recourse Communications Inc., 115
Reed Business Information, 58, 71
REENIC (Russian and East European Network
    Information Center), 219
Research Institute of America (RIA), 176
Resources for Economists on the Internet, 55
Restaurant industry, 34
RestaurantMarket.com, 34, 35
Results, xxi
    with advanced search features, 12–15
    improving, 1–2
Revenue Ruling 59-60, 57

RIA, 187. *See also* Research Institute of America
RIA Checkpoint, 187
Risk Management Association (RMA) Annual
    Statement Studies, 126
Robert Half & Associates, 115
RoyaltySource, 173
RoyaltyStat, 173
Russian and East European Network
    Information Center (REENIC), 219

St. Paul Public Library, 58
SalariesReview.com, 121
Salary and executive compensation surveys,
    111–127
    Abbott, Langer & Associates, Inc., 112–113
    America's Career InfoNet, 114–115
    Best Jobs USA Salary Survey, 115
    Bureau of Labor Statistics, 115–116
    Business Magazine Special Issues, 124
    Career Journal, 117–118
    CompGeo Online, 124–125
    eComp Executive Compensation
        Database, 118
    Economic Research Institute, 118–119
    Executive Compensation Advisory
        Services, 125
    Hewitt Compensation Center, 125–126
    The Institute of Management and
        Administration, 126
    JobStar: California Job Search Guide,
        119–120
    LIVEDGAR, 120–121
    in print form only, 112
    Risk Management Association Annual
        Statement Studies, 126
    SalariesReview.com, 121
    Salary.com, 121–122
    SalaryExpert.com, 121
    Trade Associations, 123
    Wageweb, 123
    William M. Mercer - Mercer Human
        Resource Consulting, 126
    WorldatWork, 127
Salary.com, 121–122
SalaryExpert.com, 121
Sanders, Jack, 131
Schmidt, Dennis, 192
SDC, *see* Securities Data Company
SearchDay, 15, 16
Search directories, *see* Directories
Search engines, xxi, 1–19
    advanced search features of, 12–15
    alltheweb, 5–6

AltaVista, xxi, 2, 6, 9, 11
    country-specific, 196
    crawling by, 11
    differences in, 2
    directories vs., 1
    Dogpile, 15, 16
    fee-based services, 17–19
    Google, xxi, 1–3, 5, 9, 11, 13, 15–17
    and invisible Web, 10–12
    LexisNexis, xxi, xxii, 17, 18
    Metacrawler, 15, 16
    meta search engines, 15–16
    meta vs. multiple, 16
    paid placement with, 8–10
    Patent Café IP Search Engine, 159–160
    Search Engine Showdown, 7
    Search Engine Watch, 7, 8
    Teoma, 3–5, 17
    top 10, 2–3
    WiseNut, 3–5
    Yahoo!, 1, 8, 13
Search Engine Showdown, 7
Search Engine Watch, 7, 8, 16
Search Systems Public Records Locator, 223,
    227–228
SEC, *see* Securities and Exchange Commission
Securities and Exchange Commission (SEC):
    EDGAR system, 83, 138–140
    M&A filings, 129, 138–140
    SEC Info, 94–95
Securities Data Company (SDC), xxii, 144–145
SEDAR (System for Electronic Document
    Analysis and Retrieval), 94–95, 97, 220
Segal, 112
Sherman, Chris, 11, 12, 16
Skyscraper ads, 9
SmartPros, 187–188
SNL Securities, 143–144
Social Science Research Network (SSRN), 54
Spiders, 11
Sponsored sites, xxi, 8–9
Spreadsheets, downloading to, 38, 42
SSRN (Social Science Research Network), 54
State Search, 29
State Tax Library, 189
Statistical resources, 30–31
STAT-USA, 56, 206
Stock options, 111. *See also* Salary and execu-
    tive compensation surveys
Stock quotes, 81–82
    Wall Street Research Net, 82
    Yahoo! Finance, 81

"The Straight Story on Search Engines"
    (Laurianne McLaughlin), 9
Subject-specific portals, 21
Super Searchers Cover the World (Mary Ellen
    Bates), 196
SurfIP, 173–174
Survey of Current Business, 51
Switzerland Images, 153
System for Electronic Document Analysis and
    Retrieval, *see* SEDAR

TakeoverStockReport.com, 148
Tax Analysts, 189–190
TaxBase, 189
Taxes and accounting, 175–194
    About.com, 23
    accounting news Websites, 176
    accounting portals, 175–176, 187
    Accounting Research Network, 190
    accounting scandals, 176
    Accounting & Tax Database, 190–191
    AccountingWeb, 23, 191
    American Institute of Certified Public
        Accountants, 177–178
    AuditNet, 191
    Big Four major accounting firm sites, 178–180
    Bureau of National Affairs, 180–181
    CFO.com, 191
    Commerce Clearing House, 182
    Comperio, 192
    CPA Journal, 182
    Deloitte & Touche, 178, 179
    Electronic Accountant, 184–185
    Ernst & Young, 178, 180
    Federal Tax Law, 192
    FTA State Tax Rates, 192
    Internal Revenue Service, 185–186
    international accounting information, 195
    Kleinrock's Tax Expert Online, 186
    KPMG, 178–179
    PPCnet, 193
    PriceWaterhouseCoopers, 178, 179
    regulations and standards, 193–194
    RIA and RIA Checkpoint, 187
    SmartPros, 187–188
    Tax Analysts, 189–190
    writing skills for tax professionals, 194
Tax Notes Today, 189
T-Bills, Notes & Bonds Online, 78
Tech Deal Maker, 149
TechDealNet, 149
TechSavvy, 109

10k Wizard, 84, 138–140
Teoma, 3, 17
TheStreet.com, 81
Thomas Register of American Manufacturers,
    106, 149
Thomas Register of European Manufacturers, 220
Thomson Carson Group, 131
Thomson Corporation, 176
    Derwent patent sites, 152, 153
    Electronic Accountant, 184–185
    PPCnet, 193
    RIA, 187
    Securities Data Company Worldwide M&A
        Database, 130, 144–145
    Thomson Media Group, 148
    Thomson Patent Store, 153–154
Thomson Patent Store, 153–154
Thomson Research, 65–66
Thomson & Thomson, 161
Tobacco Industry Portal, 58
Tobacco Merchants Association, 58
Trade associations, 57. *See also specific*
    associations
    ASAE Gateway to Associations, 123, 245
    directories of, 66–68
Trademarks, 151, 163, 172. *See also* Intellectual
    property research
Trademark.com, 158, 174
Trademark Electronic Business Center, 163
Trademarkscan, 161
Trade periodicals, 57
Trade publications, 58
TRW, *see* Experian

Unclaimed property, 229
U.S. Census Bureau, 49–50
    Industry Resources, 72–73
    International Statistical Agencies, 218
U.S. Chamber of Commerce, 37–38
United States Copyright Office, 161–162
U.S. Death Records, 230
U.S. Department of Commerce:
    Basic Guide to Exporting, 213
    Commercial Service, 198–199
    GLOBUS/NTDB, 206
    ITA Basic Industries, 71
    STAT-USA, 56
U.S. Department of Energy Patent Database, 170
U.S. Department of Justice, 229
U.S. Department of Labor:
    America's Career InfoNet, 114–115
    Bureau of Labor Statistics, 38–39, 115–116
U.S. Department of State Business Center, 210

United States patents, 152, 158, 172
United States Patent and Trademark Office
    (PTO), 151, 163–164
University of California, Berkeley, 53
University of Connecticut, 55
University of Georgia, 194
University of Kansas, 208
University of Maryland, 52
University of Texas:
    Copyright Crash Course, 165–166
    Latin American Network Information
        Center, 218
    The Watch File, 174
USA Consensus Forecasts, 215
USSearch, 228

ValuationResearch.com, 21
ValuationResources.com, 31, 32
ValuationResources Industry Resources
    Report, 73
Value-added information services, xxi, 17
Value Line Investment Survey, 97
Vault Reports, 109
Verification services, *see* Public records
Vickers Stock Research Corporation, 131
Vortals, 32–35
    finding, 34–35
    uses of, 33–34

Wachovia, 56
Wageweb, 123
Wall Street City, 97
The Wall Street Journal, 18
    Briefing Books, 95
    Career Journal, 117–118
The Wall Street Journal Online, 210–211
Wall Street Research Network (WSRN), 77, 82
    earnings estimates, 79
    public company data, 95–96
    stock quotes, 81, 82
The Watch File at the University of Texas, 174
Webcrawler, 15
Webmergers.com, 149

Web pages, cached copies of, 3
Webstat, 221
WEFA, 46, 47, 207
WetFeet.com, 73
Wharton Economic Forecasting Associates,
    see WEFA
William M. Mercer - Mercer Human Resource
    Consulting, 126
Winzer, Ingo, 61
WIPO, *see* World Intellectual Property
    Organization
WiseNut, 2
WiseSearch, 5
WISI, *see* Wright Investors' Service
WorldatWork, 127
Worldcom, 176
World Factbook (CIA), 212
World in Figures, 221
World Intellectual Property Organization
    (WIPO), 153, 166–168
Worldwide M&A Database (SDC), 144–145
Wright Investors' Service (WISI), 24, 84, 199
Writing skills (for tax professionals), 194
WSRN, *see* Wall Street Research Network

XLS.com, *see* Alacra

Yahoo!:
    advanced search options, 13, 14
    Bond Center, 77–78
    as original portal, 21
    paid placement with, 8
    searches with, 1
Yahoo! Finance, 31, 33
    Mutual Funds Center, 80–81
    stock quotes, 81
Yardeni's Economics Network, 56
Yellow pages, 220
York, Grace, 30–31

Zandi, Mark, 24
Zapdata.com, 109